"If you want to break free from old patterns that prevent you from embracing your gifts and talents, read this book! Sara Giita Flores uses her compassionate, soothing, and beautiful voice to guide you on a journey of healing and liberation that empowers you to play your part in using your feminine power and wisdom to heal our world."

—Amy Rose, LCSW, Delight the World

"Brimming with gentle, empowering wisdom, Unleash Your Goddess Voice is a guide to understanding, embracing, and fully expressing our true voice. Through a combination of powerful stories, encouraging coaching, and healing practices, voice coach Sara Giita Flores gives us all of the tools we need to step into our authentic self-expression, so that we feel more awake, more aware, and more alive."

—Maria Blon, author of *Hearts Blooming* and *Living Passionately*

"Sara Giita Flores delivers an approachable, loving guide on how to connect with your voice and your inner power no matter what may have happened in your life. If you feel a yearning to strengthen your voice and your connection to your power, read this book."

—Jodi McLaren, Board Certified Music Therapist, Singer-Songwriter & Coach

"This is a beautiful book about the author's journey towards healing and finding her own voice. It offers readers captivating stories of triumph plus practical guidance and actionable exercises to find their own gorgeous, unique Goddess Voice too. This book will help you on your own path so that you can heal, self-actualize, and use your voice for making positive change in the world."

—Kristine Kaoverii Weber, founder of Subtle Yoga, subtleyoga.com

Unleash Your Goddess Voice

Build Your Resilience to Speak Up,
Sing Out, and Spread Your Message

SARA GIITA FLORES

INTRODUCTION

Trusting the Fullness of Authentic Expression

"Ooohhhhhuhhaaaaa." I let out a low, slow groan. A gorilla-like groan. I sank back into the couch, relieved. I softened. I sighed. But then my self-consciousness crept back in. "That was not pretty," I said nervously, eyeing my somatic therapist, Maggie, for signs of disapproval or judgment. I found none.

"It was just right, Sara. You let your body express what needed to come through. Give yourself a pat on the back for that bravery." With her reassurance, I was able to sink more deeply into the feeling of release and relief that came from that instinctual, guttural groan.

In this moment of making raw sounds, I came home to the power of my authentic voice. In some ways, it seems strange that this was the moment I began to open up my self-expression because I had obviously used my voice in all the years prior. I talked plenty. I gave school presentations. I loved acting in theater productions in high school and had no problem projecting my voice to the back of the auditorium. I had sung confidently on stage at least 100 times, and I had finished a music degree with a concentration in vocal performance. I had even helped a few aspiring singers in my budding career as a vocal coach.

1

I had been expressing myself, yes. But all this was happening at a surface level because it felt profoundly unsafe to go deeper. As an empath who deeply feels other people's emotions, I was hyper-focused on pleasing others to avoid the discomfort of rejection. The cold feeling of someone being turned off by my quirky, expressive, emotional personality felt like too much to bear.

Adding layers of shame to my sensitivity, traumatic experiences eroded my self-worth. Having lived through sexual assault at ages five and fifteen, I had internalized the message that my authentic voice was unworthy. If I spoke up truthfully, I expected my voice to be demonized, disrespected, or dismissed. I unconsciously reacted to trauma by tamping down my self-expression to stay small, pleasing, palatable, and safe. The sounds I allowed to come through were narrow and restricted—everything I expressed had to be pretty and polished. And this directly correlated with the amount of truth I permitted myself to express in conversations and interactions with others. I disconnected my voice from the innate power deep within my belly and focused on what I thought other people wanted me to say. My life became a puppet show, and I was the exhausted but lovable puppet.

I see now how all my years of people-pleasing and performing on stage prepared me for the shift I felt as a 24-year-old on my therapist's couch. I began to tap into my deepest, most powerful voice. A voice that came from my divine power within. A voice that felt raw and courageous. A voice that wasn't afraid of the dark depths of the human experience that were waiting to be healed. By giving myself the time, space, and support to heal the experiences of my voice being shut down, I gradually began to reconnect to my authentic voice with greater frequency. I learned how to transform my habits of surface-level self-expression rooted in unworthiness and set the foundation for bringing my true voice into the spotlight. I started to embrace the fact that my highly sensitive, empathic nature brought the gift of being able to express my soul's truth.

While traumatic abuse was a big factor in how I tamped down my voice, I was also affected by a universal pattern of women learning to play small to stay safe within the confines of our patriarchal culture. Our own wounding plus the effects of cultural conditioning often cause us to restrict our self-expression and to downplay the importance of our voice, our message, and our own fulfillment as drivers of personal and collective healing. Through the process of healing those moments when your voice was dismissed, disrespected, or devalued, you can build the confidence in your voice to share your message on a bigger scale and find greater freedom, fulfillment, and leadership capacity! Woo-hoo!

The Power of Your Goddess Voice

As the process of reclaiming my voice unfolded, I eventually gave a name to my authentic self-expression: the Goddess Voice.

I believe that everyone has a Goddess Voice within them. While the sacred power inside of us is a formless energy, the Goddess Voice that it births is an outward expression that can easily be perceived by others. Your voice is the channel through which the intangible becomes tangible. Your Goddess Voice is not a single creation, and it may not even be expressed through sound or words. It is a steady stream of authentic expression that wants to interact with the world of form. Even if the flowing river of your self-expression has been dammed up like mine was, a trickle of water can still come through. And when the conditions are safe enough, you can gently remove any obstructions from cultural conditioning, past criticisms, rejections, discrimination, traumas, and intergenerational patterns of wounding.

When the Goddess Voice is coming through without fetters or filters—***Whoa, Mama!!***—you had better make some space. It holds the raw creative energy of lava emerging from a volcano. We tend to think of volcanoes as destructive, but that is only the case when the magma is sealed off with no way to vent the pressure. Then when the pressure becomes too great, it explodes as a destructive force. However, it's even more common to see constructive volcanoes. When the lava can flow out in a steady stream without blockages or inhibitions, it slowly creates mountains and volcanic islands. In the same way, your Goddess Voice has an amazing creative power to heal, to connect, and to build mountains.

Learning to tap my Goddess Voice became my life journey. In the 16 years since I first discovered how to outwardly express my inner power, I have gradually unearthed the courage to amplify my voice and increase my visibility in ways I never imagined. I followed the call to write hundreds of songs and perform them on stages large and small. I built a music career with a message of hope and healing and gained the attention of local magazines and radio and TV stations. I have been paid generously to speak and have sung in front of audiences of thousands. I incrementally built up the guts to share my story of overcoming trauma and reclaiming my voice on numerous podcasts, social media live events, speaker summits, and conference stages.

Throughout my healing journey of bringing my voice into the spotlight, I have had the privilege of helping hundreds of clients to build the confidence to speak up and get on stage themselves. For the first decade of my career, I focused on teaching voice and piano lessons in a rather traditional way. I felt the need to hide my "Woo-Woo" self—it was just part of my habit of hiding my Goddess Voice to stay safe.

But one day, my longtime piano and voice student Josephine walked in the door needing something deeper. With her shoulders hunched and her perfectly styled black hair hanging over her face, she revealed to me that she'd been going through intense depression and anxiety. Her upbringing left her with the feelings of being an unworthy sinner which made it hard for her to dedicate the time and energy needed to complete a song. Music gave her a grounded sense of joy, but since she didn't feel worthy of feeling good, she kept falling into an unconscious habit of self-sabotage. Her wounding taught her to stay small and trapped in suffering.

Remembering how much she loved hearing the resonance of the piano lid being open, I lifted the curvy triangular lid on my 100-year-old baby grand piano and rested it on the tallest support stick. I invited her to stand in front of the open strings while I improvised a calming song. I spontaneously started singing and she joined in. As we became present to the breath and sound, our nervous systems settled. The anxiety and worries melted away for a moment as our spirits started to intermingle. Through the magical experience of toning together, Josephine began to tap the power of all that is healthy and whole within her being. Spending some time every week connecting to the power of her voice gradually helped Josephine to heal her anxiety, depression, and feelings of unworthiness. She came to terms with her empathic nature as someone who deeply experiences life and is very tuned into the emotions and energies of others. She started forming new, healthy friendships and joined communities that supported her return to her authentic self. Josephine is now thriving and living a fabulous life with plenty of music and joy.

Seeing the healing power of authentic vocal expression, I knew it was time to make a shift in my career. I couldn't keep hiding my own authentic voice, my spiritual side, or my story of overcoming trauma. I began to teach my clients some of the healing tools I had been using in my own life– mindful movement, visualization, sounding, sung affirmations, inner child healing, performance techniques, and voice-energy practices. In addition to helping singers and pianists, I began coaching empathic entrepreneurs, writers, and creatives to start spreading their soulful message by landing speaking opportunities of their own. I took several trainings and courses for coaches and somatic practitioners to feel confident in safely working with people who have experienced trauma. Through six years of playful experimentation, testing, and feedback from my clients, I developed my own system for helping people to tap their inner power and express it confidently through their voices.

Resilience for Speaking Unapologetically

While I have experienced my own ever-evolving version of success as a singer, speaker, writer, and coach, I don't want you to think for a moment that it was all a breeze just because I did therapy and discovered my Goddess Voice. Just like pretty much every person who has put themselves out there, I have had a lot of failures. I have had rejections. I've had gigs and opportunities that I wanted with all my heart but didn't get. I've shared beloved blog posts and book proposals and songs that didn't resonate with others. I went through frequent periods of feeling like I had so much love to share with the world through my voice and message, but no one was listening.

And I'm not gonna pretend I let it all roll off my shoulders. Holy cow, how each failure hurts! Each failure and rejection brings up the residual pain of my voice and body being devalued. I see this pattern in so many women, whether or not they have experienced sexual trauma. Because of the subtle and not-so-subtle ways we have been interrupted, ignored, demeaned, and put down, the cumulative effect creates its own kind of traumatic stress. Yes, society has shifted dramatically in the past 100 years, and you can now find more places where women's voices are celebrated and honored. But the real-life experiences of disrespect we have experienced keep alive the millennia-old patterning of being made to feel unworthy. Because of the unique needs women experience when reclaiming their voices, I have written this book for people who identify as female. However, if you identify as a different gender and are interested in freeing your voice, you are definitely welcome here!

All the wounding that gets passed along means the process of reclaiming your voice will likely need tender, compassionate care. When speaking up and putting your voice out into the world brings up past hurts (whether conscious or unconscious), it's not as simple as following some steps and exercises. While a deep part of you may feel called to share your voice in bigger ways, most of us will have opposing parts of our psyche that prefer to stay small. These inner energies need love and healing to feel safer speaking up and being heard. By rooting yourself in confidence, you can build a sturdy bridge that allows you to live your purpose.

On a practical level, speaking up unapologetically starts with anchoring yourself in safety and healing your self-doubts (even if this is an ongoing process). Then it is super powerful to share your voice with safe people who you know will treat you with respect, before expecting yourself to show up fully in front of a large group or audience. This process of healing your voice can help you make yourself heard in any arena you choose, including:

- Speaking up for yourself with your partner, family members, coworkers, and friends.

- Setting clear boundaries that garner respect.
- Strengthening your creative voice.
- Reclaiming the joy of singing.
- Getting on stage.
- Becoming a professional speaker.
- Speaking on podcasts.
- Getting featured on media platforms.
- Launching new programs or creations and sharing them with the world.
- Spreading your message through impactful content.
- Amplifying your impact as a leader.
- Finding fulfillment through joyful self-expression.

Here's a snapshot of what the process of bringing her voice into the world looked like for my client, friend, and frequent collaborator, Maria Blon. Maria is a prolific creative writer and mentor with abundant wisdom and presence. She had already published a book, tried different business ventures, and helped start a school in Haiti when we started working together, yet she often had the experience of her wisdom and creations being unrecognized and undervalued. She had a recurring scenario which was my default for a long time as well. She poured her heart into a creative project, shared her enthusiasm with the world, and received… crickets. Other than a few enthusiastic friends praising her work, each launch brought more obscurity and silence.

Life kept reiterating a common experience she had as a sensitive, creative child. She was being called in to heal the wounds of being unseen and unheard so she could build her capacity to shine on a bigger level. When I invited Maria to participate in a writer's group I started called The Divine Author Goddesses, she felt completely seen and heard for the first time in her life. While she already knew intellectually that she was worthy of recognition, she finally knew what it felt like to have her voice and gifts acknowledged and valued. When we are seen, heard, and accepted, we can actually experience this as a grounded feeling of peace in our bodies. She gradually learned to anchor herself more in this bodily experience of connecting to her inborn capacity to thrive in communication and relationship with others.

With this deeper sense of feeling safe to express her worthy voice, Maria began to put herself out there in ways that felt aligned and joyous to her. She began communicating with her mailing list regularly. With a few simple tools, I helped her reach out to podcast hosts and she shared her immense wisdom with their audiences. She began facilitating writer's groups and a nine-month "Birth a Book" group coaching journey where people actually showed up to receive her medicine. With the confidence our collaborative work gave her, Maria also became open to learning marketing skills so more people could find her books and group coaching programs. In sharing her gratitude for how I helped her step into her vocal power, Maria expressed that she feels at home within herself for the first time.

While Maria's story may seem like a linear process, healing the patterns of smallness so your voice can shine always happens in cycles and seasons. I can say for myself that it's not about getting to an end point of never, ever having failures, self-doubts, or creative pause. I still experience a typical success rate (and the accompanying rejection rate) when going for music gigs and speaking opportunities. But the ongoing process of integrating my voice has given me the resilience to manage the emotions and triggers that arise from rejection. I can return to my blueprint of worthiness and radiant self-expression with more grace and ease.

I hope this brings a sigh of relief that you don't have to be perfect or have the correct vibration or be completely healed to follow your calling and share your voice and message with the world. You also don't have to be a "good" singer, a natural public speaker, or an extrovert, because all voices and all sounds are welcome here without judgment. You can start from where you are, with a willingness to reflect upon your life and try some new practices to help your innate worthiness and self-expression be revealed.

How to Use This Book

When you begin to navigate this instinctual forested terrain of speaking your truth in bolder, more visible ways, it's easy to make it all really deep and serious. (Cue the dramatic music!) Yet much of the inner healing comes from balancing the momentous reclamation of your power with a light, playful mindset. You will be invited to try out silly roars and deep, weighted growls. You will be shown how to embody the airiness of a fairy while also going deep into your fiery core. Embracing polarities is at the root of healing yourself as a channel of self-expression. We will learn how to bring joyful, supportive energy to meet the edges of your buried pain and unknown depths. There, we experience alchemy. Our struggles and our pleasures join together to form something that could not have been created just by skating along the happy surface.

How do we bring the two together, you may ask? Let's consult our map for a lay of the land, an overview of the concepts in this book. Each chapter weaves in wisdom, meditations, and stories from my journey and the courageous journeys of my clients. To close each topic we will explore a step-by-step practice to help you unleash your Goddess Voice.

To build a firm foundation, this chapter will offer you gentle reminders on how to use deep breathing, cognitive awareness, and kindness in your self-talk to embody more self-compassion as you explore your voice.

To heal your voice and unleash your self-expression, it's essential to honor the moments when your voice was disrespected, dismissed, or devalued (no matter how big or small). To help shine a light on the path of healing, I will also share my own story of shutting down my voice after sexual trauma.

Here we will explore how to unravel all the conditioning and beliefs that keep you small, quiet, and disconnected from your worth. In addition to recognizing these unhelpful beliefs, we will explore a powerful practice to tap into your intrinsic worth, through a visualization of your Inner Flame or source of divine power within.

By deepening your comfort in your own body, we will journey through the territory of sensations so your earthly vessel can become a beautiful instrument for your voice.

With practice, you can learn to tell the difference between your ego's voice and your Goddess Voice, or your unique upwelling of divinely channeled self-expression. By cultivating silence, listening to intuition, and releasing attachments to outcomes, we will discover how to easily step into a creative flow state.

We all have a deep human need to be seen and heard by ourselves and others, so it's important to find safe ways to express ourselves vulnerably. We will also practice speaking up and setting boundaries that garner respect.

Since sharing your voice with the world may be perceived as a threat to your nervous system, I will show you how to use trauma-healing tools to help you feel safe and stable as you increase your visibility. We will explore tools such as pendulation, titration, rewriting the story, and feeling your emotions.

What does it even mean to share your authentic voice? In this chapter, we will play with practices to ditch our filters and projections so we can express ourselves from a place of authentic wholeness.

When you want to start sharing your Goddess Voice more boldly, some scared, tender parts inside are likely to create resistance. By stepping into the role of being your own loving caregiver, you can heal your inner child so you feel safe when speaking up.

Chapter 10: *Aligning Your Energy to Make Your Voice Heard*... 257

Every time you speak or sing, your body posture and energy field are communicating to others along with your voice. In this chapter, we will explore archetypes and practices to help you call in the energy that will match and amplify what you wish to communicate.

Chapter 11: *The World Needs Your Voice*.......................... 295

No matter what, your voice creates impact and influence in the world. When you add in loving intention, your voice can become a gift that contributes to our collective healing.

As I weave my own story into the steps of healing your voice, I will issue trigger warnings for the brief recounts of my traumatic experiences. Feel free to skip over them—you will still be able to make sense of the book. Likewise, if you ever need to stop reading for a while, my wish is for you to honor your needs. Pay attention to how you feel in your body and let your breath settle into a comfortable rhythm. (I really mean this—I hope you will take pauses, body breaks, or skip over sections as a way to honor your own needs.)

When you bring in the intention of moving slowly and compassionately, you may hear a voice inside (or outside) urging you to push yourself to exhaustion. I have definitely worked with some women who were mired in the conditioning of constant pushing. But learning to let our Goddess Voices shine is not a marathon. We are not trying to beat our old patterns into the ground through intense effort.

Instead, we allow our bodies and our deep inner knowing to guide the process. We start to listen to the subtle internal nudges and rest when it is needed. We trust when it is time to take a break, take some breaths, or take a walk. We may remind ourselves to drink extra water and nourish our bodies throughout the healing journey.

Even with awareness, gentle pacing, and self-care, you may still find yourself rocketed into a state of overwhelm at times. Reading a distressing news article or situations in which I feel helpless still trigger overwhelm for me sometimes. There is no failure in this, as triggers can send our nervous system into threat response before our rational, conscious mind has time to evaluate the situation. If you need help to regain your balance, please refer to the Appendix on Calming Down from Overwhelm. And if you are ever in crisis, please don't hesitate to get help.

In the spirit of taking care of yourself, you can make this journey as light or as deep as you need right now, knowing you can always circle back to chapters and practices when the time feels right. No matter how you engage with the book and practices, just by reading you are embarking on a courageous journey. You are saying "yes" to your voice, your purpose, and the blossoming of the message in your heart. By learning to tap into your Goddess Voice, you are opening the door to greater fulfillment and joy as you create ripples of positive change through your voice and being.

CHAPTER 1

Breathing In
Self-Compassion

A spark of self-compassion
raw, knowing, fierce
meets the place of shadow and shame.
A breath of self-expression
like golden wings outstretched
Perches on the edge of flight.

Carrying Compassion in Your Backpack

Here we are at the trailhead, ready to unleash your voice and discover how to own your power. But before we set off, I want to make sure you're carrying an essential and precious resource: self-compassion. Treating yourself with kindness in your thoughts, words, and actions is a learnable skill. Very few people grew up with models of radiant self-compassion. I definitely saw a lot of adults putting themselves down, saying they "should" be doing things differently, or scowling at themselves in the mirror. We live in a culture that encourages people to feel like they are not good enough! That means that embodying self-compassion usually starts as a decision, and then becomes an ongoing learning process.

Just as you would want to pack enough water before setting off on a hike on a hot day, self-compassion is an underlying resource that you will rely upon in all phases of your journey. Without it, you will likely get parched and withered and turn back long before reaching the beautiful territory of expressing your Goddess Voice. With inner kindness in your toolkit, you can give yourself a baseline of nourishment that you most definitely deserve to receive. This sustenance will propel you through silent deserts and lush canyons with rushing waterfalls until you find that place in yourself where you have full permission to live your expressive genius in all its forms. When you allow yourself to drink from the ever-refilling water source of self-compassion, you can enjoy the experience of being worthy and just right, just as you are.

If you're not sold on the idea of treating yourself with compassion, consider the fact that our brains have pain receptors. Those receptors are going to fire like crazy if we look inside without some kindness to ourselves. Self-harshness hurts, because as far as our brain is concerned, *hurt feelings trigger the same exact pain receptors as physical pain.*

The women I work with tend to be empowered empaths who have already come far on their journeys of evolution. They are in tune with their sensitivity, emotions, and inner landscape. Yet the awareness of their potential to express themselves powerfully and shamelessly means they get hard on themselves when they are not embodying that radiant potential in every single moment. This happens to me, too. I catch myself feeling like I should be past all these old patterns by now. So the first place to soften up is by recognizing it's okay to have moments of self-doubt. Even though you have worked so hard to increase your sense of empowerment, there may be times when it feels hard to speak up for yourself. It does not mean you are a fraud or a failure! As you learn to tap your most powerful voice, you will be able to navigate these moments with greater ease and grace.

Embracing Your Voice, No Matter How It Sounds

While we're on the topic of self-doubt, do you ever judge the "quality" of your vocal sound? Oh, Sister, you are not alone. Almost every person who has walked into my studio has shared those doubts about their voice. There is a strange modern phenomenon where we judge singers as good or bad. TV singing contests thrive on harsh judges who sneer at people's "bad" voices. And when it comes to speaking and other vocal sounds, there's definitely cultural pressure to stick with what is deemed acceptable and polite. As a result, we see a widespread orphaning from the Goddess Voice within. When singing is only for the super-talented and speaking is often judged and compartmentalized, we become disconnected from the innate joy of expressing our voices.

Beyond the question of whether you want to be a singer or professional speaker, this widespread labeling of voices as "good" or "bad" has a profound impact on our speaking voices and how we express ourselves.

Let's dig into this notion of good singing for a moment. When I'm paying money to go to a concert, I do indeed like to hear a singer who has amazing pitch, rhythm, style, and expressiveness. But that doesn't mean the rest of the world shouldn't sing! While I've been helping students improve the quality of their vocal tone for sixteen years, the magic of this work is helping people love how they sound. Joy is the goal. So while I love the process of improving your singing, I'm also a big advocate of throwing off the judgments and using your voice for pleasure, connection, and liberation. You have a right to sing, no matter how you sound.

If you feel a sigh of relief that it's totally fine to sing and even to make unconventional and surprising sounds, this represents a homecoming to our ancestral legacy. Anthropologists know that humans of every culture have been singing together for millennia. Some surmise that we began singing before we began speaking. No matter the continent where your ancestors took root, they surely gathered together in song and ceremony. They lifted their voices to connect to the Divine. Singing was about connection, not perfection. I like to imagine there were probably some folks around the fire singing off-key, but their enthusiasm, expressiveness, and devotion were appreciated as a necessary part of the whole. In the past few thousand years, the majority of people have become disconnected from tribal ceremonial life. Factors like migration into cities, religious wars, witch hunts, slavery, and colonial domination unraveled the threads of tribal structures as the fabric of our communities. Yet our ancestors kept singing. At the ashram, church, mosque, synagogue, temple, or ceremonial grounds, people gathered to sing. While harvesting crops, putting children to sleep, or gathering for a party, people sang.

Then, in 1877, Thomas Edison invented a machine to record sound (the phonograph). The popularization of recorded music would eventually play a huge role in changing how we relate to our voices. While we have gained so much richness and possibility from recorded music, we have allowed our innately human need for singing in community to fall by the wayside. In revering the megastars, we project onto them the joy of vocal sounding which has been neglected in our souls. The trend of average people singing less and less is evident in some modern churches as well, where singing in community has largely been replaced by a professional band on stage. I once had a student who came to me with so much love to share through song, but they wouldn't let her on the worship team at her church. In my mind, that whole setup of needing to be good enough for the booming microphones represents perfection over connection. She had to contain her glorious voice with the rest of the congregation, who were only invited to sing a few easy, repetitive phrases of each song.

Like many cultural shifts, we can sow the seeds of change in our own lives. If you are ready to reclaim your right and need to sing, the first step is to soften judgments about how you sound. Unless you want to sing on stage, it's really not an obstacle to sing off-key, out of rhythm, or with an uncertain voice. If you can speak, then you can harness the healing power of singing and sounding. You don't have to be perfect to express something meaningful. Plus, singing has been shown to lower levels of the stress hormone cortisol. To me, that is proof that we are all born to be singers regardless of how we may sound.

Once you get comfortable with experimenting and embracing your voice on your own, you can seek out safe places to sing and sound with others (no microphones needed.) After hearing my sermon on singing for connection, my friend Nancy began to sing to her young daughters before bed. She had never given much thought before to the notion that she shouldn't sing unless she had a great voice. However, when she took the risk of singing anyway, she found that she and her daughters experience great joy through her lullabies. She describes an experience with her teenage daughter, kindergartener, and preschooler all singing together: "The four of us sang before bed while laying down, just "Twinkle Twinkle" since we all know it and it's short. It was one of the most beautiful feelings I've ever felt in my life. All of us together, two sweet little voices and my teen's now deeper womanly voice along with my own." Not only did she get to experience this heart-opening moment, but she also showed her daughters the power of enjoying your voice without judgment.

Easing Up on Self-Harshness

Embracing the sound of your voice shows how making peace with imperfection is a key component of learning to relate to yourself with deeper compassion. You get to be messy and imperfect. You also don't have to worry about loving yourself in every single moment, as self-critical thoughts will naturally still come up. Just make a commitment to being *less mean* to yourself. When you create a non-judgmental space inside, the self-love and inner power will gradually seep in. The radiance is coming! For several of my former clients, this first step has looked like refraining from apologizing profusely when they mess something up.

Once we make the commitment to embodying self-compassion, the next step is to cultivate awareness. We can gently notice when we have a thought such as, "That sounded stupid," or, "I don't have a good voice." Instead of beating ourselves up for the thought, we can remind ourselves that thoughts are not facts, and it's natural for them to come and go. Then we can speak to ourselves the same way we would to a close friend who is going through a rough time. We acknowledge our pain and what we are experiencing, saying, "It makes sense that these critical thoughts pop up because this is how I was trained. How human of me! At the same time, I know that my voice is worthy because it is an intrinsic part of the whole. It's not about being bad, good, pretty, or ugly, it is a beautiful tool for expressing something meaningful."

Notice that we are not giving ourselves a whole lawyer's argument on why the negative thoughts were wrong, or trying to believe affirmations that don't seem true. To counteract negative thoughts, we don't have to convince ourselves, "I have the most powerful and beautiful voice in the world!" If the affirmation seems too exaggerated, a part of your psyche will be looking for evidence that contradicts the thought. Then you might get a lengthy trial in your head. Self-compassion can bypass that debate entirely, as we acknowledge that it's okay for imperfections, challenges, mistakes, and negativity to come up. We deserve to love ourselves back into wholeness.

For me, forgiving myself for messing up is a self-compassion lesson that will probably last my whole life. When trauma and patriarchy infused my life with the message that the world is unsafe, I reacted by trying to be perfect. I narrowed my self-expression to try to please everybody, staying palatable and polished. I grew up with some super-harsh inner critics in my head and would often regret things I said to others. Even if I said something fairly benign or only mildly embarrassing, I would often be worried that others would think less of me afterward.

> ### *Meditation: Meeting Regrets with Self-Compassion*
>
> Think of a time when you said something that you slightly regretted. Replay the memory as if it were happening like a play on a stage. When the memory finishes, imagine your present-day self walking up onto the stage and speaking some kind reassurances to your past self. You can tell them, "It's okay, as humans we all say things that we regret from time to time. If there is something to learn from the situation, please share that now. I love you, I accept you, and I am here for you. I forgive you." To close the meditation, give yourself a loving hug.

Despite its abundant benefits, we may have some resistance to self-compassion. If you worry that self-compassion will make you lazy or unmotivated, consider that scientific studies have shown its effectiveness in self-motivation. Researcher Kristin Neff has made it her life's work to define, research, and teach self-compassion. She has found that being kind to yourself actually enhances personal motivation. Whereas self-criticism is a mechanism of fearful motivation, self-compassion inspires us to reach our potential through love. Studies have shown that when people have setbacks, they show more resilience if they know how to talk to themselves with compassion. They can acknowledge errors and weather the feelings of inadequacy that come after failures, while also treating themselves kindly and knowing mistakes are learning opportunities.

With practice, self-compassion can become our strongest inner impulse, guiding us through our healing and vocal empowerment. The shadow-loving doubts and self-deprecating thoughts may try to trip us up here and there, but we disarm them with self-compassion.

Finding a Compassionate Pace

When we let compassion guide our journey, we accept that there will be some discomfort involved. Yet we can develop a gentle pace that protects us from overwhelm and distress as we explore our voices. The first step is to distinguish comfort from safety. Though we often perceive anything unpleasant as a threat, comfort and safety are not the same thing. As we lean into our own growth and healing, we will be facing discomfort. That does not necessarily mean we are in danger, so we can look around and verify that we are indeed safe when those ingrained alarm bells go off. (Phew, there are no slimy predators of any species in my home right now!)

That being said, we all have limits in the present moment for how much discomfort seems manageable. Think of a continuum with your comfort zone being on one end. Your body may feel relatively settled and relaxed in your comfort zone. When you take a few steps outside to try something new, examine a fear, or share your voice in a vulnerable way, you may feel some discomfort. If the discomfort feels manageable and doable, you are in what I call the Zone of Growth. This is the sweet spot where you are not staying locked in your old patterns, but you are also not pushing yourself into your Zone of Overwhelm. You would know you are entering the Zone of Overwhelm if you are feeling anxious, distressed, out-of-control, numb, or shut down.

Compassionate Pacing

Comfort Zone	Zone of Growth	Zone of Overwhelm
Settled	*Courageous*	*Anxious*
Calm	*Open*	*Exhausted*
At Ease	*Facing Discomfort*	*Shut Down*

Reground in your comfort zone to create a sustainable cycle.

Throughout this book, you will learn to notice and honor your Edge, which is the transition between the Zone of Growth and the Zone of Overwhelm.

Keep in mind that we all have our own ever-evolving capacity for facing this productive discomfort. As much as possible, avoid comparing another person's tolerance to the range of what feels manageable to you today. There is no universal measure of what constitutes the Comfort Zone and the Zone of Growth. There is only what feels right to you in each unfolding moment. In my life, honoring my capacity often means taking breaks from feeling like I have to constantly be loud and proud, and letting my body take the lead to hang back when something feels too intense.

To move at a compassionate pace as you heal and express yourself more boldly, the key is to dance between the Comfort Zone and the Zone of Growth. If we try to stay in the Zone of Growth too long, we will likely tip into distress and overwhelm. We want to continually and consciously bring ourselves back to the Comfort Zone after a period of feeling stretched. A great way to do this is by focusing on a resource, which is anything that helps you feel safe, stable, and calm. For some people, this may mean pausing to notice your breath, or taking stretch breaks, or coffee or tea breaks. Focusing on a resource could also mean looking at something in your environment that you find grounding, reading an inspiring quote, feeling your feet, or smelling a delicious fragrance. If you have been focused on speaking, singing, or creating in service to others, resourcing may mean giving yourself some time to express yourself just for your own enjoyment and nurturance.

Each person will find their own unique way of returning to safety after facing discomfort and growth. My client Sandra stretched herself by bravely sharing a really tender, emotional song at a creative sharing circle that I hosted. She felt really proud of herself afterward, but at the same time felt some old emotions of unworthiness surfacing from being so vulnerable. In our next one-on-one session, we both recognized the need to give time and space for re-grounding. Rather than focusing on the next song or the next brave stretch, I asked her what would feel very nourishing for her system. She felt called to talk through the experience and process how it linked to her past. Then Sandra noticed the singing bowl on my mantle and voiced a spontaneous desire to receive some sound healing. I asked her if she wanted to sit or lie down, and she loved the option of resting and lying down. A gentle, relaxed smile emerged on her face as she soaked in the loving intention coming from my voice and the singing bowl. After 20 minutes, she felt refreshed and nourished. By leaning into support and resource, her nervous system settled into calmness after the rapid heartrate leaping feeling that lingered from her big jump into the Zone of Growth.

The idea of compassionate pacing is adapted from the practice of pendulation, which is a concept I first learned from the work of trauma-healing expert Peter A. Levine, creator of Somatic Experiencing therapy. Dr. Levine observed that moving through difficulty is most effective when paired with consciously returning your awareness to something that makes you feel safe and settled. You can swing back and forth between the rhythms of expansion and contraction by attuning to your body's needs for rest and positive resources.

A common fear is that we will be wasting time if we take a pause from the Zone of Growth or what society calls "productivity." Yet I have found that when I am aligned with my body's natural pacing, I am more focused and energized. During the pause, creative ideas and solutions have room to pop into my mind. And I help to protect my body from the pain and breakdown that always seems to come anytime I push myself to move too fast or hard. Compassionate pacing is like the beating rhythm of a healthy heart—the pressure is always followed immediately by release and pause. I daresay this life-giving muscle embodies intelligent, sustainable movement.

Choice Instead of Pressure

I began my decades-long journey of embracing compassionate pacing through the breath. As a high-schooler, I gravitated towards perfectionism and constant pushing as a way to feel slightly safer and in control. But my body gave me subtle nudges that I needed to slow down. I remember the ache in my side and the harsh coldness of the air hitting my lungs when I was trying to run the mile in high school gym class. At some point, there was no alternative but to slow down and catch my breath. In the same way, when being hard on myself brought me to my knees with exhaustion and tears, I needed to ease up on the self-imposed pressure.

Fortunately, I began to learn breathing techniques with my high school singing teacher, Tina. I only thought of deep breathing as a way to improve my singing; it took me years to realize how it also improved my life. Long before I was ready to acknowledge my pain and heal my authentic expression, I learned how to feel a little bit more grounded by taking a deep breath and turning the air into sound. These years I spent focusing on breathing were actually the beginning of my healing, without my conscious awareness that I even had perfectionism, trauma, or unworthiness lurking beneath the surface. Music gave me time and space to build myself up.

Bringing your voice into the world is not a process to be forced or rushed. Yet if you are like me, you may notice places where you are unnecessarily putting pressure on yourself. My client Cassie noticed she had the habit of playing small, and as a courageous feminist, she put pressure on herself to make an ever-increasing impact in her work as a coach. I get it, because empowering women to spread their world-changing wisdom is the undercurrent of my work and the groups I lead. But the thing is, playing small feels icky because it comes from restriction and repression. Something in our lives has made us feel like it's not safe or feasible for us to play really big. When you heal those old patterns of repression, you have the power of choice. When you feel called, you can share your voice, work, and wisdom in front of bigger audiences or in deeper, more aligned ways. But that is in no way meant to be a mandate to express yourself bravely all the time. We are cyclical creatures who also need seasons of rest and reflection. When you have the power of choice, you can contract back into moments of silence and pause that feel peaceful rather than icky and repressed.

Understanding the Role of Breath

Taking a moment to notice your breathing is truly an act of self-compassion because breath is one of the most fundamental ways that we receive nourishment. When we allow in life-giving air, it feeds our cells oxygen to live and thrive. Then we exhale the carbon dioxide that our cells no longer need, which provides just the nourishment that the trees and plants around us are craving. I know firsthand that it's really easy to take this nourishing process for granted, yet bringing awareness to how you breathe is the foundation of voice work. And as an amazing benefit, deep breathing has been shown in many studies to calm the nervous system and slow down racing thoughts.

Remembering our foundation of self-compassion as we explore, let's take a quick glimpse into the mechanics of breathing and sounding. Your breath powers your vocal sound, allowing your muscular vocal cords to vibrate with ease. The steady stream of your exhale is like a strong breeze that carries the kite of your vocal cords as they vibrate to create sound.

Each inhale starts with the diaphragm. A large muscle somewhat resembling a shallow, upside-down bowl, the diaphragm is located beneath the lungs. It extends to the front, back, and sides of our body, nestled between the outline of our ribs. When I show clients my diaphragm model, most of them are surprised by how big it is. This is one powerful muscle. When the diaphragm moves down, it creates a vacuum in the lungs, allowing fresh air to rush into our bodies. Once the diaphragm has begun its descent, breathing can be effortless. As we allow our lungs to fill with life-giving air, our abdomen will naturally expand outward. This is due to the diaphragm pushing our organs down and out gently. Your lungs expand like balloons because we are preparing for the Goddess Voice party. (Cha-cha-cha!)

Our chest and back can also expand significantly as we inhale. The intercostal muscles between the ribs facilitate this expansion, and our ribcage can easily grow bigger by stretching the cartilage that connects our ribs to our breastbone. The lowest ribs have the most room to expand. Along our spine, the rib attachments are actually mobile joints that can swing outward as our lungs fill up with air. So your ribs don't really form a cage at all—they form a flexible support system that is constantly expanding and contracting. Much like the practice of compassionate pacing, our ribs are in an ongoing dance to support our well-being.

I also want to note that your breathing naturally changes with activity level. If you're not exerting yourself, singing, or speaking in a conscious way, it's common to breathe with only a small degree of diaphragmatic movement and rib expansion. But when you want to access your vocal power, learning to fill the lower portion of your lungs and send your air outward in a steady stream will transform the quality and power of your sound.

Are you becoming hyper-aware of your breath yet? It may all make sense, especially if you've done breathwork in the past. But don't worry if things feel confusing right now or if your experience doesn't match my description. For example, my student Kathy came into vocal coaching with a common habit where she actually sucked in her belly on the inhale rather than letting it expand. She laughed nervously when she realized she had unconsciously been breathing in a way that caused constriction, but I reassured her there is absolutely no shame in having habits of shallow breathing. It was a clear opportunity for more self-compassion. If you tend to pull your belly in on the inhale like Kathy, this forces your body to only fill the upper part of the lungs, which don't have as much capacity for air. If you have this habit of shallow breathing, start by lying down on your back with a hand or an object on your belly. Slowly and consciously train yourself to let your lungs fill like balloons that push your belly outward as you breathe in.

When your muscles are untrained, it's common for your exhale to be somewhat uneven, with the air coming out in slight fits and spurts. This can create a wavering or cracking in your vocal tone. That's why I am always working with students on the skill of exhaling a steady stream of air. For some people, it's easiest to monitor this steady exhale by paying attention to the movement of their bellies. Once the inhale has pushed the organs outward, you can notice your belly slowly returning to its neutral position as the diaphragm moves upward. For other people, it's easier to focus on the movement of the lower ribs. After your ribs expand in the back, sides, and front on the inhale, you want your ribs to be slowly coming in and resting downward as you create sound. With time and practice, tuning into your big-mama expansive breath will ramp up the power of your vocal tone. (I promise!) Allowing your body to expand with the breath creates an energetic foundation for being able to play big and make yourself heard.

One more thing—speaking and singing almost always happen on the exhale. If you remember from earlier in this chapter, I mentioned that the exhale promotes our relaxation response. Since we are often making our exhale even longer than the inhale when we make sounds, we are naturally helping ourselves relax. And a relaxed body and mind will make it easier for us to access more self-compassion. How cool is that?

Breath as Receiving and Giving

Having worked as a voice coach since 2007, I have witnessed a lot of benefits from understanding the mechanics of breathing. But the disadvantage of focusing on physiology is that we can get hyper-analytical and stuck in our heads around how to breathe. It's easy to get into a pattern of trying hard instead of allowing our breath to flow naturally. We can start to get self-critical and worry if we are "doing it right." That's why I also bring in the energetics of breathing, to help us drop below our minds and enjoy the experience of respiration and sounding. This combination of bodily and energetic awareness comes together in a practice I call Open Channel Breathing.

As I mentioned earlier, inhalation is a primal act of receiving nourishment. To help connect with the feeling of receiving, I like to imagine the oxygen that enters my lungs being carried to every cell of my body, giving them all little smiley faces upon receiving this nourishment. If you ever feel like it's hard to receive so much goodness, that is a reminder to compassionately reassure yourself with some gentle words.

After you breathe in and receive nourishment, your exhale can become a gift of intention that you send out into the world. Now this doesn't mean that every vocal sound you create has to be pretty or positive. Our voice is a tool for expressing the wide range of emotions we naturally feel as humans, and it's powerful to use your voice to express anger or sadness or frustration rather than keeping it locked inside. But when it comes to what we practice and cultivate, I find that all expressions come back to our longing to embody Divine Love. So don't downplay the power of your intention as a gift. When you are speaking or singing, your vocal cords push and vibrate the air to create sound waves which can be a healing, revitalizing, tender experience for yourself and others. Thus the energetic aspects of Open Channel Breathing invite you to receive nourishment on the inhale and add the words, "send it out as love" on the exhale. If you are feeling a strong call into a different intention as you breathe out, you can speak or sing words of your choosing.

Unleash Your Goddess Voice Practice No. 1: Open Channel Breathing

Alright, Goddesses, we're almost ready to breathe in some nourishment! You can practice Open Channel Breathing silently or add sound depending on where you are. Adding the aspect of speaking or singing out loud is beautiful to practice in the morning, before bed, on a break, or to prepare for a performance or presentation. If you want to make Open Channel Breathing a regular habit, tying your practice in with another activity in your regular life will make it easier to remember. For example, you can set the intention of practicing for a few minutes right after you wake up in the morning, right after you take a shower, or on your coffee break at work. You can also use a cue, such as anytime you feel the urge to check your phone. When you experience the urge, then you know it is time to practice conscious breathing first.

Sometimes it can feel overwhelming to try to incorporate a new practice into your life, especially if you are someone who notices feelings of guilt any time you don't make time for the new habit. You may catch yourself thinking thoughts along the lines of:

"I'm bad at breathwork."

"I can never make any real changes."

"I'm not bold enough for this Goddess Voice stuff, so why bother trying the practice?"

If you have even mild versions of these thoughts, ask yourself if you would speak to a close friend the way you are speaking to yourself. Chances are you would be a lot more kind and encouraging with your friend. Remember the practice of self-compassion starts with bringing awareness to your thoughts, words, and actions, then injecting kindness and compassion into your day. It's about reminding yourself it is okay to be human and make mistakes. By easing ourselves out of self-criticism, we actually free up more motivation to try again instead of giving up.

Anytime you are beginning breath work, checking with a medical provider first is a good idea if you are pregnant or have health conditions. I also want to mention that this kind of deep breathing may make some people lightheaded at first. Feel free to stop the exercise at any time if it is causing discomfort. You may also wish to work up to filling your lungs more fully by taking just a few deeper breaths each day.

Occasionally people feel more anxious or even panicked when they are trying to breathe deeply. Our brains can get into a loop of making a lot of effort to breathe deeply and then become anxious if the opposite is taking place. If this happens to you, follow your body's impulses. You may feel drawn to making a sighing sound on your exhales, as sighing naturally lengthens the breath and can release anxiety. It is also perfectly valid to stop focusing on your breath at any time. When you are following what feels right to you, quitting can be self-care. If you are still feeling anxious, remember that you can turn to the Appendix on Calming Down from Overwhelm.

For a recording of this practice, visit saragiita.com/free

Open Channel Breathing

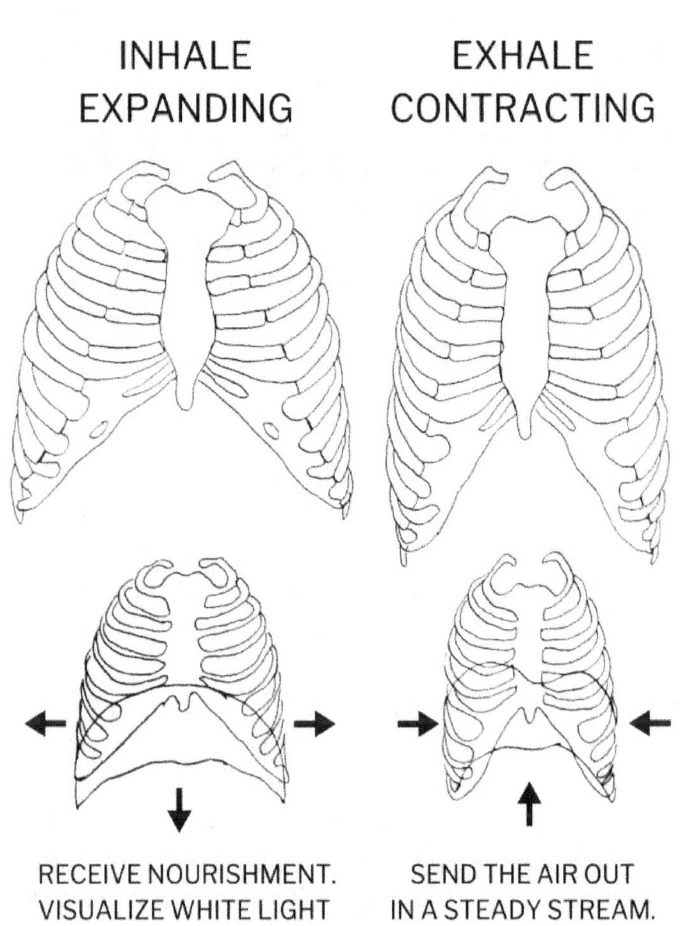

1. Sit, stand, or lie down comfortably with your spine elongated and aligned. Place a hand on your belly button and another on your side ribs. Keep your hands here as you breathe to monitor the expansion and contraction of your lungs.

2. Allow your diaphragm muscle to move downward and push your belly outward, initiating a slow, easy inhale. Notice how the ribs of your lower chest, sides, and back may also expand.

3. When it feels right, silently exhale at a comfortable pace. The diaphragm will steadily return to its highly domed shape and your abdomen and ribs will come inward again.

4. Repeat these silent breaths three or four times, and then rest with a few normal breaths.

5. Now we are going to add visualization. Allow yourself to receive nourishing white light that fills your lungs as you breathe in. Life-giving and abundant, imagining this white light is a way to invite Divine Grace into your being as you inhale.

6. As you exhale, speak or sing the words, "send it out as love." Your sound is a gift of compassionate kindness for yourself and others.

7. Continue the practice of receiving nourishment and sending it out as love for as long as you wish.

CHAPTER 2

Acknowledging
Your Voice Ruptures

I've been paralyzed, I realize,
scared to speak my mind
I've been silent, and compliant,
leaving my Voice behind,
Yes, society has taught me
Not to use my Voice
But I'm the one, when the day is done,
Who has to make the choice.

I want to sing out.

When Did You Learn to Tamp Down Your Voice?

Engaging our vocal cords is our most innate form of communication and self-expression. When a baby emerges from the womb, making a sound is the first sign of health and vitality that the little one gives to their caregivers. Everyone in the room breathes a sigh of relief when they hear that first wailing cry! As infants, we instinctively know how to scream for our needs, trusting our vocal expression to communicate and keep us safe. As our development progresses, we experience a huge creative flourishing and begin to expand the diversity of our vocal sounds. Through playful experimentation, we start to mimic the adults and older kids around us and learn to speak. We naturally have the ability to express whatever wants to arise, be it an emotion, a word, a sound, or a song.

Despite this amazing potential of our voices, most of us learned really early on to filter and tamp down our Goddess Voice. For those kids who followed a fairly typical developmental pattern, they eventually started to notice the power of their sounds to elicit reactions in others, provoking everything from loving adoration to exasperated sighs to angry shouts. Wanting to please our caregivers makes sense—after all, we needed them to survive as little children.

This external pressure may lead us to subconsciously narrow and restrict what we allow ourselves to express based on what garners approval. The toddler who burps, slurps, snorts, honks, giggles, groans, growls, howls, snarls, and screams may meet parental disapproval and later peer pressure to narrow and polish what they allow to come through their voice. Possibly combining with the pain of unmet emotional needs, this pressure to polish leads us to subconsciously splinter off parts of ourselves that become wounded inner child aspects.

By the time each child reaches age 10 or 11, they are likely restricting themselves to speaking, laughing, grunting, possibly singing, and occasionally sighing. Shouting and crying probably happen too, though people of all ages might receive some disapproval for these innate human emotional expressions, depending on their circumstances. Shouting at a sporting event is fine, but shouting at school is not. Crying in private is fine, but crying in public is not. Our self-expression becomes a dance of either fitting in or rebelling against those who tell us to fit in. Either way, it is a reaction to something EX-ternal rather than a communication of something IN-ternal. The ancestral heritage of our ancient human hearts lifted in song becomes buried and forgotten.

In addition to ongoing cultural pressure, we may experience acute incidents of our pure expression being shut down. I've given a name to these moments when we learned to tamp down our voices: voice ruptures. Whether we became hyper-vigilant to pleasing others, started trying to create safety through our communication, or learned to brace and armor ourselves, a voice rupture constricts the free flow of our Goddess Voices. It limits what we allow ourselves to express from that day forward. A voice rupture is a form of trauma.

You might have lived through a voice rupture the day you gave a presentation in school and the other kids laughed at you. Or you might have internalized the feeling of dismissal that came from sharing your heartfelt opinion with an adult and being interrupted or criticized. You might have learned self-consciousness from a car ride when you joyfully sang along to the radio and your mom said you sounded like a goat. You may have plunged into the humiliation and confusion of your music teacher telling you to lip-synch the words instead of singing with the class. These "little T traumas" are the moments when you subconsciously learned to shut down your voice. Of course, you still spoke and perhaps even sang after the rupture, but the imprint of those experiences may have created a filter that caused you to narrow your self-expression. You may have also experienced the "big T traumas" that taught you to dim your voice and play small: sexual assault, rape, abuse, neglect, chaos, discrimination, poverty, and violence.

Voice ruptures can also happen vicariously, especially during the impressionable years of our youth. When someone close to you is criticized or disrespected for standing out or speaking up, this may cause you to unconsciously limit your own self-expression. The same goes for seeing people being torn down on the news or other forms of media. When we see someone being ostracized just for being themselves, this can impact our psyche especially if we share traits with them such as gender, race, age, sexual orientation, interests, or national origin.

Inherited trauma can also lead to the repression of our voices. We live in a world where trauma is the air we breathe. It has become a normalized part of the culture, and virtually all of us grew up in family systems where there was some degree of trauma. If our well-intentioned caregivers didn't have the resources, opportunities, and knowledge of how to heal, we likely took on some of those same traumatic patterns. Recognizing inherited trauma may initially feel like a betrayal of our families, but it is not a criticism of our caretakers, who were simply doing the best they could. Acknowledging the ways our self-expression has been thwarted through the generations is the first step to healing.

In the beginning, it's often hard to see how this range of trauma from the outside culture has affected your voice. Voice ruptures can be hard to spot. That's because dimming your voice is not a cognitive decision. If your nervous system senses a threat in those moments of your voice being disrespected, your biology will make the split-second decision to go into an emergency response such as fight, flight, or freeze. "Fight" might look like putting up your fists, but it also might look like angry words or standing up for yourself. "Flight" might be actually running away, or it might look like avoiding confrontation. When it comes to the freeze response, this may take the form of immobilization, numbness, or "checking out" of stressful situations.

If you receive proper care and compassion in the aftermath to repair the situation, then your nervous system may have the chance to do what it was designed to do and come back to a healthy, relaxed, regulated baseline. When you are in a regulated state, you can respond to situations calmly. For the "little T traumas," returning to regulation can come in the form of a compassionate, nonjudgmental conversation with someone loving who reassures you your voice and self-expression are just right. For "big T traumas" the professional support of a therapist or well-trained healer can help to repair the nervous system. Either way, your resilient nature can heal any and all moments of your voice being disrespected, dismissed, or devalued so they no longer limit your self-expression.

But far too often we are left to suffer in silence and isolation and told to just "get over it." Then your body may stay stuck in that emergency response and limit your self-expression to help you feel safer. This may look like defensiveness and angry expression if you tend to default into a fight response. It could also look like a tendency to stay distracted, avoid confrontation, and opt out of any challenging social engagement if your physiology is stuck in a flight response. For my past self, defaulting to freeze mode led me to shut down and narrow my whole self-expression in order to stay small, pleasing, palatable, and safe.

To help you understand if you are living with voice ruptures, I've listed some symptoms of unhealed trauma from a video called Trauma Symptoms of Individual & Collective

Trauma by expert Amy Rose, LCSW. Keep in mind that not everyone will have all of these symptoms.

- Intrusive memories or flashbacks
- Avoidance
- Feeling numb
- Difficulty sleeping
- Difficulty focusing
- Mood swings
- Startling easily
- Individualism/reluctance to ask for help
- Minimizing your past experiences
- Difficulty making decisions
- Believing you will only be happy in the future when you get somewhere else
- Feeling a sense of urgency
- Trying to please, appease, save, or rescue others
- Feeling a sense of scarcity and lack
- Rage
- Need for control
- Domination or needing to be at the top

Body check-in: How are you feeling in your body as you consider the symptoms of trauma and the moments when your voice was partially shut down? Are there any movements or sounds that would feel good to help release tension?

If you tend to feel regret or shame about how you reacted to any trauma, keep in mind that these emergency responses are all non-cognitive. They are automatic, lifesaving biological processes that deserve to be honored and respected. So if you didn't scream or run away during abuse, or if you didn't stand up for yourself when someone addressed you with a hateful slur, I hope you can bring yourself more compassion to the way your system acted to try to keep you safe.

Why We Hesitate to Uncover Our Voice Ruptures

In addition to the ways we have reacted to trauma, our ancestral legacy can also make the process of reclaiming our voices feel like a big internal risk for women and people who don't conform to the traditional gender boxes. We are going against our training and thousands of years of conditioning that aim to keep us from recognizing our voice ruptures. On some level, we know that seeing and healing the ways our voices have been tamped down will reveal a huge, hidden reservoir of power. Once glimpsed, our powerful voices can feel scary to the people around us, and to those who wish to maintain power over us. Healing our wounds to unleash our power can also bring up internal fears. We all have parts of our psyche that would prefer to maintain the status quo.

Because of this hard-to-spot pressure, staying quiet and small has been the safest bet for women over millennia. In generations past, if women stepped into their power, they literally could have been killed through witch burnings, stonings, or wife beatings. For women of color, slavery and colonial domination drastically increased the dangers of speaking up (or even speaking at all). Those fearful patterns have not disappeared—speaking up and owning your worth can still feel like you are risking death. While we will explore how to heal those anxieties throughout the book, let's take a moment to honor the intensity of the fear we may have inherited. Given our legacy, it takes courage to even pick up this book and consider deepening your vocal empowerment. You are a warrior goddess!

In addition to the patterns of feeling unsafe, some women shy away from speaking up confidently because they don't want to seem arrogant or narcissistic. They have observed others who use their voice to steam-roll everyone who stands in their way. But this destructive brand of confidence is usually false bravado. It comes from an old belief that a person's worth is measured by how high they stand in a hierarchy. Ick. Squashing others is not my definition of being powerful. This is a new framework that leaves behind beliefs of certain people's voices being more deserving, important, or better than others. It helps us express ourselves from a place of authentic worthiness and gives us the energetic, bodily experience of feeling whole and enough. When we are connected to our expansive nature, we will be guided by humility as we recognize all beings are inherently worthy on the level of the soul. We are not tearing anyone down by claiming our radiant voice. In fact, it's the opposite: when we amplify our sense of compassionate power and worth, we uplift others with our light.

Even with this egalitarian framework, you may still have hesitations about acknowledging your voice ruptures. Seeing the ways our voices have been tamped down can almost feel like an accusation or criticism to those we love who unconsciously taught us to be nice and please others at all costs. We don't want to betray our families and our ancestors. Or perhaps we don't want to become too cynical about the culture we live in. So we repeat the mantra that the moments of being disrespected are "no big deal." Downplaying our voice ruptures is natural and is often rooted in a desire to maintain our ties to others. But it is based on a false dichotomy. When you are taught to always be nice and put others first, it implies that speaking up for yourself is selfish.

Going against those expectations of niceness could cause you to lose those you love.

One woman described to me, "In our abusive house, it was disrespectful for me to speak up because in order to do that, I had to go against my parents. Any attempt to stand up for myself or even disagree with them was insubordination. Until I graduated from college, I couldn't disagree with them. The words wouldn't come out of my mouth. I wasn't strong enough. However, I sang the shit out of the songs in choir." She found an outlet to express herself without risking upsetting her parents, which shows how voice ruptures can only partially dam up the Goddess Voice. Even if the flow becomes limited in certain areas of your life, your self-expression will find ways around the obstructions.

In childhood it may feel like being nice is the only way to preserve certain relationships, but once you reach adulthood it can be possible to maintain those loving ties while reclaiming the power of your voice. As you learn to step into your power and prioritize your own needs, most of the other people around you will unconsciously adapt and begin to treat you with even more respect. If you had relationships that depended on you subtly downplaying your needs and voice, those people may also rise to meet you at your new level of self-respect. Or they may drift away. Losing those ties can be painful, yet also liberating.

Another reason we may hesitate to uncover our voice ruptures stems from the desire to stay positive and live in the present. Many people fear that looking earnestly at their past experiences and acknowledging the wounding will cause them to become mired in negativity. I totally get it. Yet I want to be clear that acknowledgment is different than dwelling on the past, which has an element of unconsciously replaying past regrets. Acknowledgment, in contrast, is rooted in presence; you shine the light of awareness into pockets of your experience that deserve your loving attention. It's an affirmation that you matter. Healing begins when you start to recognize how you have been impacted by any and all voice ruptures. While societal notions might give us the idea that being able to ignore and brush off an incident makes us strong, that myth tends to lead to avoidance, armoring, and bypassing our pain. When we deeply acknowledge the pain we have experienced, our soul can guide us to heal and move forward.

Finally, we might disregard our voice ruptures because we have labeled our experiences as small or insignificant. I saw this pattern in myself when I compared my "big T traumas" to my "little T traumas." Once I had acknowledged my wounding through the process of therapy, it was easy to see how the two experiences of sexual assault diminished my confidence and self-expression. My voice was clearly dishonored and disrespected, so those incidents seemed significant enough to demand my attention. But I did not validate the smaller moments that impacted my self-expression, like when I sang loudly and my sister and her friend made fun of me. Or when I went to my friend's house only to have her ignore me while she talked to her crush. When I arrived, she put the phone on mute just long enough to tell me to be silent because he thought I was a dork.

After years of dismissing those voice ruptures, I finally decided every little moment was worth healing. I released my judgments about what constitutes an impactful experience. Seemingly minor incidents can have a major impact. An experience that someone else may be able to laugh off could damage my feeling of self-worth. As a highly sensitive person, I am deeply affected by each life experience. I have come to see that this trait is a strength, not a weakness. My ability to feel deeply enriches my capacity as a coach, teacher, writer, musician, and human being. Yet if I expect myself to just grow a thick skin and stop being affected by experiences of disrespect, I am left feeling like there's something wrong with me. That's why acknowledgment and self-acceptance are key steps of healing. Only once I was willing to identify where I was hurting could I begin to explore and develop the healing practices that allowed me to go from fearful and confined to embodying bold, joyous self-expression.

Beliefs, Stories, and Eye Rolls

Along with physical tension that may be stored in your body from voice ruptures, subconscious stories and beliefs may have developed around your voice. Oh, I know. We hear so much about beliefs running the show that you may have the urge to roll your eyes. But once you're done, take a look at this list of beliefs that can emerge from voice ruptures and see if any are similar to a critical voice in your head.

- "No one wants to hear what I have to say."
- "It's selfish to advocate for myself."
- "Other people's needs are more important than mine."
- "People won't like me if I don't work hard to earn their approval."
- "My opinion doesn't matter."
- "My voice sounds funny."
- "It's not safe to stand up for myself."
- "Everyone is against me."
- "I have to constantly defend myself."
- "I have to prove myself."
- "I can't handle criticism."

- "I'm not going to share my voice if no one will listen."
- "People will think I'm causing trouble if I speak up."

It usually takes some digging to uncover these kinds of negative beliefs around your voice, and Chapter 3 will give you tools to gradually shift those beliefs. For now, just imagine yourself standing with more rootedness in one of these healthy beliefs:

- "The world needs my voice."
- "I deserve to express myself and be heard."
- "My needs are equally important to everyone else's needs."
- "I can safely stand up for myself now."
- "My voice is just right."
- "I am strong enough to handle people's unconscious reactions when I speak my truth."
- "I don't have to earn anyone's approval."
- "My Goddess Voice is a gift to myself and others."

Honoring the Ways we have Held On

Acknowledgment comes in its own time. Until we are ready to recognize the ways our powerful voices have been constricted, we will still find ways to carry on. For me, trying to be good and please others was my primary coping mechanism after my voice ruptures. With my self-worth and sense of safety based entirely on other people's opinions of me, dimming my Goddess Voice was a subconscious strategy to be accepted and liked. Fear ran the show throughout my teens and twenties. Though I never would have admitted it, I was desperately terrified of not being good enough.

On the surface, it was a different story. I would have told you that, sure, I was good at plenty of things. I had friends, I had skills, I had talents. (Watch me do jazz hands! Listen to me sing!) Yet underneath there was a voice saying I was bad. I was *bad, bad, bad,* and I needed to hide it. I thought that no one could see the darkness inside as long as I worked hard to be perfect. As long as I kept everything buried. Looking back, I feel proud of how well I hung on. Painting on a smile when I was screaming inside showed a certain resilience, which served me at the time.

When pain hits, we all have coping mechanisms. I spent some years beating myself up for my "unhealthy" patterns, and I want to highlight the message that our coping mechanisms usually develop without our conscious awareness. So let's forgive ourselves for how we held on. You are worthy, no matter what bedraggled journey led you to the doorway of unearthing your Goddess Voice. I don't like to categorize coping mechanisms as "healthy" or "unhealthy," because that implies unkind judgment on a pattern that emerged to help us survive. Why waste time beating ourselves up about the sometimes illogical ways we have sought self-preservation? Rather than judging coping mechanisms as "good" or "bad," I prefer to see them as stages in a journey. Burying my past experiences of being devalued worked for a while, until I had grown strong enough in other areas of my life that running away no longer felt like an option. I realized that avoidance was hurting me, and with time I moved into more helpful strategies, like self-compassion, acknowledgment, and inner child healing.

In the spirit of honoring our journeys, I share my story of childhood and teenage sexual trauma in the upcoming sections. Your story of learning to dim your voice may be very different than mine. It might have been a slow drip of poison rather than an intense shock of shame. What matters is that we recognize our resilience. We have adapted to difficult circumstances. We have carried on. No matter what experiences led to your voice ruptures, I hope this story helps you bring love and acceptance to any pockets of shame from the past. And if reading about overcoming trauma does not serve you right now, I wish for you to honor your needs and skip ahead to the practice at the end of the chapter.

In the Time Before the Pain

Once upon a time, I lived without shame. I sang and danced and dressed up like a queen in a purple satin dress. Whenever my best friends Mirabai and Jonnah came over, we would twirl and climb trees and run through the sprinklers. I played. I painted. I danced. I knew what it felt like to be radiant.

One day in preschool, the parents came for a special program to hear us sing. Folding chairs filled the crowded classroom; the walls were covered with the ABCs and our glitter-encrusted artwork. Parents and grandparents and siblings shifted in their chairs, waiting expectantly. We obediently sang a few songs as a group, and then we joined our parents in the audience.

Next, the teacher asked if anyone would like to come up to sing a song by themselves. I forgot to raise my hand. I was too busy leaping out of my grey metal chair and running to the front of the room. When I turned to see all the faces, I hesitated. But once I started singing, my face lit up with enthusiasm again. I was all smiles and joy.

The Day I Lost My Voice (Trigger Warning)

But then it happened. The pain. The sweet bedtime story stops here, as silence and shame are imposed on the innocent girl. I was five years old. Almost six. My mom gave me permission to walk home and play with my kindergarten friend and her sister after we got off the school bus. In 1990, no one thought twice about children walking along the sidewalk without an adult in sight. We skipped along, past the one-story frame houses. We ventured through the dark tunnel of the underpass. We turned right, down the street, and into their clapboard house.

We were supposed to be quiet at her house because her dad was sleeping. But we were children, so we were laughing and giggling and making noise. Awakened and angry, he marched us into the basement and said he needed to punish us. I huddled in the corner, watching in terror as he "punished" my friend and her sister. Then I found myself naked on the basement floor, lying helpless on the orange shag carpet. He was on top of me. I was gasping for breath. I felt pain between my legs. I am going to die, I thought.

As I look back on the scene, the other details blur together. I cannot reliably recount the order of events, or say with certainty what caused the pain that got trapped in my tender body. But I do know this: I survived. I survived! I SURVIVED!

Afterward, he told me it was my fault. He threatened to punish me again if I told anyone. He told me they would know how bad I was if I let anyone see what had happened. Then he let me go home with his threats ringing in my ears.

I walked home and curled up in my bed. I vomited. My mom gazed down at me with affection as I told her I was sick. She put her hand on my forehead. "Hmmm, no fever." She brought me a towel, and helped me change my clothes, and she climbed onto the bed to pull the corners of the clean sheets around the mattress. The sunlight streamed through the curtains she had made herself, as I stared up at the faces in the wood grain of the bunk bed that I shared with my sister. Part of me wished I could tell her what happened. But I was too scared. *She will be mad at me. Everyone will hate me if they know. And then he will hurt me again.* I believed it was better this way. It was safer to curl up silently, and have my mom pat my shoulder and tell me that she needed to go cook dinner, but that I could call her if I needed her. *I need you, Mom. I need you,* I wanted to scream.

But I had no voice.

Left in fearful silence, I wondered, "If I never think about this pain, will it go away? Can I bury it so deep that no one will ever know?" Allowing myself to forget may have been my salvation. My psyche knew how to adapt and cope-thank goodness repression is possible when we don't yet have the support for healing to be an option. I pushed the images and memories back into the murky recesses of my mind, like dark shadows. I floated outside of my body because feeling sensations might mean stepping on a land mine. But the shame. That I could not push away. Shame poisoned every area of my life, the runoff permeating my once-clear waters.

Soon after that horrible afternoon, my dad got a job in a new town and our family moved to a new neighborhood. *Goodbye, little rabbits in our backyard. Goodbye, weeping willow by the bus stop. Goodbye, mean man who knows how bad I am.* I never saw my friend or her father again, making it easier to pretend the abuse never happened.

Wearing a Mask after Voice Ruptures

I developed an unconscious motto after having my voice shut down: Do not let the darkness show. Be absolutely perfect in every way, because slipping up will cause something horrible to happen again. Be good, wear a mask, and hide your true self. As a child hiding an unspeakable trauma, being perfect meant trying to please the adults in my life. I lived for praise. I would sing songs and make up dances for my mom, performing on the scratched brown linoleum floor in our new suburban home. "You are so charming," she would say. I remember the feeling of making my mom smile and basking in her approval.

Once I entered the murky waters of adolescence, I felt the need to fortify my mask, creating an over-achieving persona that I could show to the world. And the mask of perfectionism worked for me, most of the time at least. I could buckle down and study like crazy. I could practice my piano songs diligently before the competition. I could wake up early before school to spend some quality time with my makeup and curling iron to look as pretty as possible. If I worried and fretted enough, I could be in control about 80% of the time.

But, oh, the painful 20%. The tears and shame and flopping about like a fish out of water when life spiraled out of control. When my best friend and I would get into a fight, or when I didn't get the part in the school play, or when an angry red pimple became all I could see in the mirror—then there was no way to keep the darkness at bay. Then I was left with a tear-stained face to show the world. Crying made me feel weak and out of control, and I was ashamed that I could not truly hide my vulnerable side.

This is how it goes with masks. Voice ruptures may make us feel like we have no choice but to show a curated image of ourselves to the world. But life will bring the moments when our masks are torn down and our authentic emotions peek through the cracks. Mostly, those glimpses of my authentic voice made me feel out of control. But my true self found one way to peek out from the mask and express herself: through music. When I was seven years old, I had begged my mom to let me take piano lessons. By the time I was a teenager, the piano had become more than a hobby. It became a source of solace. I could express my emotions in an abstract way, letting my wounded deeper self receive praise and validation. I could be seen and could shine on stage in a way that felt safe.

I Said 'No' (Trigger Warning)

In other areas of my life, I was not so confident. As a teenager, I felt desperate for male attention. I thought having a boyfriend was my ticket out of childhood. Deep down, I wanted the validation, the reassurance that I was worth paying attention to. I was still a long way off from discovering how to give myself that validation and love. In my high school, I felt like I was too smart and too high-strung to attract any guys. So, I soaked up the attention of anyone I could find outside of school.

When I was fifteen, my parents went out of town for a few days to celebrate their anniversary. My eighteen-year-old sister was left in charge, and my parents had every reason to trust us both. We showed them only our best-behaved, overachiever faces. But my sister was getting bolder as she neared high school graduation, and she decided to invite over a dozen friends for a Saturday night party. Her flamboyant friend Darren had ambitions to become a chef and was mixing his own cocktail creations. All her friends knew not to invite anyone beyond their immediate friend group; it was to be a small party.

My sister did allow me to invite two of my own friends, though. I called up Debbie and Melissa, friends of mine since elementary school. And they brought over three guys they had met at the ice arena earlier that day. The guys were assholes; I could tell. They had a fifteen-minute conversation about Britney Spears' boobs. Yet one of them was cute. And he seemed to like me. Me! I ignored his sexist comments, for the word "sexist" was not even in my vocabulary yet. I convinced myself he might have a better side, and I sat with him alone at our wooden dining room table as he chugged his alcohol from a large bottle. I slowly sipped a fruity cocktail, for I was still a good girl, who had tasted alcohol but had not yet been drunk.

We talked, flirted, leaning in closer. And finally, we began kissing. My heart raced with the thrill of kissing someone new, the third boy I had ever kissed. And then he asked if there was someplace more private we could go. I hesitated. Well, there was my room. But was that a good idea? I wavered before answering. I liked him. And he seemed to like me. So I convinced myself: I'm not one of those low self-esteem girls who is afraid to speak her mind. I can say "no" if he wants to go farther than I do.

Up the stairs we went. "Click" went the lock. Off came the clothes. And I thought I could say no. And I did. But I was unprepared for my dozens of "No's" being met with his shaming words and attempts to convince me to perform oral sex. I was a frigid bitch. I was a prude. I would never know until I tried. Like a broken record, I said, "No, I'm not doing that" as he pushed me down toward his genitals. Each time I spoke, I grew less sure of myself. His insults penetrated deeply. But my words still came, murmured through my purple braces: "No." So he gave up, and I got up and turned on the light to find my clothes.

I thought we were done, and we were leaving it at "frigid bitch refuses to help the guy get his needs met." But then he came up behind me and pushed me against the bed. And I went into freeze mode. I did nothing. I said nothing. My throat was tight, mute. I stayed as still as a possum, playing dead, as he attempted to penetrate my anus. Stabbing, jabbing, pushing, my knees cutting into the hard wooden bed frame. Over and over again. My comfy bunk bed, my haven, became a painful place. And all I could do was tighten my muscles, keeping him out, silently praying for everything to be over as quickly as possible.

Why didn't I scream or struggle or run away? Why did my voice leave me? I have asked myself this question so many times looking back. And here is the answer: because all the training I ever received in life made it clear I should do what was expected of me. I should please others. And he wore me down so completely that I had no strength left to refuse him. I became the girl he expected me to be: a girl who felt so worthless that she would become an object for sexual gratification. At age fifteen, I was unable to acknowledge that I had been assaulted. All I knew were the maxims of rape culture: "It's a girl's fault for wearing slutty clothes or for getting herself into that situation in the first place. It's unfair to get a guy worked up but not help him reach orgasm. A girl's job is to make everyone else happy." I didn't even realize that sexual assault could happen from someone you liked. I had heard about rape: that was when a stranger attacked you and violently forced you to have sex. Vaginal sex. But disrespectful behavior, treading over my boundaries, shaming me into complying: that was just The Way Guys Are. Years later, I learned that this assumption is part of rape culture, or the cultural attitudes that condone sexual violence against all genders.

Since I was experienced at burying my pain, I did not tell my friends about the icky, confused feeling I had afterward. I did not tell them about how he kept pushing me down, or pressuring me, or calling me a prude. I just told them that we made out, and that is how I left it in my mind. I told myself it was simply a weird experience that I did not want to think about. Two years later, a friend of mine was raped and decided to press charges against the perpetrator. I have a deep respect for survivors who report the crimes and fight for justice. But that doesn't make it easy. The legal process was agonizing for my friend, and the perpetrator was found not guilty. I did my best to support her, but never once associated my own experiences with what she was going through. I could not even bear to consider the fact that I had been sexually assaulted.

The Rupture is the Catalyst

If you look at your life as a story, your voice ruptures may be an important catalyst that can set you on a path of healing. Before they are acknowledged, you may have a lurking worry that recognizing your wounds would be the end of the story. Somehow, we fear that awareness would define our story as a tragedy. Yet if we learn to zoom out, each voice rupture is an important event in a much larger timeline of our evolution towards greater freedom and joy.

The story often begins with innocence. You may (or may not) have memories of a time in early childhood when your Goddess Voice had the freedom to play, create, and explore. Taking yourself back to this "time before the pain" can bring tremendous healing. Even if you experienced pressure to dim your voice before reaching the age of conscious memory, you can use your imagination to envision a moment of feeling free to express yourself as a baby. Or perhaps you want to travel back even farther to find that innocent version of yourself, and imagine yourself as a soul existing on a different plane or in a different lifetime. This "time before the pain" represents your natural blueprint of health, or your innate capacity for thriving. Resilient and patient, this blueprint is always within you, even when wounding makes it hard to access. In the same way, your Goddess Voice can never be taken from you.

When voice ruptures pull us away from our soul's innocence, at some point we need to allow ourselves to grieve. It's a tender process when we acknowledge our experiences of our voice being disrespected, devalued, or dismissed. *Mama Mia,* it's easy to accidentally hit the pause button and worry that this moment of struggle is the entire story. Our worst fears will chant, "I am doomed foreeeeevveerrr!" Yet if we are brave enough to accept the invitation, the rupture is the catalyst. Experiences of being disrespected call our attention to the fact that we matter and deserve to reclaim our power. From this point of being broken open, our soul can shine through the cracks and start to guide our journey. Healing, wholeness, and unapologetic self-expression emerge through the process of overcoming.

In reality, there's no end to the story. But if there were, it would be a more nuanced story than simply "happily ever after." The fall from innocence, catalyst, struggle, and healing bring us to greater wholeness. We create more space for our Goddess Voice to be expressed through our being. And we build the resilience to know we can handle the challenges that may come our way in the future. While the mind may still wonder why the voice ruptures happened, all along our soul has maintained a big-picture view of what experiences would guide us to liberation. Our eternal Self guides our healing when we are brave enough to dip below the surface and recognize our voice ruptures as worthy of attention.

Unleash Your Goddess Voice Practice No. 2: Love Letters to Yourself

Now it's your turn, Goddesses! In this practice, you're invited to write two different love letters to yourself: one that acknowledges your voice ruptures, and another that strengthens your awareness of the part of you that is already healed, whole, and radiant.

1. Clear some time and space for journaling. Perhaps light a candle or put on some gentle music.

2. Write yourself a love letter acknowledging the voice ruptures that have come into your awareness. Be sure to soften judgment and bring loving acceptance of all the feelings that arise, knowing no moment of wounding is too small or too big to acknowledge.

3. Next, write a letter from the stance of your soul. What loving words would your soul like to offer the part of you that was hurt by voice ruptures? What vision can your eternal Self communicate to help you know that you can simultaneously be broken open as well as healed, whole, worthy, and free to speak up boldly?

4. If it feels good, read your love letters out loud to yourself.

5. Finish by giving yourself a hug or any act of nurturance that seems doable right now.

CHAPTER 3

Unearthing Your Innate Worth

I am much more than
Who they told me to be
I find my wholeness
Underneath the debris.
I am the ocean,
The volcano, the trees.
Cascading expression,
A voice for all beings.

Tapping Into Your Divine Worth

While you breathe in self-compassion and acknowledge your voice ruptures, you may start to hear the whispers of your Goddess Voice. But don't despair if you're not feeling your glowing vocal power just yet. Our radiance often gets clouded over by the party-crashers of cultural myths and lies we have been fed. Every single one of us has unconsciously absorbed beliefs about ourselves and our voices which may leave us feeling unworthy. So let's get clear on one thing: Your worth is brilliant. Inherent. Unshakable.

There is nothing to earn or prove because you are already enough. Wholeness is your true nature. No matter what level of abundance you are experiencing with relationships, success, money, creativity, or happiness, you are enough. No matter how many people like your post or read your book or see your art or hear you speak, your worth is unchanging.

This sounds really good in theory, right? But in practice, how do we get a felt sense of our worth underneath our self-doubts? I spontaneously began using visualization one day, and the imagery which I received intuitively has brought huge results for myself and my clients. Bringing in my background in yoga and chakra work, I imagined a divine Inner Flame at my third chakra, or the area from the navel up to the diaphragm. This image of the Inner Flame represents our deepest identity as healthy, whole, connected expressions of Divine Love. When you are connected to your inner truth, you know that your voice matters. The beliefs and attitudes that serve your highest good and the highest good of all can shine through. I call these your Inner Flame beliefs.

Once we can find our way back to our Inner Flame of worthiness, the beliefs that keep us in smallness are bound to surface. It's a dialogue that goes back and forth. When you are aligned, you start to feel in your cells that you are a radiant, worthy expression of the Divine. Then a voice or body part or dream or emotion pops up and says, "Umm, excuse me, what about all the times you've been ignored and what about all these places where you don't measure up, and what about all those past failures? Don't expect me to jump right on the worthiness train and sing into the sunset."

That's where opening a dialogue and getting curious can help to unlearn your conditioning. You can learn to ask yourself if a belief about your voice is true, or if it is a distortion that was absorbed from fear-based, outside influence. These are the questions of unlearning your conditioning:

- Where does this belief come from?

- What thoughts and feelings are my own?

- Is this belief a universal truth, or something more transient and pliable?

- Was this viewpoint given to me by individuals and/or a society that view me as an object rather than a fully expressed human being?

- Does this belief serve my highest potential and the good of all beings?

- When I think this thought or engage with this belief, do I feel scared, angry, or helpless? Or do I feel open, connected, and honored?

- What perceived benefit comes from holding on to this viewpoint? (The belief might offer a sense of safety, risk aversion, familiarity, group belonging, etc.)

Recognizing your limiting beliefs is like plugging in a fan to clear the smoke out of your house so you can finally see clearly. Underneath all those hazy patterns and beliefs you have inherited, you will find that you are whole and worthy just as you are. You are a joyous being who deserves to feel, sense, create, and express without the choking restriction of self-doubt.

However, changing those beliefs takes more than an intellectual awareness. It is often a process because some part of our subconscious mind will be scared to let go of the old belief. Let's take the example of my perfectionism. When I asked myself what perceived benefit I received from trying to be perfect, there were a few answers. First of all, I believed perfectionism would reduce the amount of criticism I got from the outside. Since criticism felt like a terrifying monster knocking on my door, I wanted to avoid it at all costs. The second reason I was hesitant to let go of perfectionism came from my belief that my worth had to be earned or proved. I wanted to feel like my life mattered, so my pattern of perfectionism gave me hope that in becoming perfect, I could feel worthy someday in the future. And that third reason… she is a doozy. When I wait until my writing or my songs or my speeches are perfect, that gets me off the hook from actually sharing what I create. It allows me to stay in the cozy, familiar zone of creative flow, without the risks and courage it takes to shine and be seen. Yep, perfectionism and smallness are good buddies.

Though it's still a lesson in progress, I have gradually loosened this belief that perfection equals worthiness by reminding myself that my soul holds unconditional value and importance as an intrinsic part of the whole. Then I am free to let go of the self-harshness of trying to be perfect, while keeping the positive side of the trait: striving to achieve and excel. I can still pursue excellence while giving myself plenty of room to make mistakes, take breaks, and be messy and imperfect. I can remember that what I create is essential to the world, not because it's perfect, but because it is an honest and vulnerable expression of the Divine. The process isn't always easy, but I find I can bring in more lightness and ease as I gradually shift my beliefs. And the more that I anchor myself in my Inner Flame beliefs that align with self-love, the more my creative floodgates open. Perfectionism choked my self-expression, whereas gradually growing into a sense of my worth has ramped up my creative inspiration and joy.

Opening to Truth is a Brave Act

Disentangling our limiting beliefs takes courage. Out of fear, many people spend their whole lives allied with the destructive patterns they grew up with. The old viewpoints provide a familiar ground on which to stand, a comforting reason to never look within or express your deeper truth. We subconsciously understand that when we tap into unlearning our conditioning, there may be some personal wounding and transformation brought to the surface.

As we question the harmful beliefs that keep us small, we may recognize more deeply the suffering and oppression on planet Earth. On the one hand, this lets us know we are not alone. On the other hand, we may feel there is no end to the lies we have ingested from outside influences. While this reckoning is part of our natural evolution, there's no denying that it hurts. And then it's beautiful. And then it hurts. And then it's beautiful. That's the nature of tapping into and expressing our truth. We have to let our old preconceptions and beliefs burn away. This is the destruction before the rebirth. And I'm not gonna pretend that entering the fire of transformation is always blissful. But the reward of sifting through the inner and outer pain is deepening our sense of inner belonging and wholeness. We develop steadiness. We can feel grounded even amid chaos.

When we are intentional with the process of unlearning our conditioning, we can ensure that we don't stay mired in the resentment, anger, or discouragement of seeing how our voices have been tamped down. The key to empowerment with this process is to focus even more attention on the Inner Flame. Connection to our radiance can reveal the beliefs, ideas, and societal structures that are nourishing, truthful, and supportive of ourselves and all people. So if you love saying "F-you" to those who keep people silent through patriarchy, racism, homophobia, rape culture, or capitalism, that is part of the collective awakening. But we need to devote even more energy to allowing a higher level of consciousness to build new ways of being—first within, and then without. We need to consciously nurture positive beliefs and new, empowering systems as they take root.

Throughout this chapter, we will explore how to create these islands of reclamation, compassion, and grounded wholeness. We're going to dive into some of the harmful distorting patterns that make us doubt the worth of our voices, so bring your self-compassionate pacing along and get ready to meet your radiance underneath the muck. And if you're not in the space of unlearning your conditioning, you may consider jumping to Chapter Four on Expressing Yourself Through the Body or Chapter Five on the Voice of Intuition.

Reclaiming our Worthy Voices in Community

Here's another piece of good news: we don't have to examine the forces that keep us small all on our own! Since we're talking about collective patterns, doesn't it make sense that we get to unravel them in community? This can be on a small scale, like having discussions and sharing our voices with a trusted friend. Unlearning our conditioning in community can also look like taking a group course or joining a discussion group where all voices are valued.

I got my first taste of questioning beliefs in community as a college student. Before that, I was a devoted worshiper of the cultural myths about what would make me worthy. Questioning my beliefs was not really on my radar as a high schooler trying to fit in. Yet I eventually grew itchy trying to squeeze myself into the boxes of being pretty and perfect. I longed for a fresh start, so I decided to run away from my home state of Colorado to attend Lewis & Clark College in Portland, Oregon. I realized I wanted more from my life than masks and fitting in. I hit the jackpot of self-esteem boosts when I signed up for a 12-week Self-Defense for Women class. We met in a windowless basement workout room covered with mirrors and practiced our moves in slow motion with partners. To close each class, we sat cross-legged in a circle and pounded our hands on the padded rubber floor. As the rainstorm of drumming intensified, we shouted in unison, "I am a strong and powerful woman! Yes!"

Was I really strong and powerful? I was plagued with self-doubt. Yet I shouted along with the other young women, exploring my voice, my body, and my power. In a supportive circle of sweaty women, I began to question why I believed myself to be weak, fragile, and inadequate. I saw that the beliefs I grew up with did not have to be a fixed set of ideals that I lugged around with me for my whole life. In this community where we showed up authentically, I began to worry less about what other people thought of me.

More unlearning came from a class with a significant focus on gender roles. Learning about stereotypes of women in the media blew my mind. How had I never seen these patterns that were in plain sight? How had I never noticed that women were most often portrayed as an accessory with the sole purpose of orbiting around men? How had I never noticed those images of women as silent, emaciated sex objects rather than empowered, autonomous humans who deserved to be heard? And how about the incessant message that we need to either change ourselves or buy something in order to belong? Of course I felt crappy about myself! At times looking at my unexamined conditioning was a bit overwhelming. I definitely wanted to pull my hair out and scream when I realized how our beautiful human sexuality is so often manipulated for the sake of trying to sell us things. Yet I wasn't alone in the process of unraveling. In addition to discussions with my classmates, I ranted and wondered with a new friend about all these harmful messages we had ingested. I experienced the power of speaking up with my opinions and questioning mainstream doctrines in a safe community.

That's not to say there was never disagreement or dissent. Unlearning your conditioning is not about finding a group of people who agree with you so completely that you never have to question anything. And it's definitely not about becoming so entranced with a group or leader that you start to believe everything they say or every online article they post. Coming back to self-belief is a gentle process of being willing to listen inside and ask which beliefs resonate as sacred truth, serving your highest good and the highest good of all. We all have different roads to uncovering the beliefs that disconnect us from our Goddess Voice. Sometimes the momentum of societal movements may spur us to examine the beliefs we were handed. For my vivacious aunt (who is white, as am I), the protests of the Black Lives Matter movement inspired her to enroll in numerous racial justice courses and share nuggets of what she's learned with her friends and family. For others, seeing a friend go through oppression or abuse may highlight the harmful patterns that need to be dismantled so all voices can be heard. A well-timed book, article, or teacher may also be our eye-opener.

No matter how you start examining the beliefs which affect your self-expression and sense of worth, it is a cyclical process. Just like our greater healing, reconnecting to our

Inner Flame beliefs is not a one-and-done event, but it is a process that naturally comes in waves. We may start with a little nugget of the belief that's making us feel unworthy, and decide to discuss or write about its origins. Then we can reconnect to our Inner Flame and ground ourselves in more healthy beliefs. After some rest and more life lessons, we may find ourselves circling back to the same beliefs with the ability to go even deeper in our healing.

The Belief that Restores Our Sense of Worth

Now that we get a picture of how to examine beliefs in a way that feels supportive rather than draining, let's go straight to the root of what inhibits our self-expression: the wound of unworthiness. On a collective level, the wound of unworthiness is birthed from a subconscious belief that we are isolated units that operate separately from All That Is. This is called "Separation Consciousness." Separation Consciousness leaves us feeling lonely and scared deep down. When we feel disconnected from the wisdom and grace of the Universe, humans tend to scramble and fight for any scrap of perceived security. We stay stuck in our evolutionary survival habits of cruelty, impulsivity, and selfishness. Then we try to take others down, so it's them and not us who take the fall, and the wound of unworthiness gets passed along. Think of the kid who gets mistreated at home and then becomes a bully at school—she is simply hoping for some pain relief by passing it along.

Cultivating empathy is the pathway that leads us to Unity Consciousness, or the understanding and experience that we are inextricably connected to everything around us. On the level of consciousness, all beings form one unified whole. When you tap into Unity Consciousness, you know your voice is worthy and needed. If this sounds pretty abstract and your eyes are starting to glaze over, consider looking at Unity Consciousness through metaphor. We can envision ourselves as part of a great tapestry. At first glance, it appears that every person, animal, plant, and object is separate and distinct. If we look closer, we will realize that we are all woven from the same infinite threads. The billions of atoms in our bodies contain particles from the explosion of stars long ago, the composted leaves of ancient ferns, and water that once was part of the vast ocean. We are all part of one whole.

Unity Consciousness sounds like a nice idea. But it becomes real when we actually experience the energetic interconnectedness of All That Is. I received my first taste of feeling one with the greater whole during my second year of college, when I was deep into unraveling my old habits of trying to be perfect to earn my worth. I would vacillate between moments of self-acceptance followed by an onslaught of self-criticism and pressure. In this fertile ground of unlearning, I was ready for a shift. So I signed up for a fall break backpacking trip in the redwood forest of northern California and allowed Mother Nature to work her magic on me.

On our second day of hiking in the forest, we staggered our start times on the path climbing up to a ridge so everyone in the group could experience a solo hike. The dappled sunlight streamed through the towering trees as I found my walking rhythm. I became acutely aware of every deep, oxygen-rich breath. My mood became more euphoric as I climbed higher through the breezy forest. When I paused to catch my breath, I suddenly became aware of a divine presence in the trees. I experienced each redwood tree as a part of my being. I felt the oneness in my cells. The rest of the hike was an enchanting experience as I rejoined the group and descended through a lush fern canyon opening up to the

Pacific Ocean. When I heard the ferocious, roaring waves, I dropped my day pack and ran along the sandy trail to the beach. I stripped off my socks and hiking boots to dip my feet in the cold waves of the ocean, acutely aware of every sensation in my body. The late afternoon sunlight graced the rolling waves, leaving me mesmerized. There I was, a tiny speck before the most magnificent painting, living a perfect moment.

I don't want to lose this feeling, I thought, and with that fear, I descended back into Separation Consciousness. In a predictable pattern, I began to cling to that elevated happiness that came with my experience of oneness. Yet the more I grasped, the farther it slipped out of reach. My old patterns of smallness, fragmentation, and unworthiness were waiting at the door, ready to rush back in whenever I opened up a little bit of space for expansive connection. At the time, I was very hard on myself for losing the elation of expansion. But after a 20-year journey, I can look back with gratitude and compassion. That moment of awakening to Unity Consciousness in the redwoods gave me a taste of what was possible. The longing for Divinity propelled me to learn to express the wholeness of my Inner Flame with greater frequency and ease as the years went on.

I hope this story illuminates how Unity Consciousness is more than a philosophy. Oneness already exists as a lived experience that we can start to access when we invite more empathy, love, and uninhibited self-expression into our lives. While the glimmers may seem fleeting at first, we can gradually cultivate more and more moments of flow, divine connection, and oneness. Accessing Unity Consciousness is also the key to owning our inherent worth. We understand that we are the cosmos and the oceans and the powerful volcanoes, so of course, we deserve to receive the beautiful flow of support, wisdom, and nourishment that is available to us. Simultaneously, we feel humble knowing that all beings carry the same Inner Flame of worthiness.

Domination vs. Universal Empowerment

When enough people come to experience that we are all one, the destructive, outdated model of superiority and inferiority of beings can be laid to rest. Think how much blood has been shed through human history from people believing their religion, race, nationality, or economic status makes them superior to others (while secretly fearing they are inferior). In the model of either being the dominator or the dominated, patterns of pain get passed along through the generations. We repeat the same wounds over and over, creating patterns that disconnect us from our inherent worth. Voices get squashed. Creativity gets devalued. Ancestral songs are forgotten.

All this fear and wounding ties back to what I call the "culture of domination." The culture of domination encompasses patriarchy, capitalism, colonialism, heterosexism, white supremacy, and domination over the Earth's ecosystems. If it's based upon one group of people trying to claim superiority over another group of people or the natural world, it's part of the culture of domination.

While there have always been pockets of love, goodwill, and cooperation, the overarching power structures have been based on hierarchy and oppression for millennia. All of these systems benefit a few people at the top of the hierarchy by bringing oppression and destruction to the people, plants, and animals that are viewed as inferior. Thanks to colonialism and globalization, the culture of domination has spread around most parts of the world, leaving billions of people feeling insecure, powerless, and voiceless.

Though the dominant groups definitely benefit materially and physically from being near the top, this system is not good for anyone's mental or spiritual health. Even if you fit the hierarchical definition of being worthy, you will suffer from the fear of losing your wealth, power, and privilege. When our self-worth is viewed to be conditional and scarce, it is constantly under threat. That is why I always start the work of reclaiming your voice with the premise that we are all worthy of respect and empowerment. We can speak up from a place of having power *with* others rather than power *over* others.

Body check-in: how are you feeling in your body as you read about the culture of domination? Take a moment to breathe and notice what is present for you. If you like, spend a few minutes doing a full body shake to release any heaviness or tightness that no longer serves you.

Thankfully, the systems of domination are already being dismantled by countless courageous crusaders for equality and balance. While the dominators desperately cling to power, people are deconstructing patriarchy, economic oppression, racial discrimination, heteronormative thinking, and environmental destruction. We are witnessing the culture of domination's slow, groaning collapse. That being said, I want to honor and acknowledge the suffering many people are still forced to endure every day due to the systems of oppression. The pain is not over yet, but the light of our Inner Flame offers hope for a loving, connected, sustainable way of being.

While remembering that we are divine beings connects us to our inherent wholeness, we need to be careful because the larger view of interconnectedness can be used to bypass or gloss over the very real suffering on the physical human level. For someone whose experience of oppression is ignored or refuted, this bypassing can be downright hurtful. Our goal is to keep the bird's eye view of Unity Consciousness in mind while also deeply acknowledging the pain of others and ourselves. We keep part of our awareness in the connected consciousness that witnesses the suffering, and we also open our hearts to heal the collective wounds we have inherited.

I want to say one more thing about the leadership that is arising in small pockets as the culture of domination is dismantled. Rather than perpetuating status roles and the myth of some people's lives being more important than others, the new paradigm is built upon true leadership. The foundation of true leadership is respect for all people's voices and beings. Have you ever had a teacher, mentor, or boss who was comfortable in their leadership role, yet also could bring out the talents, wisdom, and sovereignty in the people they lead? Like a gardener watering the seeds lying dormant in the soil, a true leader will have the wisdom, vision, and knowledge to see what others need to flourish. They offer help in a way that respects autonomy and sees each person's gifts as essential to the thriving collective garden.

How Our Nervous Systems Allow Us to Move Beyond Domination

For a long time, I felt that the energy of domination was 100% bad. But I developed a more nuanced view of this human tendency from reading, *The Call of the Wild: How We Heal Trauma, Awaken Our Own Power, and Use It for Good* by Kimberly Ann Johnson. In this accessible and insightful book, Kimberly dives into the physiology of predator and prey responses that are available to all humans. Countless generations of inherited trauma have encouraged a rigid, either/or relationship with the predator and prey responses that are part of our human nature. Either you are a predator (aggressor) who dominates and conquers, or you are the prey (victim) who is dominated. When we only see polarized role models, we subconsciously identify with either the predator or the prey energy. We use our voices to try to control others or to try to appease others. Fun, right? For those who allow their predator instincts to dominate, there is a lurking fear of losing their power in any moment of so-called weakness. For those who have been pushed into the prey role, there's often a feeling of being stuck in helplessness on the body level, even if the mind is aligned with empowerment.

In my experience, we can move past these calcified roles by embracing our wholeness. As human beings, we are all predators and prey simultaneously. We have fangs and claws and strong muscles and cunning instincts that enable us to have a fight response. We have booming voices to warn off any threats. At the same time, we also have legs that can run for many miles to flee a predator. If neither fight nor flight seems like a viable option, our systems will collapse into freeze or "play dead," which is an intelligent and natural survival mechanism. The freeze state allows us to dissociate from our bodies and feel somewhat numb from the pain and hopefully get the predator to leave us alone as quickly as possible. When we embrace that these non-cognitive capacities are part of our wholeness, we can release shame and judgment around how we've responded to perceived threats in the past. Your nervous system is intelligent and you are worthy no matter what threat responses your body has chosen! As we gradually make peace with our mammalian instincts, we can reclaim the power of choice in each situation that arises. We can embody the firm, determined power of our inner predator when setting boundaries, speaking up for our needs, or defending ourselves and others from attack.

Taking inspiration from animals is a powerful way to integrate these parts into our whole self. One of the most potent ways to unlearn our conditioning and embrace our predator energy is through animal imagery and sounds. My clients have imagined inner wolves, tigers, lions, panthers, and bears to build their resilience and power of choice. A primal power reawakens when we take a deep breath and let out some playful growls and roars! At the same time, we can benefit from embracing our prey nature by relating to herd animals such as antelope, buffalo, zebras, and horses. I first experienced this power through an audio course by Dr. Peter Levine, creator of the Somatic Experiencing method of trauma resolution. He encouraged listeners to imagine the bodily sense of safety from being in the middle of the herd, attuned to the movements and the nervous system state of the other animals. This helps you sense how our human nervous systems are designed to derive a sense of safety or unsafety from sensing the levels of relaxation or activation in those around us. Put simply, we are wired to feel safer when others around us feel safe.

All of this is to say that being human is a both/and experience. The inner predator and prey can be embraced without shame. When we make peace with our physiology, we can step outside of the rigid "conquer or be conquered" mentality of the culture of domination. We can make our voices heard, knowing we have the resilience in our bodies to handle other people's reactions to our truth.

Building a Culture of Mutual Empowerment

Choosing when to step into predator energy as self-defense as well as attuning to the needs of the species as a whole allows us to move beyond domination and create a new/ancient way of relating. If you look in the right places, people are building a culture of mutual empowerment right alongside the flailing, destructive systems of oppression. The culture of mutual empowerment is based on equality, respect, compassion, and unconditional love.

To get a view of how the culture of domination compares to the culture of mutual empowerment, I like to think of a potluck dinner party. In the culture of domination, only the hosts would have free access to the food and drinks, even though everyone's labor contributed to the abundance of food. The guests would get meager portions, and if they complained, they would be shamed and blamed for their circumstances. It's hard to imagine a party actually going this way, because in small scales among people we trust, we have experienced the culture of mutual empowerment. I'm grateful to have been at many parties where each guest was welcome, honored, and invited to participate in the equal sharing of resources. While the host may not be able to gorge on those delightful desserts, they will likely have a lot more fun and fulfillment in sharing resources and power with friends in the cooperative party.

When we take the metaphor of a party and apply it to the whole world, this shows the possibility of a culture of mutual empowerment. All people are valued and are free to express themselves and contribute to the most positive experience for all. The foundation of the culture of mutual empowerment is recognizing the beautiful Inner Flame that exists in abundance within all living beings and Mother Earth herself. When we tap into this interconnected divine radiance, we understand we are all worthy. We all belong. We all deserve respect. We all deserve to be heard. Even the dominators who have violently torn others down for their own material benefit are part of our big human family and deserve the opportunity to rectify their behavior and receive love.

Now I realize this may be triggering, especially if you have been traumatized by domination and exploitation. Seeing perpetrators as worthy of rectification, forgiveness, and love might not feel accessible or even healthy at some moments in the healing journey. So please remember you are always invited to work with what resonates with you and leave the rest. If seeing all beings as one big, interconnected family seems unattractive or even threatening, you can still bring in threads of the culture of mutual empowerment as you reclaim your inherent worth.

I am well aware that the framework of the culture of mutual empowerment may seem like a pie-in-the-sky idea. Yet I want to emphasize that this is not a vision of a utopian society that could happen someday in the future. The culture of mutual empowerment already exists as a mindset and experience in numerous hearts and minds. You can find people creating a loving, compassionate culture of mutual empowerment on every continent. As more and more people wake up to our shared radiance, the power of this mindset and way of interacting continues to grow. We see the evidence in people of all colors raising their voices in protest to dismantle systemic racism. We see it in sustainable urban farming projects and women singing into the Earth and men camping out in trees so they won't be cut down. We see it in non-binary and transgender folks bravely showing up and living their truth. If you need more evidence, look at people volunteering in their communities and contributing to crowdfunding campaigns and making friends with people across the world and empowering the survivors of crimes perpetrated by the culture of domination. We are already building new ways of being rooted in cooperative, sustainable power. More and more people are seeing that every single voice matters.

Releasing Comparison to Others

Constantly measuring where we stand compared to others is a habit most of us learned from the culture of domination. I'm no stranger to comparison, and there is no shame in having this habit pop up. But at the same time, comparison to others most definitely keeps us in the realm of playing small. We subconsciously limit how we express ourselves when the lurking fear of how we compare to others is running the show. Years ago I coached a woman named Dana who had a beautiful singing voice and massive stage fright. Her husband loved to get on stage and sing karaoke after a few beers, and she wished she had the same comfort on stage. Unfortunately, her subconscious comparison to an imagined standard of how her body "should" react to singing in front of a crowd just layered on more pressure. It made it even harder for her to share her voice with anyone because she felt shame for being where she was at.

We began by acknowledging and normalizing her anxiety and stage fright as a natural bodily reaction that could be worked with, rather than demonizing it just because others don't experience the same anxiety. With compassion and encouragement, I helped Dana to build confidence in her voice and feel safe to sing in front of a small audience. She released some of her comparisons and started to celebrate where she was at.

The road to loosening these persnickety patterns is a mental discipline. We notice when we are comparing ourselves to others, and we remind ourselves that our worth is inherent. Even if someone appears to have more success, abundance, or opportunities that does not make them inherently better. We carry the same radiant Inner Flame. We are part of the same beautiful whole and we can shimmy back into the space of inherent worthiness. Sister, you deserve to applaud your own beautiful, just-right voice and journey regardless of how polished and amazing someone else seems.

I want to point out that letting go of comparison doesn't mean we have to throw out all forms of healthy competition. For those who are naturally motivated by striving for the blue ribbon, there is still plenty of room for competitive events, sports, games, and contests that encourage excellence and peak performance. The key is to remember that the worthiness of our deepest soul is unchanged, no matter if we get 1st place or 437th place. Our failures and setbacks are a part of the human experience, and it's a tragedy for anyone to get stuck in silence from these necessary experiences that fuel our growth.

The Invisible Beliefs of Capitalism

Yes, I'm going there. I brought up the "C word." Now, if you were raised by hippies or activists, had a radical economics professor in college, or happened to make friends who love to "stick it to the man," then you are probably familiar with at least a few of the collective beliefs of capitalism. For the most part, however, the gospel of corporate capitalism is an unseen, stealthy force that easily erodes our sense of inherent worth.

You may be somebody who believes that unmitigated private ownership of trade and industry (i.e. capitalism) is the best way to organize an economy. I am not here to convince you otherwise. I am here to help you see how the unspoken beliefs of the world's dominant economic model may be contributing to how you view the worth of your voice and creativity. Remember we want to bask in the abundant vitality of our Inner Flame, so sometimes we have to be willing to do the dirty work of scrubbing away the mucky personal and collective beliefs that keep us stuck. Let's start the cleanse with this list of some beliefs that could use a healthy dose of questioning:

- Achievement equals worth.

- Resting is a sign of laziness.

- Creativity is a waste of time.

- Speaking up equals causing problems.

- Fame is the defining factor that makes a voice worth listening to.

- Ancestral songs are less important than mega-hits.

- Wealth equals superiority.

- Poverty is the fault of the poor.

- Unearned privilege equals proof of hard work.

- Greed and hoarding are inalienable rights.

- Being constantly busy means you are leading a virtuous life.

- Pushing your body equals being strong.

- Working tons of hours is the only way to be financially abundant.

- Paid labor is more important than unpaid labor (parenting, caregiving, housework, volunteering).

- The quest for constant economic growth is more important than the sustainable use of natural resources and human resources.

As you read through this list of beliefs, notice if there is one that stands out to you as being significant in your life. For me, it was a total game-changer to realize how much I berated myself for being lazy when it was time to rest and have fun. Recognizing that this belief doesn't come from inside but is something that I absorbed helps me distance myself and respond with compassion when those fearful thoughts still arise (and the self-criticism still does come up sometimes after my afternoon nap.) Of course it's going to take years to completely unlearn this kind of persistent indoctrination. I mean, it took years to convince me that I should feel guilty for indulging in the healthy, joyful, innate tendencies of rest and playfulness, so it makes sense to give time to the process of unlearning these beliefs.

Once you identify a belief that resonates with one of your own patterns, read over this list of Inner Flame beliefs and try on a new perspective for just a moment.

- Worth is a facet of your inherent, divine nature.

- Rest is healthy and nourishing.

- Creativity is a vital, essential human need for expression.

- Speaking up means you are valuing your needs and the needs of others.

- Fame is a way we collectively create belonging by becoming familiar with common people.

- Ancestral songs are just as vital and worthy as recent hits.

- Wealth equals an opportunity to be an agent of collective abundance.

- Poverty is a persistent cycle that we need to collectively heal in order for any of us to experience liberation.

- Unearned privilege is something to recognize with humility and self-compassion.

- Greed and hoarding are mental diseases with a fearful energy, rather than the free-flowing lightness of true abundance.

- Being constantly busy is an opportunity to affirm your value by practicing more self-care.

- Pushing your body is potentially stimulating in small bursts, while giving yourself plenty of time to recover.

- Working tons of hours is an intense way to focus your human resources in only one area of your life.

- Paid labor is just as important as unpaid labor, personal relationships, and what brings you joy.

- The quest for constant economic growth is a reflection of our innate thirst for limitlessness, which is possible on the spiritual plane but not on the material plane.

After writing this, I got the urge to jump up and dance the Macarena. Seriously, I just did that. So take a moment to move your body or write something down or shout something out loud to help you integrate the possibility of a new belief. What does it feel like in your body to realize you can throw off the lies imposed on you by this traumatic economic system, even if only for a moment? What does it feel like to recognize that wealth is an overflow of resources that can allow you to be even more impactful as an agent of collective abundance? It may feel like the absolute freedom of naked dancing. Or it may feel pretty terrifying. Remember that whatever you experience is just right for this moment of your journey. I applaud you for the courage to face and unravel even a tiny drop of these big, unwieldy beliefs. And if you feel ready to dive in and create some whole new bad-ass systems that serve the collective good, search up some info on PROUT or Doughnut Economics. Learning about new economic frameworks and perspectives is a good reminder that we are already building a beautiful culture of mutual empowerment right alongside these destructive systems created by the culture of domination.

Healing Outdated Patterns with Love

Before we explore a free-flowing process to loosen the patterns that keep us small, I want to shower you with the loving awareness that it is completely fine to have these limiting beliefs. We all have them! Part of being human seems to be a tendency to believe things based on our experiences and outside influences, even if they are not true. If you have been in the self-transformation game for a while, bringing compassion to your limiting beliefs is especially important. Every once in a while, coaches and teachers may weaponize the idea of limiting beliefs, suggesting that the teacher's methods don't work for someone because the student hasn't worked hard enough to let go of their negative thoughts, beliefs, or self-aggression. Many people are left feeling anxious that they are "blocking" good things from coming into their lives because they haven't mastered their mindset yet.

This perspective shifts when we remember that healing is a cyclical, ongoing process. Healing your beliefs, or anything that is causing you pain, is not a linear process where you get to a fairy-tale destination of being completely "fixed." We get to be messy and imperfect and honor that we are always in the right stage of our journey. Our beliefs and patterns arose as a form of protection, and we can most definitely evolve into living by new beliefs that better serve our highest potential. With this cyclical model, there are five components of healing distorting patterns that disconnect us from our radiant Inner Flame. While the journey is non-linear, I still find it helpful to spell out five general components of the process of anchoring new beliefs.

Component One: Unlearning Our Conditioning

Through inquiry, we can start to unravel a little piece of a limiting belief. Back when I was building a music career in 2017, I struggled with the belief that no one wanted to hear my music. Every time I invited someone to come to one of my concerts, deep down I assumed they wouldn't actually want to come. They might show up just to be nice, though, and that was my desperate hope. Seeing how much I agonized with the fear of having no one in the audience, I realized I needed to shift my beliefs. Assuming that no one wanted to hear my music came from a deeper belief that my voice didn't matter. Yet when I asked myself if this was a universal truth, it clearly was not. With more inner inquiry, I saw how the belief emerged from my own wounding: traumas, criticisms, frequent interruptions, and my opinions being dismissed throughout my life. I also started to see how my own belief that my voice was unimportant could not be separated from the larger cultural context of women's voices being frequently demeaned, devalued, or ignored.

When I asked myself what perceived benefit came from holding onto the belief that my voice didn't matter, a deeper possibility of healing emerged. I saw how the parts of me that were terrified of rejection preferred to expect that others would spurn me and my work. This gave me a sense of preparation for any potential letdowns, rather than allowing my sensitive heart to get her hopes up that my voice would be accepted, valued, and celebrated. The thing is, the perceived benefits of viewing my voice as unimportant were based entirely on my negative past experiences, while ignoring the positive evidence that my voice does in fact matter. Throughout the years, I had received plenty of experiences of people genuinely wanting to hear my music, yet I focused on those who didn't "get it." I had to accept that putting my voice into the world was not going to work if I needed every single person to like my music. Instead, I had to focus on my ideal audience: the highly sensitive, spiritually attuned people who relate to my introspective wisdom.

Furthermore, the possibilities of joy, wholeness, and personal fulfillment are worth the risk of letdown that comes every time we put ourselves out there. By digging deeper into my psyche's reasons for playing small, I was able to release the gripping attachment to believing that my voice was unimportant.

What limiting belief do you wish to shift so you can speak up, sing out, and be heard? You can ask yourself: is this belief a universal truth, or something more transient and pliable? Does this belief serve my highest potential and the good of all beings? When I think this thought or engage with this belief, do I feel scared, angry, or helpless? Or do I feel open, connected, and honored? What perceived benefit does my subconscious get from holding on to this viewpoint? Through the process of questioning, we gain awareness of why we are experiencing pain, self-doubt, or a feeling of unworthiness.

Component Two: Anchoring Your Inner Flame Beliefs
The next component of shifting your limiting beliefs comes from strengthening the positive beliefs that you wish to embrace. Remember that your inner truth-teller is always alive underneath the muck of cultural conditioning and harmful beliefs. Anchoring in your Inner Flame beliefs allows you to connect to values that feel positive, empowering, and serve the greatest good of all (including you!) I visualize this process as creating, joining, or strengthening islands of

positive reclamation. Even when the negativity of the culture of domination seems ubiquitous, you can seek out places in yourself and in our society where healthy, loving, encouraging, bad-ass ways of being are nurtured and cultivated.

When I realized I could shift my belief that my voice didn't matter, I started by writing down affirmations and hanging them on my walls. Every morning when I woke up, I would read, "The world needs my voice," and "My voice matters." I also had fun singing the affirmations, even though at first I didn't fully believe them. Another way I anchored my Inner Flame beliefs was through Emotional Freedom Technique (aka Tapping). As I followed along with various Tapping videos, I experienced the powerful combination of stimulating acupressure points while speaking out loud. The more I practiced, the more I was able to bask in the sunshine of valuing my voice.

With this second aspect of healing, keep in mind that grounding in your Inner Flame beliefs is a practice that seeps in over time. Repetition and frequency are the keys to shifting a pattern. Neuroscience has affirmed the potential of repeating positive thoughts as a way to increase happiness. Every time we think a positive thought or engage in a healthy habit, we are widening the neural pathway associated with it and making it easier to go down that trail in the future.

Component Three: Cultivating Simultaneous Awareness

Once we have built a robust foundation of truth-connected beliefs that support our highest potential and the good of all beings, we can start to play with simultaneous awareness. If you are wondering what the heck this means, simultaneous awareness is being able to hold our attention on two (or more) different feelings or thoughts, even if they seem contradictory or paradoxical. It's a practice I first learned through a course with Rachael Maddox. Cultivating simultaneous awareness is a "both/and" approach: the pain of limiting beliefs, personal wounding, and the culture of domination has permission to be present. At the same time, we can cultivate worthiness, cooperation, and life-giving energy right alongside the difficulty. We can call in Divine Grace to witness, support, and hold us in our wholeness.

When you allow the limiting beliefs to peacefully coexist with your Inner Flame beliefs, a magical alchemy takes place. Here's a metaphor to help us understand the effortless shift that can arise. Have you ever heard stories from disciples or even been in the presence of a spiritual master? Just by being in the presence of the master, the disciples cannot help but be uplifted. In the same way, your limiting beliefs will naturally shift when allowed to sit next to the loving, nonjudgmental presence of your light. Fears, shame, and outdated frameworks start to soften. Self-confidence has space to seep in.

Going back to my experience of worrying that my voice didn't matter, simultaneous awareness helped me trust the value of my voice for the first time. When self-doubts emerged, I allowed my awareness to rest on the polarities of worthiness and inadequacy coexisting within my being. In this way, I eased off of the tendency to shame myself for having the unpleasant emotion, and let it be acknowledged. But I sure as heck was not gonna let that icky feeling fill the whole frame of my awareness. I learned I can split my screen and turn on my sense of worthiness right alongside the difficulty. With time, I began to open up to a divine presence that embraces all of my contradictions and complexities. Allowing grace to move through me helped the self-doubts, shame, and limiting beliefs soften. Rather than feeling like the negative beliefs and the positive beliefs were at war with each other, I could see them peacefully holding hands. The self-doubting side began to understand that I am worthy.

When you start out practicing simultaneous awareness it might be easiest to start with two seemingly contradictory feelings that feel fairly neutral. Let's save the heavyweights for later once we've built up our strength. For example, you could stand with both feet on the floor and become aware of gravity pulling you downward. At the same time, you could imagine a sense of upward directional pull along your spine bringing you to your full height. You are bringing simultaneous awareness to the downward pull and the upward sensations that coexist. Here's another pair of opposites you can play with: the feelings of stillness and motion. As you sit or lie down, notice what it feels like to let your muscles rest and be motionless. At the same time, see if you can tune into a sense of motion, perhaps through your breathing or your heart pumping blood through your veins. With practice, simultaneous awareness can be pretty darn magical whenever the old limiting beliefs or negative thoughts pop up. The point is not to make those distorting patterns go away, but to know they no longer need to dominate your awareness. Eventually, the light of your Inner Flame glows so brightly that it colors the whole landscape, just as the sun outshines distant stars in the light of day.

Component Four: Inner Embrace
In order to create lasting change, I have found it essential to acknowledge and take care of the inner parts that are scared of letting go. When you slow down, tune in, and listen, you will likely find a buried voice inside that feels like it's safer to stay small and quiet. The process of meeting these tender parts with loving, open arms is what I call Inner Embrace. In chapter 9 we will gently and playfully get to know our inner landscape of voices. If this sounds a lot like inner child work to you, then you are right on track! Sometimes, one profound experience of acknowledging and reassuring your scared parts

makes a huge difference. But most of the time, the healing of inner embrace is a practice of showing up consistently to care for and reassure your inner children and inner critics.

Component Five: Offer the Pattern to Divine Love
In a sense, the previous four components of healing limiting beliefs are ways to loosen the attachment to the old ways of being so that you can finally let go. The real healing comes not through practice or effort, but through Divine Grace. The sweet nectar of grace can be called in through prayer and meditation as we offer the old beliefs and patterns to Love. Whether you relate to any spiritual masters, deities, or angels, or feel more comfortable with a formless energy, you can invite the divine presence to take each outdated belief. You can offer it in your hands outstretched, and say, "Please make this yours," and allow it to be burned away by the benevolent force of love which lies within and without. This is where profound shifts can happen. It may seem like you spend months or years in the grip of a limiting belief that causes suffering, and you offer it to Divine Love day by day. Then, suddenly, it lifts away. All the time devoted to questioning the old beliefs, anchoring your Inner Flame beliefs, cultivating dual awareness, practicing inner embrace, and offering it to Love prepared you to let the old pattern be miraculously dissolved by the divine presence within.

Unleash Your Goddess Voice Practice No. 3: Two-Minute Inner Flame Meditation

Now that we have a broad picture of how to shift limiting beliefs, let's play with a practice to establish yourself in your Inner Flame beliefs. It's quick and powerful to connect to your Inner Flame through visualization and affirmations. Rather than trying to bypass the limiting beliefs and suffering that may be present, we are allowing our radiant divine power to be anchored as a loving presence right alongside the beliefs that keep us small.

When you wish to anchor yourself in your holy inner power, the challenge is that it does not have any defined form. Worth is not something we can pin down that will be experienced in the same way for every person. In order to discover your Inner Flame, you have to let go of some of the rational, left-brain analysis and be willing to step into the right-brain experience of lighthearted experimentation.

Because each individual may experience the energy of their worth differently, I invite you to play around with how you visualize your divine core. Throughout this book, I use the metaphor of a flame because it evokes associations of power and light. That being said, you could also imagine the energy as a sun, an ocean, or a wise grandmother tree. You could imagine your worth as a glowing orb of any color that feels right. Your experience of where the worthiness is most potent in your body can also shift and evolve. You can also bring in your own affirmations to anchor in your Inner Flame beliefs. There is no right or wrong way to relate to your own powerful, vibrant, connected sense of completeness. It is vast and changing like the ocean, and also rooted and solid like the Earth. It is always burning like the sun and also tiny and contained like the potential of a seed. Your Inner Flame is vast and indefinable. We use images and metaphors because it gives us something tangible to relate to.

While I encourage you to experiment, the practice that follows is based on the wisdom of the yogic chakra system and has brought powerful transformation for myself and my students. We will be focusing on the third chakra at the navel, which is the center of personal power. This part of the belly is related to the element of fire, and tapping into the inner strength that resides here can light up our whole being with authentic self-expression.

Yes, that's right, we are owning our right to shine by connecting to our power and fire. And if you have complex feelings about tapping and showing your inner fortitude, that is totally okay. We can have all kinds of misgivings about becoming more powerful—and most of them come from the ways power is abused in our culture. But remember we are not aiming for the pseudo-power of domination over others. We are cultivating our inner authority to stand our ground. The key lies in strengthening our own power alongside our compassion for ourselves and others. You got this, warrior goddess!

For a recording of this practice, visit saragiita.com/free

1. Place your hands over your belly button as you sit, stand, or lie down.

2. If it feels good, gently rub your abdomen in small circles or from side to side. You can also let your hands rest if you prefer.

3. Imagine a giant candle flame underneath your hands, in the midline of your body. The base of the flame rests behind your navel, with the flames fanning up into the area beneath your diaphragm.

4. On your next inhale, imagine your flame growing bigger.

5. As you exhale, speak or sing, "I am worthy."

6. Play with allowing your flame to grow even more as you inhale a few more times. If expansion feels difficult, let your light stay at its current size without forcing or pushing.

7. Continue repeating the affirmation, "I am worthy" on your exhalations. Inhale and amplify, exhale and affirm.

8. If it feels good, move your hands outward around your body in any way you like. Imagine the feelings of worthiness and peace as rays of light that radiate through all parts of your body and into the space around you.

9. If you become aware of limiting beliefs or voices of self-doubt that protest as you practice, invite in simultaneous awareness. The doubts and patterns of staying small can coexist with your radiant, divine Inner Flame beliefs.

CHAPTER 4

Expressing Yourself through the Body

Can I rest in here for a minute?
Can I feel inside with compassion?

After years of hovering
in the detached periphery,

I want to come in,
accept what I find
and gently inhabit my body.

My amazing vessel
For sound and silence,
You now have permission
To release your roar.

Finding Benevolent Beliefs about Our Bodies

Given how much pain has collectively been passed around from the culture of domination, befriending the body is a lifelong exploration. Our bodies hold a rich topography of waterfalls, forests, seas, mountains, and deserts we can experience when we have the right tools to move, sense, notice, and explore. This sensitive territory requires compassion and care. It is also a powerful doorway into your vocal power: after all, your muscles, tissues, and breathing mechanism create all vocal sounds.

When you learn to get in touch with the physical joy and pleasure of creating sounds in your body, self-expression will naturally flow with greater ease and authenticity. Let's not gloss over the fact that I just used the word "pleasure." It's such a loaded word in our society, but why? Because we've been conditioned to stay drowsy and detached, believing happiness resides in the fulfillment of material desires rather than in the joyous expression of our dancing, breathing aliveness. That's why it is a radical act to befriend the body, even if our internal awareness only lasts for a few seconds.

Before diving into the somatic work of noticing sensations and creating more freedom in the body, there is often some underlying belief work to unlearn our harmful perceptions of our bodies. If you've been around the self-empowerment block more than once, you've heard about the benefits of loving and accepting your body as it is. But reducing our critical thoughts and views of our physical form is a tricky process. This makes sense, given that we have been programmed by millennia of religious doctrines that shame our flesh and innate sexuality. When you layer on top the inundation of messages about how a "good" body should look, it makes sense that this is an area of struggle for many women. Even when we highly value female empowerment, it's still easy to be influenced by the message that women should always try to make themselves look younger, thinner, prettier, and less hairy.

Here's where cultivating awareness of the Inner Flame can help. We don't need to completely root out or eradicate our negative beliefs about our bodies. We just need to bring awareness to those thoughts implanted by consumer culture, and choose to focus instead on fortifying what feels healthy, expansive, and connected to our Inner Flame. It's not about never having another negative thought about your body, it's a process of gently expanding your sense of appreciation for your physical form. The momentum of the healthy beliefs you seed will gradually grow into a strong default of self-love. You can ask yourself: is there one thing in my body that I can feel appreciation for right now? Perhaps you can thank your ears for working well, or your feet for supporting you, or your heart for beating steadily and keeping you alive all these years. Finding one little thread of gratitude for your body is the perfect starting point. Then, you can play with reading out loud these body celebrations:

- All bodies deserve equal respect, power, privilege, and opportunities, including bodies of all colors, ethnicities, sizes, shapes, abilities, ages, genders, and places of birth. I know all bodies are worthy, and that most definitely includes mine.

- The look of each body is worthy and respectable in its natural, unaltered state. While people can choose to alter their appearance if they find it enjoyable, that doesn't mean that fulfilling an external standard of beauty makes any body more valuable or acceptable. This means my body is just right as it is.

- Every body is an important, intrinsic part of the whole, regardless of what it can do or achieve. I honor all the phases and shades of health and ability that my body may experience.

If you would like more support in learning to love your body, I highly recommend the book, *The Body is Not an Apology* by Sonya Renee Taylor.

I want to acknowledge here that while nearly all women face similar messages regarding their body image, these obstacles show up on a spectrum based on your experiences and identity. The more marginalized your identity, the greater the chances are that you have experienced more layers of harmful messages about your body. (Marginalized identities are those that have historically and currently been cut off from power and privilege.) Remember that seeking out community can bring more lightness, hope, and ease to the process of reclaiming the radiance of your AMAZING, VIBRANT, WORTHY body!

When looking at how we can feel more comfortable in our bodies, we also have to consider the harmful beliefs we may have absorbed from rape culture. Just from the name, you can tell that these myths will not be invited to the Goddess Voice celebration! But for clarity's sake, I will define rape culture as the collective attitudes and power structures that normalize, condone, and perpetuate sexual violence against all genders. Victim blaming, slut-shaming, sexual objectification, excusing the behavior of perpetrators, non-consensual pornography, and the silencing of survivors are all part of the culture that perpetuates sexual violence.

Body check-in: let's pause and acknowledge that this is heavy stuff. Can you feel your feet right now? Can you tune into the rhythm of your heartbeat? Look around the room. Is there anything that catches your eye as a source of calmness and stability? As you notice your body, it's a good time to check and see if examining these harmful beliefs about bodies is a helpful practice at this moment or not. Are you ready to continue down this path?

In my own journey, the process of waking up to understand that my victim experiences were not my fault unfolded over several decades. Like many, I initially had no alternative to believing the lies. Now I can understand that the man who sexually assaulted me at age five needed to frighten me into silence so he would not get caught. He lied when he said it was my fault. He lied when he said I was bad. But unfortunately, I did not have any framework to understand that he was the one at fault. At the time, there was very little information for parents or teachers to train children that it's safe to speak to a trusted adult if someone is hurting them. Without the necessary training to understand I deserved bodily sovereignty, I was left in the dark hallway of believing the lies.

As I reached adulthood and gradually began to receive the message that a survivor is never to blame for their violation, I saw how those lies I ingested could survive only in a cage of silence. We have all heard harmful untruths, either from those who have taken advantage of us or from society at large. Which lies have you heard? That it was your fault? That your clothing or curves or words provoked the violation of your bodily sovereignty? That your body and needs are shameful or inferior to others? Did you learn that it is your job to be nice and please everyone? When we recognize that the messages we received are not true, this is the first step of healing. There may be torrential feelings of anger, disappointment, or abandonment that arise when we fully acknowledge the impact of the harmful beliefs that have been thrust upon our bodies. Remember that all experiences are welcome here, including all your emotions. You get to be a whole human being, sister! When we intend to release shame, we can accept the emotions and give them space to be expressed and released.

You know by now that we are not going to stop at the stage of acknowledgment, but we are going to also cultivate more empowering beliefs about our bodies. Luckily, the path has been paved for us by countless courageous individuals, groups, and organizations creating a culture of consent. Consent culture is based upon mutual respect and clear communication. Rather than normalizing coercion and boundary crossing, consent culture affirms every person's right to be asked if they want to engage in any form of sexual touch, and to have their wishes respected. Here are some of the empowering pillars that encourage respect for all bodies:

- Any person initiating a sexual act has the responsibility to obtain clear, affirmative, enthusiastic consent from their partner or partners.

- A person can change their mind or withdraw consent if things are not feeling right for them.

- Just because a person gives consent to do one particular intimate act, that does not mean they are consenting to another. For example, if a person agrees to make out with someone else, that does not mean they are agreeing to oral sex or intercourse.

- When the person initiating sexual contact is in a position of power, true consent cannot be granted. This is relevant in situations where a victim may say yes to something they don't want to do because they are underage, or they are in fear of losing their job or another opportunity.

- Humans do not exist as objects for other's gratification, but as sovereign beings that deserve respectful treatment.

- Each person has the power to control their sexual urges—and this goes against the stereotype that men can't help themselves if they are turned on. Even if they are aroused by someone's choice of clothing or flirtatious behavior, they can responsibly manage their turned-on feelings if the other person does not want sexual involvement.

- Human sexuality can be beautiful, healthy, natural, and pleasurable in all its expressions when enthusiastic consent is given.

When hearing these possibilities, some people protest, "But asking for consent during a sexual interaction would make it boring or mechanical." In my opinion, consensual sex will only be boring if you view it that way. It can be a major turn-on to be fully tuned in with your partner and know they are enjoying the sexual interaction. When everyone involved is empowered to speak up about their needs and desires, sexuality can become a more authentic expression that aligns with what you are feeling inside. We can create a respectful foundation so we can feel comfortable in our bodies.

The Habit of Distance

Once we start to cultivate benevolent beliefs about our bodies, we can gently explore the territory of sensations. Yet we may find it difficult to tune in somatically if we have learned to cope with life's storms by distancing ourselves from our bodily sensations. Speech, sounding, and singing may also become detached as our attention becomes centered in the mind or even "checked out" of our being entirely. Very often, we become separated from our bodily sensations due to trauma in our lifetime or inherited trauma from our family lineage. This is called dissociation, or feeling detached from our inner sensory experience. When it no longer feels safe inside, we keep our focus on the external. We hover outside, staying distracted and disconnected. This can be a blessing if we are trapped in an intense situation with no escape— we become somewhat numb to the pain. Even long after a traumatic event, we may be experiencing dissociation without even realizing it. As with all coping mechanisms, there is no shame in ignoring the body. However, the downside of blocking out the pain is that we also block out the potential for pleasure in our bodies. We are turning the volume down on all sensations and making it harder to feel what wants to be expressed through our beings.

Up until college, I was used to ignoring my body. Only the most intense physical experiences would catch my attention; I was unaware of the subtleties of pain and pleasure. I lived very much in my head and my thoughts, which was a pattern I learned from my parents and our society. Yet I was gradually called back into my body through voice lessons, sexual exploration, experiences of feeling the strength of my body in nature, and a challenging injury. I began to notice the sensations in my muscles, the sensitivity of my skin, and the roar of my beating heart. During the time that I was exploring my physical sensations, I also learned to be a little more accepting of the roller-coaster emotions that had been the norm for me since I was five years old. Emotions are often stored in the body, so it makes sense that they will intertwine in the process of reclamation.

My Wake-Up Call

Since perfectionism was still my well-worn path of coping with shame, my body was a tangle of tension as a college student. The stress of always running from my past left me with shoulders like a rock, a neck in constant pain, and hands that could no longer perform. Yet during my second year of college, my pain grew from a gentle murmur to a panicked scream. I finally dragged myself to the school health clinic, and I was diagnosed with tendonitis. Suddenly I was a piano major who could no longer play piano. I was a straight-A college student who could no longer type an essay. If I wasn't perfect, who was I? One afternoon I sat on the hard, black piano bench in one of the music building's practice rooms, praying no one would peek through the square window to see if it was occupied. I stared at my palms, willing them to just *work.* But all I got was more pain. As my chest began to heave, my sobs melted into the cacophony of bellowing trumpets, cellos, drums, and pianos from neighboring practice rooms. I had always felt fragile, and now I had been pushed over the edge. I was left broken, crumpled, hunched over the piano keys. Playing piano, my safe place of self-expression, was no longer safe.

As my pain increased with each day, I spiraled into depression and despair. I felt myself unraveling. At the time, I did not know that unresolved trauma can impact our health. Heck, I didn't even realize I had unresolved trauma. Now there is research as well as many anecdotal stories about how Post-Traumatic Stress Disorder (PTSD) can disrupt sleep, digestion, and elimination. Many chronic disorders have also been linked to trauma, as well as the experience of pain that may not be linked to an obvious physical cause.

With the wisdom I've gleaned in the 20 years since that initial onset of shoulder and hand pain, I now understand physical and emotional pain as having a role within the context of my life. One function of pain is to make us slow down and reflect, and possibly change the trajectory of our lives. When I was 19, I needed to learn to look within with love. The methods I sought to relieve my physical pain were ultimately what brought me to heal my victim experiences. The pain led me to switch my major to vocal performance, and the emphasis on singing gradually opened up a deeper layer of authentic self-expression through my voice. In this way, the screaming pain became a catalyst. Tendonitis was my call to wake up. The message was clear: this body is not to be ignored. This body is for feeling and loving and expressing.

Re-inhabiting The Body

The beautiful thing about coming undone is we have an opportunity to build a new foundation for our lives. In the hidden places where we previously held ourselves together with distraction and patched-up coping mechanisms, we can create a restful base of awareness and compassion. Coming into our bodies is one of the most powerful ways to feel at home inside. I call this re-inhabiting the body. It is a process of gently bringing our attention within and being open to what we notice. Most of us knew how to inhabit our bodies when we were babies and small children, learning to roll over, pick up an object, draw, skip, and run. Our cells know how to do this, even if our conscious mind has forgotten. No matter how many years we have spent with our awareness hovering outside our bodies, it is never too late to peek back in. At our own pace, we can explore the long-neglected rooms and learn to love and appreciate our beautiful home.

I began exploring the territory of my body by practicing yoga on my dorm room floor. I didn't even have a yoga mat.

I just had a square of grey industrial carpeting in between the two built-in Formica desks. It was enough space for me to flop into a forward fold, letting my neck release and my worries lessen. Then I would curl up in child's pose on the floor, breathing deeply. For years I had been detached from my body, but with each breath, I let in the possibility that it was safe to feel. I let in the possibility that it was safe to love myself.

When we bring in our loving awareness, it is like shining a flashlight into the cobwebbed rooms of our inner world. By asking the question, "What do I notice in my body?", we turn on the light. When we feel ready to ask, "What does this part of my body need?", we clear out the dusty corners and begin to settle in. Over time we learn to notice and give ourselves what we need more consistently. This is the process of re-inhabiting the body, which can be summarized in three steps:

1. Noticing the sensations and experiences inside the body without judgment.

2. Asking what our body needs or wants to express.

3. Finding ways to meet those needs with compassion and care.

Let's look into the first step of noticing what we feel. Through movement and stillness, we may become aware of sensations of tightness, ease, contraction, lengthening, heat, cold, dullness, tingling, restlessness, or restfulness, to name a few possibilities. When what we experience feels manageable or pleasurable, we can breathe into the rightness of accepting what we feel. When it is too much, we can pull back and bring our attention to something that feels easier or more restful. A key to exploring our bodies in a healing way is to welcome whatever arises. We soften judgments of what we previously labeled a "bad" sensation or a "bad" part of our body. We hang up an inner banner that promises: all are welcome here. If something touches into overwhelm, it doesn't mean the feeling was bad—it just means that being immersed in it felt too intense. We can give ourselves a lot of compassion for what arises, and avoid being hard on ourselves when feeling guilt, shame, or pain. There are no "shoulds" when it comes to moving and experiencing our bodies. That includes thoughts like, This should feel easier, or I should be past these blocks by now.

The second aspect of coming home within allows us to notice what may be needed to help our body feel more nourished and whole. This can be very practical, like noticing when we are hungry, thirsty, tired, hot, or cold. We may also feel an urge to move, and let our bodies guide us through stretches, movements, changes of position, and breaks in activity. We can ask, "What direction is this sensation leading me in?" We may notice our neck wants a stretch, or our hands want to shake out, or our legs want to jump. We may notice we want to curl up in a ball, hug the floor, or twist to feel the two sides of our body integrating. When exploring movement, remember that this is not about cultural injunctions that we "should" exercise in order to have an "acceptable" body. We are listening to what feels good for our own unique organs, muscles, joints, tissues, and bodily systems as the moment unfolds.

The keys to our nourishment can also arise on the level of imagery, sound, and metaphor. Once we notice the objective aspects of our sensations, we may notice emotions or energies that want to be expressed. Is there a color that comes up? A shape, object, or animal? Do we feel the urge to groan, growl, cry, or sing? Is part of our body longing for a hug, or kind words, or for you to unlock a cage and open the doors to freedom? I have uncovered many energy patterns in my body by digging them out from layers of leaves, rocks, and soil. Through imagination, we can let the stuck places have a voice to be seen, heard, and honored.

Honoring the Needs of Our Bodies

Once we have noticed what is going on inside and asked our body what it needs, the final aspect of re-inhabiting the body involves meeting those needs to whatever extent we are able. As we learn to hear the subtle messages from within, we can grow more consistent with giving our bodies what they yearn for. Right now as I tune in, I am feeling a little thirsty and am going to honor that with some warm water to drink. This is a straightforward example of a need that is easy for me to meet. At times it is harder, like when one part of our body is screaming out for some loving massage, and another aspect of our being is afraid to shine the light of attention on that dark corner.

If you feel these complex fears or hesitations, you can start exploring your body by noticing what functions well or feels good inside. Even a part that feels neutral can be a place to rest our awareness. It's easy to focus our laser vision on what is not working so well or what we're not happy with in our bodies. Yet that does not necessarily boost our health or feelings of being nourished and whole.

Here's how this works. We start with the intention of creating a loving home inside by noticing one organ, bodily system, or body part that works well or feels neutral. For example, even if your digestion feels problematic, you may notice a sensation of gratitude for your well-functioning heart or eyes or vocal cords or feet. Even if it seems as though your whole body is suffering, perhaps you can find a fingernail or a toe or a spleen that seems to be doing ok. Then we can feel into the sensations in that part of our body and notice them with curiosity and presence. We can invite in gratitude as we explore the parts of our body that keep on truckin'. By focusing on what feels good or neutral in our bodies, we boost our overall health. This has positive effects on the parts we may have trouble with. When we rediscover that our bodies have the capacity to feel great, it's like bringing in a perpetually optimistic, jovial person to spend some time with a grumpy curmudgeon. Even if they won't admit it, the grumpy one can't help but be affected by the laughter and good cheer.

When living with tendonitis, I learned to focus on movements that felt good rather than always pushing myself to "fix my problem spots." With significant pain in my neck, shoulders, and wrists, I could make myself more tense by focusing my attention there. I slipped into self-loathing and self-harshness when I did not like the sensations of pain and tightness. Yet it seemed miraculous how I often had the experience of opening my legs and back during yoga, and by the end of the session, my shoulders and neck felt a bit better. The positive sensations in other parts of my body opened up the possibility of ease in my whole being. By grounding ourselves in positive sensations, this doesn't mean we cut ourselves off from the sensations that feel hard. It's not helpful to try to pretend pain doesn't exist or to push away what feels difficult. I like to think of dipping a toe into the places that hurt or feel scary. You can let the pain have a voice and be witnessed, without letting it run the show.

If you feel drawn to developing bodily awareness in a class setting, pay attention to the atmosphere of the class and how the teacher honors and respects individual needs. If you resonate with being a trauma survivor, you may wish to seek out a trauma-informed yoga class. Teachers with this special training will offer choices, respect all ways of engaging with the class, and encourage participants to honor their own needs.

If you are interested in or engaged in a class in one of the many other mind/body movement modalities, you can similarly gauge the atmosphere of the class. Is the teacher subtly or overtly encouraging competition or perfection? Is there a false belief that young, flexible, muscular, or able bodies are superior, and all those who don't fit that model should scramble to try to mold themselves to that norm? Or do you feel that all bodies are welcome, and the teacher offers modifications or invitations to make it feel comfortable and right based on individual needs? An atmosphere of pushing is more likely to lead to injury and makes it harder to make peace with our bodily sensations. That doesn't mean we can't challenge ourselves, but that we want it to be on our own terms. If the goal is to re-inhabit the body, we want to gravitate towards joyous consent with our bodies, enjoying what feels good and listening when a movement feels like too much.

What Do You Mean, Crying is Good?

In my journey of reclaiming my body, it took time and patience to love all parts of myself (and the process is still finding deeper layers). In the beginning, I could love my back while I stretched out in a spinal twist on the floor. But it was harder to love my hands. They were filled with memories I did not wish to face. I could not love my neck. It was holding on too tightly. I could not love my tears; they proved how I was never in control.

Embracing the body goes hand in hand with expressing our emotions. We cannot fully embody one without the other.

Growing up, crying was my biggest shame. I was pretty good at wearing my mask, until an unexpected incident stirred my insecurities. As soon as I felt the "I'm not good enough" worry rising in my throat, I would begin crying, often uncontrollably. I was so embarrassed by my tears and painfully aware of how the 15 minutes of crying seemed out of proportion to the situations that brought on the tears. I remember one morning on the bus ride to middle school, a boy said something rude to me. My shame was triggered, and the tears began. I gradually pulled myself together, but my puffy, pink eyes told the story of my tears. When I arrived at school and greeted my circle of friends, one said, "Oh, no, what's wrong? Are you okay?" I began sobbing again.

In my mind, crying was a sign of weakness. It was something shameful to be avoided at all costs. Yet after my nineteen-year-old hands were hit with tendonitis, I found myself crying in a piano lesson and being met with complete love and acceptance. I told my piano teacher, Carol Biel, that I was sorry I was crying. "Don't be sorry," Carol replied calmly. The gentle Portland rain smattered the window as I looked at her disbelievingly. "It's good to cry. I always feel more relaxed after a good cry. It's such a cathartic way to release pent-up emotions. You certainly don't want to bottle up your stress, pain, and feelings. Your body sheds stress chemicals through your tears, so let them flow and appreciate the release." As I left the music building after my lesson, I walked into the rain and felt the drops on my face. I turned upward to the sky and appreciated the cleansing and renewal. Thank you, Carol, for a potent lesson in self-acceptance. I was so used to hating my pain, pushing it away at all costs. You showered me with love as you suggested it is actually helpful to feel the pain and give it an outlet to be expressed. Allowing the pain creates space for new possibilities. After a rainstorm the earth is renewed, plants are nourished, and the sunlight reappears.

The Creative Power of Sexuality

Tears, physical therapy, hurting hands and endless studying made me ready for a break. I found it on a semester abroad in Ecuador during my third year of college. I was 20 years old, trying desperately to release my stress and perfectionism. Gratefully, I discovered it is hard to feel stressed when you are hiking up a mountain. It's hard to cling to perfectionism when you are learning a new language and have the vocabulary of a small child. Looking back, I see that I was building my capacity to be mindful and present while experiencing intensity. I was developing confidence, resilience, and my ability to experience pleasure. I learned that I could speak up and protect myself in new situations. I tried on the identity of a wild and adventurous *viajera,* a traveler. I learned the joy of naked swims and boat rides in the jungle. I stayed overnight in grimy bus stations with friends and spent many nights salsa dancing in crowded clubs. Sometimes I even went home with my dancing partners, learning to speak up for my needs and embody the life force energy that is awakened through sexuality. I was reclaiming my right to trust my instincts and give expression to my desires. When my hips and my gut told me I was dancing with a safe person, I learned to trust that intuitive voice. When I desired a closer interaction, I enjoyed the power of consensual expressions of our human sexuality. Rather than fearing instinct, I found outlets for it to be felt in my body.

And, my oh my, there was a lot of Goddess-given power and life force energy that came through experiencing my hips and pelvis and genitals as a place of sovereign self-expression. When you think about it, pleasurable sexual interactions are a microcosm for building the confidence to speak up and shine in your Goddess-given self-expression. You can learn to be seen and heard. You learn to tap your life force energy from the depths of your pelvis and become a channel for something bigger to come through. You can practice noticing and speaking up for your needs and desires. You have the opportunity to use your voice unapologetically through any sounds or words that emerge like a geyser from the Earth.

By the way, I am not just talking about the power of embracing your sexual energy with a partner. In many ways, it is more powerful to practice attuning to sexual pleasure on your own as an act of self-love. You can see and hear the parts of yourself that feel ashamed or embarrassed by the creative life force energy that sexuality embodies. By listening to your needs and desires, you can build the confidence to know that you matter and that you belong as you are.

Regardless of whether you feel called to open your voice through exploring sexuality, remember that the power that creates LIFE is alive in women of all ages. This also applies if any of your reproductive organs have been removed or if you were born with different organs. Trust that your upwelling of energy will find the right way and the right time for you to create and share with abandon.

Following Impulses

Part of expressing our Goddess Voice comes from attending to the impulses we feel in our bodies. When you hear the word "impulsive," what comes to mind? Drivers flipping each other off? Violent outbursts? People who make poorly thought-out decisions only to regret them later? In my mind, these kinds of eruptions that we think of as impulsive come from denying our inner impulses for too long. When our unconscious mottos are: Don't feel the anger... Try to keep everything locked inside... This body needs to be controlled... Dominate instead of feel... Then eventually the dam will break. The suppressed impulses explode into the world with a loud SPLAT!

If you have ever seen the first "Frozen" movie, the main character Elsa attempts to conceal her ice powers in a classic example of repressing emotions. She was taught to shut down her emotions so that ice and snow would never again come out of her hands at the risk of hurting someone. But of course, repression cannot succeed indefinitely and her power erupts unexpectedly at her coronation ceremony. As Elsa eventually learns, embracing moderation helps you unleash your power as a gift to yourself and others, rather than as a potential danger. In the same way, we don't have to try to control or tamp down our bodily impulses. There is another way to relate to the urges that naturally arise within: to slow down and listen.

Through movement, we can create containers to safely feel our bodies' natural desires as they arise. Instead of trying to control or suppress the inborn urge, we give expression to it through movement. Once we are more practiced at knowing it is safe to feel these innate impulses through movement, we can trust our deepest impulses to be voiced out loud at the right time, with the right volume and the right message. For me, starting a solo morning yoga practice was my doorway to honoring my impulses. While holding one yoga pose, I waited to feel what my body wanted to do next. I would often start on the ground and move my way up to standing poses only once I felt ready. If I stretched and moved enough, I could step outside of the chronic pain in my neck, shoulders, and hands for at least a few moments. I saw that my body could become a beautiful vehicle for expression instead of a burden.

Yoga was my way to reconnect in the mornings, and dancing often became my way to feel free at night. I first discovered the joy of un-self-conscious dancing when my lovely friend Mariel and I had an impromptu dance party to celebrate the end of the year. In previous dance experiences, I was always a little worried about how I looked and what people thought of me. But as music-lover Mariel put on an eclectic soundtrack, we let our bodies be free. We danced crazily and we danced slowly, often with our eyes closed, letting the music carry us into a flow state beyond all worries. We were sober, yet in a trance. And I discovered that my body held so much potential for joy and freedom when I took the time to listen to my impulses.

Finding Your Unique Bodily Awareness Styles

When you start to notice what you feel inside, a whole new territory of self-expression starts to open up. You gain the capacity to notice what is present and tune in to what is needed to feel more nourished. When you start to hear your body's yearnings you can learn how to follow through with movements, sounds, and self-care practices that feel sustaining and healing.

Moreover, I have observed from teaching yoga and body-oriented voice and piano lessons that each individual will have a unique language for their bodily sensations that correlates to their dominant learning styles. These include verbal, visual, auditory, kinesthetic, and logical modes of exploration. If you tend to draw upon multiple learning styles, you may have fun exploring the territory of internal sensation from multiple angles. As always, I recommend experimenting with a playful spirit. You may be surprised by which modality is most potent for you. For example, verbal and visual styles are more potent for me compared to auditory input, even though I am a professional musician, and all of my work is around the voice.

While tapping into the pleasure of movement will most definitely carry over into your vocal freedom, I find it helpful to give some time for open-ended movement. Instead of reaching for a goal, the invitation is to experiment with just being in your body and feeling what movements or sensations of stillness wish to arise. This is the practice of Body Listening. You're really not trying to get anywhere or make anything happen.

As a lead-in to this spacious practice, we are going to look at how you can deepen your bodily exploration through any of the five lenses—verbal, visual, auditory, kinesthetic, or logical modalities. If you find that one language is more powerful for you, you can also modify other practices in this book to harness your flow.

Bodily Awareness for Lovers of Words

Someone who is a highly verbal person may love expanding their vocabulary to notice and name sensations. Here is a list of words for possible sensations, and you can experiment with keeping this list open and looking for words that describe what you're feeling when you practice Body Listening.

Sensation Words

smooth	light	reaching	open	dull
rugged	heavy	huddling	burning	slow
bumpy	deep	sharp	prickly	fast
tingly	superficial	dispersed	shaky	tender
numb	buoyant	floaty	tense	airy
warm	grounded	bubbly	empty	strong
cold	flowing	pleasurable	spacious	depleted
neutral	moving	sore	contracted	full
jumpy	stuck	compact	relaxed	nourished
fluttery	frozen	expansive	knotted	welcoming
settled	jittery	queasy	sensitive	invigorated
easy	calm	buzzy	hungry	pulsing
receptive	releasing	sensual	burdened	alive

For a verbal approach, it is helpful to either speak out loud or write down a description of what you're feeling inside a particular part of your body. Once you have named the sensations you're feeling, you can follow up by asking questions such as: "What is a metaphor for the tension in my shoulders? What message do my shoulders wish to tell me? What does my body wish to express? How can I follow through on giving my body what it needs?"

Visual Metaphors for Internal Sensations

If you are a highly visual person, you will likely respond to colors, images, and visual representations to deepen your experience of sensations and tap what wants to be voiced. Some ideas for experimentation include:

- Pick a color that suits your mood and find an object or image of that color. Invite your body to harmonize with the feeling that color evokes in you. For example, you could choose aquamarine and play around with what movements or sounds would express the lightness and vibrancy of the color.

- Imagine a beautiful place in nature or a serene indoor location. Let your mind fill in all the details of what would feel lovely and nourishing. Then draw a picture, write a description, or make a quick recording of the imagery. As you listen to the recording, look at the picture, or read your writing, feel the bodily sensations that are stimulated by your visualization.

- Watch yourself in the mirror as you move your body. If your mind goes easily into criticism when looking in a mirror, try to imagine your body as a beautiful work of art (because it is!) Focus on the curving of a finger, the shape of an eyelid, or the texture of a toenail. Explore the reflection of your body not as something deficient or imperfect, but as a living, breathing masterpiece of cells working in harmony.

Once you are tapped into the impulses of your body, you may enjoy exploring movement in a visual way through scribbling. Yes, scribbling like you did when you were two years old! Grab a colorful marker or crayon and a blank sheet of paper. Then ask your arm how it wants to move and let it express itself. You can even create vocal sounds as you let your hand move across the page without judgment. It's not about making "good" art, but a mindful practice of self-expression through the body.

Exploring Sounds to Deepen Bodily Awareness

If you are a person who is more oriented toward sound, you may find it harder to find words to describe your sensations. You may also feel like visualizations don't do that much for you, and that is just fine. You can find your doorway into the body by listening to music or tones and finding how your muscles wish to move or vocalize in collaboration with the sound. Here are some ideas to befriend your body using the auditory modality:

- Use a singing bowl, gong, or musical instrument to create long tones. Notice how the sound waves feel in your tissues. Even if the vibration of the instrument is less noticeable than booming bass notes that shake your whole body, every tone still creates sound waves that can be felt in the body.

Notice if certain parts of your body respond differently to changes in pitch or loudness.

- Put on music that you love and invite your body to move in any way it wishes with the sounds. This may not look like dancing at all, as you could find yourself stretched out on the floor or curled up in a ball or jumping up and down. Let your awareness move back and forth between the experience of the sounds and the feel of the movements internally.

- Explore body percussion, such as clapping, snapping, or tapping parts of your body gently to make sounds. Feel what parts of your body would just love to get in on the music-making.

- Let vocal sounds emerge as a healing offering to any part of your body. Keep in mind the vocal sounds do not need to sound beautiful or musical. Growls, grunts, sighs, purrs, barks, yells, and whispers are all valid ways to express your inner self.

Exploring a Kinesthetic, Hands-On Approach

If you are a kinesthetic or tactile learner, you may spend a lot of time moving your body already. Your process of expressing yourself through your body may be about deepening your awareness of sensations and making the connection to what instincts want to be given form or expression. You may wish to try:

- Moving freely with the goal of noticing sensations for a few minutes. Follow what feels good, safe, relaxing, or invigorating.

- If you are accustomed to goal-oriented movement, give yourself time to move that's not about pushing yourself, growing your strength, or achieving anything. Create designated times to just run or move or dance in a way that feels good to your body and then stop when you get the urge to rest. Let yourself just lie on the floor if that's what your body wants to do. There is no such thing as laziness when practicing Body Listening!

- Play with texture and touch. You may wish to try self-massage, oils, baths, swimming, tapping, warm or cold packs, or noticing the feeling of lovely fabrics against your skin. See what needs or impulses want to be expressed through touch (while always honoring consent with others, of course.)

I recently witnessed my friend Christy coming into free-flowing kinesthetic self-expression in an online group circle. After a few minutes of us sending metta or healing energy to each other, she described her experience with such radiant, integrated movements that I knew her Goddess Voice was coming through. More than being movements to accompany her words, she was embodying the energy of her vision of her highest self. Her arms, shoulders, neck, and face were lit up with a pure expression of love and possibility brought into momentary form. Interestingly, when I told her how much I was basking in the energy of witnessing her movements, she said she usually feels caged in her body. Yet the safe environment of the circle let something freer emerge. Her spontaneous embodiment shows the potential of our bodies as conduits for a greater power to come through. What was intangible became knowable through her body, voice, and energy as she shared her true self with our circle.

Integrating Logical Frameworks to Speak or Sing in Alignment

When I was recovering from the repetitive strain injury in my hands and wrists, I was first introduced to the concept of Body Mapping. This is taking a permanent marker and drawing a detailed map on your face. Just kidding! No Sharpies are needed here. Body Mapping is the practice of learning the details of your anatomy and integrating that awareness into your movements. Knowing how your bones and muscles actually align can reduce tension and bring more ease to your movements and vocalization. I consider this a way of using the logical framework of understanding your anatomy to become more acquainted with your bodily sensations.

I have been using anatomical diagrams throughout my 16+ years of vocal coaching, and for some people, the insights feel nearly miraculous. Understanding that the head can balance effortlessly on top of the spine or that we don't have an anatomical part called a waist really blows some people's logically oriented minds. Other students find the logical insights helpful but not quite as earth-shattering. Either way, I encourage you to experiment with some of the anatomy insights and movements here. They provide a framework for optimal bodily alignment that supports your voice. When you can continually return to a point of balanced poise while speaking and singing, your tone will be stronger. Your lungs will have greater capacity and your throat can act like an unbent flute transmitting your sound.

If you are interested in going deeper, I invite you to play with these practices that I have adapted from my study of body mapping and the Alexander Technique. These practices can be used to explore your sensations or to align your body as an open channel for free vocal sounding.

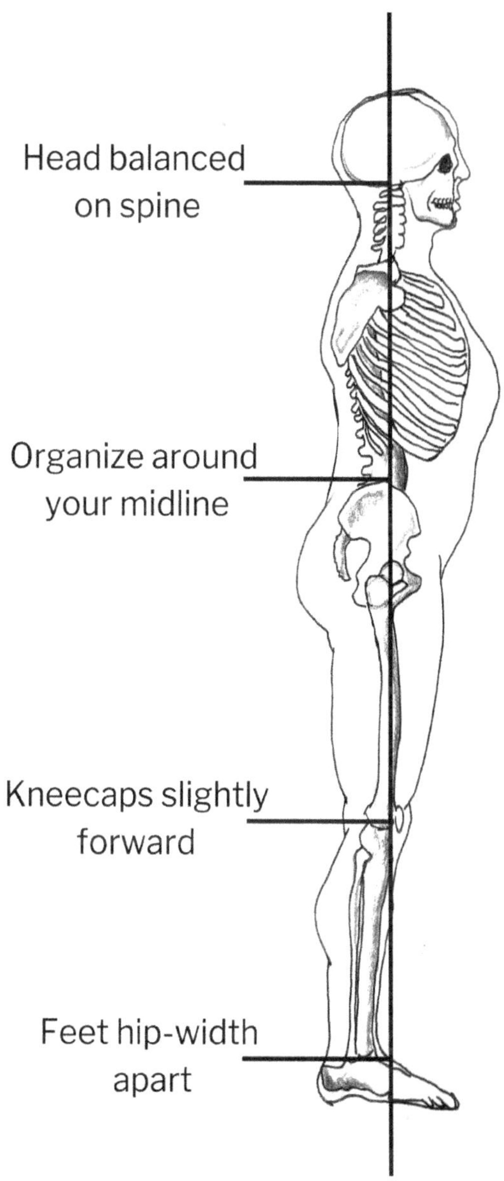
Head balanced
on spine

Organize around
your midline

Kneecaps slightly
forward

Feet hip-width
apart

Meditation: Exploring Your Alignment

1. Plant your feet as wide as your hips for a strong and easy posture. When speaking and singing, think of balancing the strength of your muscles that hold you upright with a sense of openness so you can be a conduit for sound to emerge with ease.

2. The weight of your body is transferred into your feet not at the very back of your heels, but a little closer to the center of the foot where the leg bones (tibia and fibula) meet the feet bones (tarsals and heel bone). To integrate this knowledge, play with bringing a little bit more of your weight onto the balls of your feet rather than centering on the heels.

3. Your knee joint is behind and below your kneecap. When standing, lots of people tend to lock their knees backward so the kneecap is underneath their hipbones. But this is not good for circulation or weight distribution. Try keeping the protruding kneecap a little forward so the leg bones can balance on each other. Now sing everyone's favorite kids' song, "Head, Shoulders, Knees, and Toes." (Hahaha!)

4. Your spine is not a skinny little column going along your back. It is really wide! What we can feel with our fingers is the bony process along the back. But the weight-bearing part of our spine is deep within our body, inside the ribs. The part that goes along the back does not bear any weight! In the lumbar or lower back region, the vertebrae are so big that the weight-bearing part of the spine is in the center point between the front and the back. If you drew a line down the midline

of your body, it would touch the weight-bearing part of your lumbar vertebrae. To feel this core support, I find it helpful to stand with your feet hip-width apart and gently rock your hips back and forth. As you move, visualize the core support of your weight-bearing spine in the center of your body rather than along the back.

5. Your skull balances on top of the spine. It connects at a joint called the Atlanto-occipital joint which is located right between the ears. This is a lot higher and more centered than most people imagine! Try placing your fingers in your ears and imagining the location of that joint as you gently look around the room and let your head follow with easy movements. This exercise can help you tune in to the point of balance, so your neck and shoulder muscles can relax. Think of it like this: you can balance a bouncy ball on top of a Crayola marker cap when the marker is aligned. But if you tilt the marker instead of holding it upright, which is akin to habitually bending your neck forward or backward, then your bouncy ball head will fall off. Oops! Luckily, our neck muscles, ligaments, and tissues and all that good stuff keep our heads on. But the shoulder and neck muscles will have to work overtime if the spinal balance is off, and this can cause tension in your voice.

6. When breathing and vocalizing, lots of people constrict their throats by engaging the exterior muscles that are actually for swallowing. When these swallowing muscles are unnecessarily engaged, the inhale will be audible, like you're gasping for air. Try relaxing the muscles of your throat as you breathe and vocalize. The inhale will be nearly silent when everything is loose instead of tightening up.

So how do you feel? Is your head floating like a balloon? Are you feeling tall, aligned, and free? Or is your mind spinning with all this information? I want to acknowledge that while a logical framework for how to align your body can bring more ease, it's also possible that it takes you into over-analysis. If that's the case for you, perhaps start by choosing just one of these six practices and set the intention of playing with it rather than mastering it. Aligning your body and creating ease is a process of noticing sensations and getting curious rather than achieving perfection or doing it "right." Optimal alignment is less about how things look on the outside and more about the state of the muscles and the internal sensations. If your body feels tall yet relaxed, then your physical alignment can allow you to be an open vessel for your voice.

All of these doorways to coming into your body create the space for you to become a channel for your message, voice, and creativity to come through. I think of attending to the sensations in your body as preparing the soil for the seed of your Goddess Voice to germinate, sprout, emerge, and flourish. Yes, our voices are resilient and can survive in some pretty harsh conditions of tightness, slouching, self-loathing, and distance from our bodies. The Goddess Voice will find a way through even the most depleted soil. But that spunky little sprout of self-expression can grow into a lush, deeply rooted tree if we give our bodies the right nourishment. We can recognize that everything we create, say, and do emerges through the vessel of the body. When we make it a place of open alignment and self-love, the soil is loose enough for our divine purpose to take root. So let's explore how to tend the soil together in our next practice.

Unleash Your Goddess Voice Practice No. 4: Body Listening

As we explore our voices, we can learn to listen deeply to our bodies by stripping away all the goals and practicing movement for movement's sake. We can build trust by attending to our body's impulses and urges. In the exercise below, I recommend starting with shaking your body to loosen up and release tension. This can be gentle and slow or vigorous and fast. Then you are invited to drop your awareness into your body to notice what movements and/ or sounds wish to emerge. As long as you move in a way that does not cause pain, there truly is no right or wrong way to move when practicing Body Listening. Focus on tuning in to your sensations and trusting the impulses that arise.

Chronic pain is another obstacle some people encounter. If you have a health condition or are experiencing pain, check with a health professional before trying this exercise. If you get the green light, focus on the areas of your body that feel less discomfort. For example, if you feel pain in your back but lying on the floor feels comfortable, you can lie down and move your ankles, neck, and fingers freely. Even if some parts of your body feel uncomfortable, you can still feel trust and joy through Body Listening.

If stepping into your bodily sensations with wild abandon feels like too much of a free fall, consider breaking down the exploration of your body into very small, doable nuggets. Keep in mind that you can start with a part of the body that feels relatively settled or comfortable and ask yourself what you notice. As with all practices, remember the goal is to stay within your individual Comfort Zone and take steps in and out of the Zone of Growth. If at any point you are feeling overwhelmed or have had enough, give yourself permission to take a break or stop entirely.

For a recording of this practice, visit saragiita.com/free

1. Find a space where you can move freely without bumping into furniture or objects. If it feels right, close the curtains to create a feeling of privacy. You may also wish to turn on some music that you enjoy.

2. Stand with your feet slightly wider than your hips. Gently stretch your neck, arms, back, or legs to warm up.

3. Imagine a cool stream or a warm campfire in front of you, whichever sounds more comforting.

4. Begin to shake your hands. Let all the excess worry, tension, and unpleasant emotion fall out through your hands, into the stream or bonfire.

5. Bounce your knees so your whole body begins to shake up and down. Keep your jaw loose as you bounce. Continue letting the tension flow out of your muscles.

6. If you like, try sighing loudly on each exhale. You may even find yourself laughing at the sounds that emerge as you shake.

7. Let your body be still and rest for a few moments. Drop inside to feel the sensations, bringing acceptance to whatever you are feeling.

8. Ask yourself the question: How does my body wish to move right now? Be patient as you allow the answer to arise.

9. Follow the sensations to move in any way your body wishes. Remember there is no right or wrong in Body Listening, only comfortable or uncomfortable. You may hear the call to run or leap or dance. You may feel the urge to lie on the floor and stretch. You may wish to curl up in a fetal position. You may wish to massage your body. You may wish to scream. Give yourself the gift of trusting

that however you find yourself moving is just right for this moment.

10. Continue expressing yourself through movement for as long as you wish.

CHAPTER 5

The Voice of Intuition

The Small Voice
grows louder
the Truth Knower
grows stronger
Listening within,
I hear the tinkling of bells
a Divine upwelling
waiting to be expressed.

Intuition and Your Goddess Voice

Your Goddess Voice, the stream of self-expression that is both uniquely yours and divinely channeled, emerges from the territory of the intangible. It is hard to pin down and impossible to quantify. We are meant to access it not through intellect, but through a more ancient way of knowing: sensing what feels right. This is the land of intuition, the fertile ground from which your Goddess Voice can be heard and expressed outwardly.

You may hear your intuition as a whispering voice. You may hear it not in words but through movements. You feel pulled forward towards something that calls to you and repelled backward from something that doesn't feel right. You may feel it in a particular organ or part of your body where you tune in and notice the sensations that arise as you contemplate action. You may be someone who needs a lot of time to slow down and clear your mind through meditation and silence in order to tap your inner knowing. No matter how intuition emerges for you, your true knowing holds gems that are ready to be brought into the light through your beautiful, just-right voice.

When you are tapped into intuition and the Goddess Voice that it births, you will feel yourself in the flow. The song lyrics pour out. The Divine speaks through you on stage. Your hands instinctively know which lines to make on the page. Your self-expression feels natural. Mother Earth wants you to create and bring joy to the world through your gifts, and you can revel in the flow. It's amazing when your Goddess Voice emerges spontaneously. But how can we tap that flow more consciously and consistently? Let's dig in and start exploring.

Discerning what is Ego and What is Intuition

One of the big challenges with tapping into your intuition is discerning what voice is speaking in your head. Many of us ask, Is this my ego talking or my intuition? When you take the time to get to know the different voices within your psyche, that radiant voice of intuition becomes easier to spot. At first, the different voices or subpersonalities such as inner critics, inner protectors, and inner children might blend together like the dozens of instruments in an orchestra. But it's helpful to study them and recognize what distinguishes each voice.

When I was taking a music history class in college, we had to identify a list of songs solely based on listening to them for each test. As someone who has never played an orchestral instrument, this was more challenging for me than for some of my friends who had spent thousands of hours in an orchestra. Luckily, my study partner Ashley was a harpist who was super tuned in to hearing the lovely plucking of the harp amid the many sounds of the dancing ensemble. Since not all orchestral songs include the harp, anytime we would be listening to the song list and she would notice her instrument, she would cry out with glee, "Harp!" By spending time listening with Ashley, I also grew adept at tuning in to the harp, which helped me ace my tests. In the same way, by paying attention, we can start to map out the different energies that dominate our psyche at different times.

I consider all of our different sub-personalities to be under the umbrella of the ego, or the part of our mind concerned with survival and decision-making. Our egos are primarily driven by fear. They try to find things or people on the outside to blame. They also tend to ruminate on worries and fear-based thoughts. The ego is not bad; it's just a product of the way we evolved in order to stay safe. The trick is to learn how to stop identifying with the thoughts of the ego and to step into the voice of the wise Self. I think of the overarching Self as an expansive, restful state of consciousness. It is the voice of our Inner Flame, connected to all beings and infinite wisdom. You could also call it Consciousness, the Inner Divine, the Essential Self, or the Soul. Going back to the metaphor of subpersonalities as instruments in an orchestra, the Self can become the conductor who guides all the ego's parts to make something beautiful rather than fearful.

When we embody the stance of our Self, we become a compassionate witness to our thoughts, emotions, and the outside world. We take a break from being identified with the fearful parts, the angry parts, and the vulnerable parts of our psyche. Yet we are not denying our human suffering or the struggles of others. If we try to ignore, bypass, or bury our human experience then we will probably drive ourselves crazy (my hand is raised because I've been there!) The goal of identifying with the Self is not to deny or exile the parts of the ego. The goal is to know that we are more than the small, fearful mind. We are the expansive Universe; we are the witness of life's craziness. We are the deep, beautiful energy of the Self which acts as a wise leader for all the other voices in our being.

Tuning into your Self is an intuitive process. For most people, the Self does not speak through thoughts in the mind (though you may find that yours does speak in words.) Don't get me wrong—thoughts are fine. They are part of being in a body. As I mentioned earlier, we don't have to eradicate them or stress about every single negative thought, because that obsession can distract us from hearing the deeper, slower voice of our intuition. Intuition is the communication system of our Self. We can learn to interpret this deep knowing as sensations of expansion and contraction in our bodies, which is the focus of the practice at the end of this chapter.

Cultivating Silence

In order to slow down and hear what our intuition wants to express, we need to give ourselves some moments of spaciousness and silence. These moments can happen in any setting, when you're walking in nature, taking a shower, making soup, practicing body listening, or creating art. But because we tend to be so busy and distracted these days, many people also find it helpful to cultivate silence intentionally through the ancient practice of meditation.

My journey with meditation practices has been like an internal game of tug-of-war. A wise part of me feels drawn to quiet reflection, and another part kicks and screams every step of the way. I spent my early years avoiding meditation. My parents were avid meditators of the hippy generation, and they tried in vain to sell me on the practice. As a teen, I would find myself sitting with my parents and sister around the dinner table, eating our tofu. My mom would ask, "How was your day?" leading me to complain about my current sore throat or an upcoming test. When my dad managed to look away from the Wheel of Fortune show playing on the TV, he would often respond with some version of, "You know, you wouldn't get sick as much if you just meditated. You wouldn't get so stressed out either." He was always trying to convince me that meditation would solve all my problems, and I did not want to prove him right.

But eventually, I grew desperate. As a senior in college, I was still searching for the winning ticket to take away the pain I continued to experience in my hands, neck, and shoulders. I began to wonder if meditation might help me to release my tension. I felt like I should give it a go, but I struggled to meditate regularly. Yoga was easy to practice daily because it felt good. But meditation did not feel good yet. I worried that I was doing something wrong because I could not concentrate. My mind worried and wandered. My legs fell asleep. I would soon abandon my attempts every time I tried to meditate. Finally, I decided I needed to jump in. No more half-hearted attempts to meditate. It had to be all or nothing. I got my chance after I finished college, and I hopped on a bus full of traveling, singing yogis with a tour of concerts lined up throughout Mexico. Whether in a park, on the bus, or at a host family's home, we sat down to meditate at least three times a day.

The Ego Will Have its Pushback

Even though I had chosen to be on that crazy tour through Mexico, I resisted every step of the way. I argued with the tour organizer about why starting the first round of singing and meditation at 5:00 am was a horrible idea. I stayed in bed but never managed to fall back asleep after the wake-up call. I was too busy fuming about how I was deprived of my eight hours of sleep.

Given my tendency toward harsh self-discipline, I struggled to embrace the practice of quiet reflection. My deeper Self was guiding me toward getting comfortable with resting in a state of being rather than doing, but at times it felt like I was forcing myself to be still and silent. If you've tried seated meditation, I'm sure you have experienced how it can feel like our stressful thoughts are screaming at us through a bullhorn. It can be a steep learning curve to suddenly begin sitting quietly for over an hour a day (starting with five minutes a day probably would have allowed me to be in consent with myself more often.) Yet, even despite this pushback, I did start to notice inner transformation. I discovered there was no place to hide from myself or my lifelong desire to feel "in control." My impatience often ran rampant, as yogi time meeting Mexican time meant 9 pm dinners and growling stomachs. I was used to burying my helpless feelings through planning and control, but that went out the window on this tour.

One morning we hustled to pack our bags and move on to the next city, only to discover our old, lotus-adorned converted school bus had broken down. The mechanic told us it would be fixed *ahorita*, which I thought meant "right now." However, in Mexico, the term is used more as a vague, "sometime in the near future." I experienced a profound shift during the following two days of waiting. We didn't do any sightseeing or even take a walk in the summer heat since we expected the bus to be ready "any minute now." At first, I struggled. Though I had loosened up a bit from dealing with tendonitis, my ego still tried to create a feeling of safety through control. I still tried to avoid situations where I would not be in charge of my time. Waiting on the hard floor of a walled-in home in Monterey, Mexico definitely qualified as one of those out-of-control triggers. I battled my racing thoughts and sat through my feelings of frustration. By day two, I acknowledged that I never was in control of my time to begin with. Perhaps it was safe to go with the flow. The act of acceptance was the key, unlocking a hidden treasure chest of patience. I taught my friends how to salsa dance in the barren meditation room, deciding to make the best of our existence in limbo.

From this experience and others to follow, I learned that ego resistance has a pattern. First, we notice that we are fighting against something that would bring our expansion, such as looking within, taking creative risks, or getting in front of audiences to share our work. We fume and fight inside, or perhaps dismiss and shut down the idea that would bring our expansion. However, we begin to shift when we recognize that the resistance is trying to protect us in some way. Many of our ego patterns are just really crappy attempts to stay in the realm of the safe and familiar. Acknowledging the desire to stay safe shifts us into self-compassion. Then we can accept where we are at in that moment and open up the possibility of change. We can tell ourselves, "I am accepting that my thoughts are anything but peaceful. I am accepting that I feel nervous. I am accepting that part of me wants to cling to smallness, control, and familiarity."

When we bring in the disarming power of loving acceptance, we invite resistance to move away from the steering wheel and settle down in the backseat. We may still hear a few self-defeating comments from back there, but our wise, eternal Self gets to be the driver.

Entering the Creative Flow State

I followed the whirlwind bus tour with a six-week intensive retreat in Mexico and found a doorway into a blissful creative flow state. Lyrics and melodies began pouring into my head during meditation, as I played with rhymes and formed full songs. When I got the chance, I would rush to my little yellow notebook and write everything down with colorful markers. I had previously believed I could not compose songs. I was so self-critical that I would question every line as it came out. Is this too cheesy? Does this line sound stupid? Meditation taught me to enter the flow state, where ideas can arise, and judgment is softened. I discovered how to truly express myself as an act of healing, bringing meaning and hope to my struggles as I channeled my emotions onto the page.

Entering a flow state comes from allowing, not making effort. And that can make us want to scream sometimes when the flow seems out of reach. Aaargh! Yet I have found that the more you cultivate silence and offer yourself in surrender for what wants to come through, the easier it becomes to enter creative flow. Practices like moving your body, making sounds with your voice and visualization can also help take you out of racing thoughts and over-analysis into the realm of creative communion.

When you become a vessel through which deep intuitive longings can be brought into form, at some point you will bump into a paradox. Your Goddess Voice is so uniquely yours and no one else can bring it into being in the same way. And at the same time, it does not belong to you one bit (sorry, ego!) A flow of something much greater is being expressed, and there is humility that comes along with recognizing that what you create belongs to the Divine. One great piece of news is that this paradox can help take you out of writer's block or creative paralysis. When you get too far into the side of feeling like "everything I create belongs to me," it may dam up your creative flow. And that feels icky, am I right? Then you have the opportunity to embrace the other side of the paradox: if you can offer all the results and give all the credit back to Spirit, then sacred expression may move through you like a flowing waterfall of grace. You become a steward for what wants to be expressed through you.

If you're wondering how to access this feeling, my favorite methods are prayer and play. If you want to invite creative flow through prayer, give yourself a few moments to get quiet and breathe deeply. Then offer up your own version of the meditative phrase, "Please open me up and make me a conduit for the Highest Good." You can pray to your Self, your version of God, or the Goddess of Pottery (I just made her up, but if she really exists somewhere I would love to hear about this!) I believe what matters most is your intention to become a humble vessel for a higher power to guide your actions.

The other way I love to access humble expressive flow is through play. Take a moment to move your body, make some sounds, or get wacky. Throw out the need to create something good, or to create anything at all. Just let yourself play around with self-expression. Then, imagine that the thing you feel called to create is its own energetic entity that wants to speak through you. For example, when I write a song, I often feel like the song already exists and shows up to give me nudges for how to bring it into being on this plane.

You can imagine the creation with a form, like a flower or a colored shape that speaks to you. You can play with it already existing somewhere in your body. Let your imagination flow as you interact with a potential creation as an energetic entity with its own message, aesthetic, form, and trajectory. Then your process of expressing your Goddess Voice becomes a lot less like trying to muscle your way into a state of inspiration, and a lot more like taking dictation from a river that is flowing through you.

Meditation: Letting Creativity Flow

Imagine that what you feel called to create already exists as a brilliant sun shining above your head. Get a feel for what is the just-right distance for where it hangs out above your crown. Then imagine that you can open your crown chakra so the joyful rays of inspiration flow right in. You don't need to make any effort or come up with ideas on your own; the creation can speak through you as an ever-flowing, abundant waterfall of creative energy.

Releasing Attachments Brings Just-Right Outcomes

The river of creative inspiration that allows us to belt out our Goddess Voice is truly glorious. It is also ruthless in its power to wear away our attachments. You thought you could control the outcome of your concert? Speech? Launch? Difficult conversation? At times it might even seem nefarious (or comical) how the divine flow erodes these attachments again and again. Yet a deeper peace and authenticity begin to emerge through the process of releasing clinginess so we can feel whole and complete just as we are, with or without the fulfillment of our deepest desires. Like removing the big rocks that slow and alter the course of the river, releasing attachments helps us become open channels with plenty of spaciousness for our life purpose and soul's expressions to be made manifest.

As a perfectionist, you can imagine that I spent quite a few years as the queen of clinginess. Trying to control outcomes gave an aspect of my ego a shred of perceived safety. Yet I experienced a shift during my six-week retreat in Mexico. In this quiet atmosphere, I began to experience the power of offering my attachments to Divine Love. Most of all, I understood I had to stop looking for solutions outside of myself. No person or accomplishment or material possession could fill the void within. Only self-love could make me feel whole. At the retreat center, we slept on the floor. We rose early to practice chanting and meditation, followed by yoga asanas and preparing our breakfast. We learned to revel in the small pleasures of a juicy mango or a refreshing swim in the river after a sweaty walk along the rural roads. On one of these walks, it dawned on me that I had spent most of my teens and early twenties longing for a boyfriend to fill the chasm I felt inside of me. I longed for someone else to make me happy. I longed for someone else to make me feel safe. How powerless that left me, depending on others for happiness! In that moment, swatting away insects, I felt complete all by myself. I felt complete because I had tasted the nourishment of my Inner Flame, and I was learning to feed myself daily. I saw that staying attached to the desire for attention from another person kept me stuck.

As often happens when we release clinginess and offer ourselves as conduits of divine expression, we create space for the just-right outcomes to come at the right time. This is true in our creative expression and our personal lives. I got my taste of divinely orchestrated magic when I fell in love. It was head-over-heels, tumbling-deeper-and-deeper, no-turning-back love. Plenty of times we may experience some waiting for the divine timing to line up, but in the case of my love story my soulmate was plopped in my lap. I found the just-right relationship to help me learn to speak up for my needs and step into my sovereignty. Here's how it all unfolded:

After completing the retreat and feeling like a new person, I returned to Monterey, Mexico and stayed with a lovely family for a few weeks. I wanted to volunteer at one of the service projects run by the yoga society, and I was waiting for the organizers to figure out where to put me. More and more delays and problems kept popping up, keeping me in Monterey. It felt like fate was keeping me there so I could meet Paco. He came for a meditation class I was teaching one morning in the same, stuffy meditation hall where I had been waiting on the bus tour two months prior. It was the best meditation class I ever taught, for I was aglow in the attentive presence of my new student. He stayed the whole day, even eating the burned beans I made on the old gas stove. I could not believe how natural it felt to talk to him. His dark eyes seemed to glow in the dim dining room where we shared a humble meal.

Despite being from different countries, we found so much in common. Our getting-to-know-you conversation slipped between English and Spanish, as we discovered shared tastes in music, books, food, and philosophy. As night was falling, I felt an ache in my chest. I wanted nothing more than to be close to him, to see what could blossom from these loving feelings. But did he feel the same? I knew we had a connection, but I was not sure if he saw me as more than a friend. When we said goodnight near the front gate, I moved in to hug him. I noticed that he was slightly taller than me and slender. His belly touched mine, and I did not want to stop hugging him. But we finally broke free, and he gave me three short kisses on the lips. Ahhh. Confirmation! The romantic feelings were mutual!

We found an excuse to see each other almost every day after that. We wandered the streets of Monterey after sunset, holding hands, our heads and hearts a rush of hormones and excitement and love. One evening in front of a grandiose, colonial museum, romantic music suddenly filled the plaza as we kissed. We laughed about our perfect movie moment. Every moment felt like a gift from the Divine, a gift I was only able to receive after releasing attachment and trusting the flow of the unknown.

When Deep Certainty Arises

In these times of feeling immersed in the flow, we may experience moments of deep intuitive certainty. An idea comes into our mind, and we know from our core that this is part of our path to live authentically. That's how it felt one summer evening when I asked Paco to marry me. We were enjoying a humid summer night at a yoga retreat center in the Ozarks ten months into our relationship. I was not planning on proposing, but we were talking about our future and him moving to Colorado with me and visas expiring, and it just made sense. As soon as I got the idea to propose right then and there, it felt right from the depths of my being. Grinning from ear to ear, I bent down to pick some long-stemmed clovers and fashioned them into rings. Kneeling on the damp grass, I asked him to marry me, and he laughed and said "Yes!"

Developing our intuition can increase our feelings of safety because we don't have to fear taking a "wrong turn." We begin to trust that when we feel guided to take a risk, it means we will learn something from the experience. Sometimes the outcome will be much different than we imagined. Sometimes our intuition will guide us through difficult terrain. And sometimes we will be guided to situations that leave us beaming and ecstatic, just like the night of my spontaneous engagement. No matter where we find ourselves, we can trust we are right where we need to be.

Interpreting the Messages of Intuition

Clearly, it's awesome to be alive in those moments when our intuition is so loud and clear that we know with certainty what path to take. But what do we do when our deep knowing shows up as a quiet whisper rather than a booming voice? Usually, intuition doesn't show up as words or thoughts, but through sensations in the body. We can also receive intuitive messages through symbols, dreams, signs, and meditative states of consciousness.

Essentially, following your intuition can be a process of interpreting sensations in your body. You ask a question and imagine one option you are considering as an energetic entity in front of the right side of your body. Then you can imagine another option to the left side. When the answer is clear, you will either feel a joyous expansiveness to one side that signifies "yes!" or a contraction and heaviness that signifies "no." You may also feel a pull to lean your body or reach out toward one side.

There are plenty of times, however, when the answer is not yet clear. Confusion can signify that our Self is saying, "Wait until the conditions are ripe and ask again." In this case, there is something we are meant to learn from being in the state of not knowing. That's easy enough to accept if you are firmly grounded in trusting your soul's timing. But when the ego gets a say, you'd better believe it is NOT going to like being told to wait! The ego generally wants answers RIGHT NOW! This often leads to the mind filling in answers and getting attached to possible outcomes.

Here's an example. A few years ago I wanted to know what direction to take in my career, as my youngest child had just started full-day kindergarten and I suddenly had more time available. My intuition said, "Be patient," as I needed to take my healing to deeper levels and build my inner resources. However, my ego was not down with this whole waiting-for-answers thing and stepped in to provide some solutions: "You need to go back to school," "No, you need to get a job at the health food store so you're busy every hour that you're not giving lessons," "No, you need to stick with your current path of coaching and learn how to market your offerings more effectively." Every day I found myself grasping at a different solution, trying to fill the void. Yet, now I am thankful I was able to continue working part-time and do the healing and inner work that was needed. The period of waiting brought opportunities and growth.

Another hang-up we may experience happens when we initially get a clear, intuitive answer, but a part of our ego is really scared to take that choice. Then we get an internal tug-of-war. On some level we know what we must do, yet we hear an onslaught of thoughts trying to convince us to stay small in familiar territory. I experienced this push and pull when I was contemplating ending a professional musical collaboration. My divinely connected Self knew it was time to stop working together. That message felt settled, clear, and right. Yet a part of me was really scared to let go. We had so many meaningful interactions together and a strong friendship. It seemed like a waste to throw away all our work based on a feeling in my abdomen! And then I worried that I would never find a better collaboration. And then I worried that I would hurt her feelings and she wouldn't be able to recover (which was an ungrounded fear since she is a resilient badass). I delayed. I fretted. Finally, I called her and said, "Let's take a break and focus on independent projects for now." Eventually, nature took its course and we went our separate ways with no hard feelings. I learned that my intuition did know the answer, but that I needed more mechanisms to soothe the tender parts of my ego that said, "I'm too scared to go this route!"

Start with Easy Decisions to Get into the Flow

While these are situations of significant life decisions, it is easiest to start hearing your intuition with smaller decisions and questions: "Should I take a walk right now or sing a song?" "Am I meant to send a pitch to this podcast host?" "Is this a good course for me to take?" When you start hearing your intuition for smaller messages, the language gradually becomes second nature. With time you will become practiced enough to hear the promptings of your inner knowing for the big decisions, deep messages, and creative channeling.

If you are contemplating trying a practice from this book, that can provide a great opportunity to ask a question of your intuition. Using the upcoming process of Noticing the Sensations of Intuition, you can ask, "Is this a good time for me to try Body Listening (or any other practice)?" If you feel the expansive openness of a "yes," you will likely find yourself being pulled to take action. This may look like moving into the room where you wish to practice, turning to the appropriate page in the book, or starting the matching recording. When the timing is right, the right actions will often unfold effortlessly.

By the way, just because your intuition tells you to take an action does not mean you are locked into carrying through with it indefinitely. You could get a message that says, "Yes, it's time to do x, y, and z," but later on start to feel overwhelmed and have the urge to stop. Perhaps your intuition wanted to give you that experience of honoring your needs by taking a break or stopping.

These experiences of asserting our needs can serve our empowerment. I once felt a very clear call to work with a natural health practitioner and purchased a package of sessions. However, by the third session, it was definitely not working for me, and I was sliding into helplessness. I took a break in the bathroom to get a feel for where my inner knowing was guiding me. I realized I was getting an amazing opportunity to say, "I need to leave," and honor my needs. After many experiences of my voice being ignored or undervalued in the past, I received the gift of being respected by myself and the practitioner. He gave me a refund for the remaining sessions without complaint and wished me well, as I left feeling empowered to use my voice. My intuition was guiding me to just the experience I needed, even though it didn't come the way I imagined.

Unleash Your Goddess Voice Practice No. 5: Noticing the Sensations of Intuition

As we dive into a method of communicating with your deep inner knowing, remember that this is not a mental process but an exploration of sensations. While ego-based thinking will keep us in a loop of ruminating over possibilities, let those patterns rest for a moment while you tune in to what feels joyous and open, and what feels contracted or repulsive. I recommend you begin the practice with a specific question in mind and find a way to phrase it as a "yes or no" question. Alternatively, you can keep two options in mind and feel which one you are drawn to.

For a recording of this practice, visit saragiita.com/free

1. Imagine you are speaking to your ego soothingly and letting it take a little nap. You can even say, "Don't worry, I'll make sure we stay safe while we talk to our inner knowing."

2. Step into the stance of your wise Self by offering a prayer or affirmation. "May all aspects of this process belong to my eternal Soul. May I let the grasping of the ego rest as I tune in to whatever messages I am meant to receive." If it feels good, hold your hands open, palms facing the sky as you offer your intention.

3. Bring your awareness to the question you wish to explore. Designate a space on one side of your body that represents a "yes" answer. Imagine yourself taking the actions that an affirmative answer would bring.

4. Now designate the space on the other side of your body as representative of a "no." Imagine yourself in a situation that may come along with a "no."

5. Alternate between the space of the yes and the no, noticing the sensations in your body. Does one side feel lighter or more expansive? Do you feel yourself wanting to reach or lean to one side? Then that is the pull of your intuitive answer.

6. If you get a clear message, write down what you observed.

7. Remember that if you don't receive a clear answer, it could mean you are meant to wait. The right options perhaps need more time to line up, or the seemingly agonizing decision could take care of itself in the future when more information becomes available.

If you are not able to discern any sensations or messages through this practice, don't despair. Learning the language of intuition is a skill that is developed over time. You may wish to try the same question another day or try asking a question that seems simpler. Some people also like to state the intention of receiving answers through another medium such as a dream or signs, and then look for symbolic interpretations. No matter what messages we receive, listening to intuition means trusting that we have something to learn from every situation. Saying, "Show me what I'm meant to learn here" can help us feel empowered even through the difficult periods of waiting and tug-of-war. Then when the right actions become clear, we can act with decisiveness and clarity. We can trust we are moving forward in alignment with our highest good and the highest good of all.

CHAPTER 6

Learning to Be Seen
and Heard

I see you.
I hear you.
I believe you.
Every emotion,
Every voice rupture,
and every success,
Deserves to be witnessed,
acknowledged,
held,
and loved.

Why We Need Acknowledgment from Others

We all deserve to be listened to with presence, attention, and compassion. This is often called "holding space," and it can feel like a rare thing to receive these days. Amid all the noise of modern life, we have grown accustomed to being seen and heard on a surface level. We are social creatures, and our deep need to be seen, heard, and known by others is often unfulfilled. When we are used to skating on the surface, it can feel scary and unfamiliar to be deeply seen and known publicly, beyond the few close relationships where we may have allowed ourselves to be vulnerable and authentic. The good news is we can intentionally increase our capacity to be seen, heard, and celebrated, which makes it a lot easier to share our authentic voices on any scale we choose.

To stretch that ability, we first have to recognize that acknowledgment from at least a few other people is essential to feeling fulfillment and belonging. There is a big push in the self-help movement to be completely self-validating and never seek outside approval, but it often leaves us downplaying our human need for connection through speaking up and having our voices witnessed and received by others. Don't get me wrong—we absolutely do need to cultivate an inner sense of worthiness and positive self-evaluation that is independent of what others do or say. Yet at the same time, it is hardwired into our human psyche to want acceptance from others. It is natural and healthy to want to receive praise or acknowledgment from our fellow humans, especially when we pour our hearts into a creative project or feel called to share an impactful message.

This understanding really clicked into place for me when I heard a recorded lecture by Harvard psychology professor Tal Ben-Shahar on three aspects of self-esteem. The first facet of feeling good about ourselves is called "dependent self-esteem." It stems from how other people and external circumstances influence our sense of worth. When we enjoy success or someone praises our work, we feel buoyed up. When we fail or someone criticizes us, we feel deflated. And when we see someone else rocking the spotlight, we are likely to compare ourselves (and end up feeling crappy). Ben-Shahar emphasizes that this kind of self-esteem is not bad, and that experiencing it is a necessary part of being human. But if it is our only basis of feeling good about ourselves, we will likely feel lots of painful ups and downs and be lacking in self-confidence.

Because of these pitfalls, it's ideal to also develop the second aspect of self-esteem, which Tal Ben-Shahar calls "independent self-esteem." This is the ability to positively evaluate our own actions and achievements, and to react with resilience and self-compassion when we experience failure. I am cultivating this with my writing—when I look over something that I have written, I am conscious of noticing and enjoying the parts that came out really well. With the phrases which come off as awkward or unclear, I take the attitude that those sentences just need some more time and attention. In other words, independent self-esteem is not based on what I guess other people might say in reaction to what I do or create. It's about praising myself for following what feels meaningful to me. In addition to evaluating ourselves positively, independent self-esteem also comes from making decisions based on our own values and developing a sense of our individual sovereignty, or self-government.

The third aspect of self-esteem is called "unconditional self-esteem." Ben-Shahar describes this as a state of being where you internally feel whole and enough. In my own language, I call this "inherent divine worth" that springs from the Inner Flame. In many ways, this experience of unconditional self-esteem is beyond the ups and downs of feeling shiny confidence or deflated self-doubt. When we are connected to our inherent divine worth, we know that our soul is always worthy and complete. We sense that even through failures and losses, there is a perfect divine order bringing us just the experiences that we need. We are always enough at the deepest level.

Here's the key to how these aspects of self-esteem progress: you must develop the first aspect (dependent) before it's a possibility for you to develop the second aspect (independent), and you must have a robust, positive experience of the first two before you can develop unconditional self-esteem. That being said, we don't leave behind the earlier aspects as we grow into independent self-esteem and unconditional self-esteem. They are all part of a healthy human psyche and experience.

While dependent self-esteem will develop naturally in childhood with the right conditions, we can also do repair work to build this type of dependent self-confidence as adults. When we never got to fully inhabit our worth through the eyes of others, the most potent medicine is to consciously seek out environments where we can be witnessed, acknowledged, encouraged, and praised. This may happen through therapy, coaching, group coaching programs, or close relationships with trusted friends. Only once this intrinsic need for being supported and accepted by others is fulfilled, can we more deeply cultivate independent self-esteem and unconditional worthiness.

One of my clients, Judith, was able to repair her dependent self-esteem around her creative voice through the container of piano and voice lessons. I taught her lessons as a child, and she had a natural desire to play, experiment and compose songs. But her natural creativity was discouraged frequently by her father. While she was in earshot, he would tell me things like, "I'm not paying money for her to just mess around on the piano. I want her to play REAL songs."

As you can imagine, this broke my heart, but I was a young teacher who didn't know how to tactfully advocate for my student's creativity.

When all this discouragement built up, Judith stopped trying to compose songs for several years. When I would encourage her, she would say, "I don't want to make up songs anymore. I'm not very good at it anyway." Swimming in the environment of her creativity being shamed, she did not have robust enough dependent self-esteem to start to evaluate herself positively based upon her own values. Luckily, her parents did support her continuing lessons and I was able to gently and consistently praise her creative voice and encourage her to do the same. A few years after moving out of her parents' house, Judith came back to me for lessons and started composing beautiful songs. With the baseline of having her creative voice praised and acknowledged in our sessions, I witnessed and supported the blossoming of her independent self-esteem and unconditional worthiness. I received the privilege of hearing Judith's Goddess Voice emerge as its own tour de force.

When it comes to sharing my own voice with the world, I have found that I needed to develop these three aspects of self-esteem for each creative avenue that I pursue. For example, with singing, I received robust encouragement and praise that gave me confidence and ease around how I sound. This dependent self-esteem grew in the nurturing container of taking voice lessons for seven years, with teachers who gave me honest positive reflections, as well as compassionately worded suggestions for improvement.

But when it came to songwriting, I never had that kind of safe, supportive nurturance. When I started writing songs, I began to share my voice in a way that felt more vulnerable, and I definitely received some criticism and rejection. After experiencing that painful criticism, for a while I was subconsciously focused on seeking approval and praise, as my dependent self-esteem was not robustly developed. Then at a certain point, I grew exhausted by caring about what others thought. I steeled my inner determination and went to the other extreme, trying to convince myself that wanting any kind of outside acknowledgment was a sign of weakness. Never seeking feedback, I went into hyper-self-reliance mode and tried to make myself an island.

In recent years I have gradually come to embrace more of a both/and approach that incorporates how essential it is for us as social creatures to have our voices be heard and respected. Rather than keeping us hooked on the opinions of others, being seen and heard helps us build a robust foundation so that we can more easily access our independent sense of worth and our unconditional self-esteem that come from within.

A Framework for Empowering Your Self-Expression

Being comfortable with being deeply seen and heard is a skill that develops over time. When we haven't had the opportunity to develop robust self-confidence, when we have had voice ruptures, or simply from observing others being taken down publicly, we may unconsciously associate being seen and heard with danger. (Cue the alarm bells: Danger! Danger!) The risk of rejection feels really daunting when we have experienced rejection before, even if the context and our own sense of personal power are totally different now.

How can we transform these places where we are unconsciously staying quiet, small, or limited? How can we develop our capacity to be seen and heard? It begins with a foundation of awareness. When it comes to staying silent or expressing ourselves, there are four main ways that internal feelings can present themselves on the outside. To help explain this, I like to imagine self-expression as a train ride. There are two modes of staying off the train (staying silent), and two ways of hopping on a train (expressing yourself). Here's a handy chart to show you the four ways we may show up at any moment:

The Voice Empowerment Framework

Repressed Silence Staying small or quiet out of fear or unconsciousness	**Repressed Self-expression** Limiting what you say or how you say it out of fear or unconsciousness

Empowered Silence Staying small or quiet out of empowered choice

Empowered Self-expression Expressing yourself freely and with empowered choice

Let's look more closely at these four modes of showing up. When the fear of speaking up or taking risks drowns out our power, I call this repressed silence. Think of someone who is in a meeting at work and feels a call to speak up with an unpopular viewpoint, knowing their perspective could help the group take a closer look at the ethics of the decision in question. Let's give this person a name. (I'm going with Pat.) If the overwhelming fear of being judged closes down Pat's throat chakra, the urge to make themselves heard gets interrupted. Being seen and heard feels dangerous and out of reach. Repressed silence is like being in a hot, stuffy waiting room at the train station. You don't have the cash (empowerment) to get a train ticket at that moment. This is life at the "stagnation station."

Repressed silence goes hand in hand with repressed self-expression, or limiting what we say or how we say it due to fear. This is the realm of people-pleasing, watering down your truth, letting self-consciousness shape how you present yourself, or constantly speaking in defensiveness or reaction to others. Basically, if it feels kind of heavy, stifled, self-deprecating, or icky when you say it there's probably an element of repression going on. Repressed self-expression is like being stuck on a train that keeps circling back to habits of fear and unconsciousness. You're expressing yourself, yes, but it's not in a way that feels good or furthers your journey of evolution. And you are probably being seen and heard on a surface level rather than allowing others to deeply see, hear, and know you in just-right ways.

I am a big advocate for standing up for oneself, so I want to make a distinction about defensive or reactive self-expression. This usually emerges out of the nervous system's fight response. When our nervous systems are allowed to unwind, heal, and come to a baseline of regulation, we can hold our ground in a strong, centered, thoughtful way. We can respond with confidence when people are out of line, instead of reacting from a place of fear and wounding.

Another place where wounding can cause repressed self-expression is when the "flock" response is coming up. In addition to fight, flight, and freeze, Polyvagal theory identifies several other emergency responses available to the human nervous system, including the tendency to flock with a group when experiencing a threat. With emotions running high, people stuck in a flock response tend to spew out the group beliefs rather than digging deep to find their own values. Allying with the herd brings a sense of safety. We see this happening a lot in politics these days, as fear and reactivity are the dominant emotions behind a lot of what's being said.

The potential to grow into confident, grounded self-expression shows where we are headed in our journeys of evolution. We can learn to ditch the repressed habits and dance between empowered silence and empowered self-expression. Empowered silence is staying small or quiet out of empowered choice. We have the cash (empowerment) for a ticket on the self-expression train, but we might not choose to ride it every frickin' minute of every day, because chilling under a tree outside the station and recharging is awesome too. We may experience these moments of empowered silence when we choose to do quiet practices such as meditation, journaling, or allowing ourselves to just "be" without trying to get anywhere.

We may also experience empowered silence in situations that from the outside look just like repressed silence. Let's go back to the example of Pat who is sitting in a meeting when the fear of being judged prevents them from speaking up and encouraging the group to consider ethical implications. If they are experiencing repressed silence, there's a kind of freeze and shutting down of the voice that takes over so the option of speaking up isn't available. However, if Pat has dedicated some time to self-empowerment they can evaluate if there is a real threat to their safety by speaking up. They may look at recent evidence and see that their boss and team have the willingness and capacity to work through different viewpoints respectfully. But if there is evidence that their boss or team members will retaliate harshly and unjustly, they may decide that it is wise and self-preserving to refrain from speaking up until they've spoken to someone for support or even found a new job. On the outside, this looks the same: Pat is staying quiet. But the difference is that in the second scenario, they make an empowered choice about whether to speak up or stay quiet. It arises from conscious contemplation rather than an unconscious shutting down of the voice. It's about finding the wise use of your energy that feels aligned with your highest good.

Empowered silence can also look like refraining from saying unhelpful things, even if a part of us really, really wants to spurt them out like a geyser. For example, if a friend of mine has just gone through a bad breakup and calls me for support, there may be a part inside that's just dying to tell her all the things I hated about her ex anyway and all of the ways that she got too attached, etc., etc. But my wise, compassionate Self may realize that it would be a lot more helpful for me to sit with her, cultivate presence, and help her to feel seen and heard. In this case, I am holding my tongue, but I'm doing so out of the choice to be more compassionate.

Now for the golden ticket: empowered self-expression. Like a glorious train that takes you exactly where you want to go, empowered self-expression happens when you feel the urge to speak up, make something, or express yourself and have the choice and freedom to follow through. While fear and unconscious habits may still pop up as thoughts in the mind, they don't have the power to hit the brakes or turn the train around. What wants to be expressed can come through with ease and flow because you are tapped into the power of your Self, which is the engine of the whole operation. During a workshop where I invited participants to journal about what they felt in their bodies during a moment of empowered self-expression, these are some of the experiences they shared:

feeling alive, powerful, bold, free, strong, grounded, and confident.

As you gradually tap into your empowered self-expression, you can cultivate the capacity to be seen, heard, and known on a deep level. The key is to start by sharing your truth with safe people so you can give your system the experience of equating being seen with being safe.

Becoming Whole Through Being Seen

I started to understand the importance of being seen and heard back in 2006 when I was at a women's meditation retreat. One evening during group meditation I felt myself straying from my mantra repetition and recalling the young man who assaulted me as a teen. I broke into sobs, my body remembering what it felt like to be frozen in fear. After meditation, I confided in my newly found soul-sister, Alejandra, that I had been taken advantage of at age fifteen. I struggled to find the right words. Did I deserve to call it rape? Did my experience count? I was unsure. But we always spoke in Spanish together, and the only word I knew for rape was *violada*. Violated. That fit. "I was violated," I told her. "He made me feel so worthless and helpless and the memories are flooding me right now." Alejandra hugged me and nodded her head, being fully present with my vulnerable truth-telling. I felt so raw and tender inside, yet at the same time being witnessed in my pain gave me a sense of wholeness that I had only managed to glimpse before. Rather than feeling like only a splinter of me was alive and visible to the world, I saw that my deeply wounded inner aspects also deserved to be seen and heard.

After witnessing my pain and supporting me, Alejandra bravely shared her own story of being raped by a former boyfriend. We saw each other, understood each other, and became more whole through each other's stories. That night, in laughter and tears and hugs we began to heal. Alejandra put her favorite songs by The Cranberries on the CD player and we danced with abandon in the big meditation hall. The crickets joined us in our outpouring of self-expression and self-love. We had no air conditioning, so we allowed the oppressive summer heat to cleanse us like a sweat lodge as we chose to rebirth ourselves. We danced and danced, and with each step we deepened our commitment to healing and reclaiming our power to speak up for ourselves.

It turns out there is a neurological reason that we feel safe when we are deeply seen and heard. Our brains evolved for us to survive in tribes or groups. We subconsciously read other people's facial expressions and posture, and our mirror neurons gather information. Am I safe with this person? Am I safe with this group? Do I need to modify my behavior to match theirs so I am accepted? Most of us learn from a young age what is safe to express and what causes others discomfort.

When we are speaking vulnerably and have the gift of seeing love and compassion reflected through the body of our listener, it promotes a deep sense of security. We learn that we don't have to hide certain feelings anymore in order to be accepted. We learn that our whole self is worthy of love. A sense of safety is communicated not just through words but through nonverbal cues as we are witnessed in our fullness.

Selective Sharing

Telling my story to Alejandra brought a beautiful gift of transformation, but some friends and family members I later confided in reacted in ways that were not super helpful. This brings up why it's important to have discernment and use our intuition when sharing vulnerably. While speaking deeply and authentically can bring a lot of benefits, it doesn't mean we have to feel bad if there are times when it really does not feel right to spill our guts and expose our hearts. We can choose empowered silence.

What I came to learn the hard way is that you don't have to share your story with everyone when you are still feeling raw, confused, or traumatized. While everyone intended to help me when I talked about being sexually assaulted, they did not know how. That's why I have written down some "red light" behaviors and "green light" behaviors to help you gauge the relative safety of sharing a vulnerable truth with someone. If you encounter someone who does the "red light" stuff, it doesn't necessarily mean you have to cut them out of your life. You may still love hitting the rock climbing gym with this person or sharing a meal with them. It just may not be the most trustworthy relationship for practicing the art of being deeply seen and known.

Red light: The person says judgmental things about you or others.
Green light: The person tries to understand other people's perspectives and experiences.

Red light: The person gossips and takes pleasure in other people's downfalls.
Green light: The person usually stays in their own lane and shows compassion to others.

Red light: The person immediately turns conversations around so the focus is on them the majority of the time ("I went through something JUST like that.")
Green light: The person is comfortable listening to and acknowledging your own story and your unique feelings.

Red light: The person tends to squirm, shut down, glaze over, or change the subject when you test out speaking vulnerably or sharing your emotions.

Green light: The person can maintain some presence and interest in deeper subjects.

Red light: The person wants to patch up your pain by laying on some quick and easy advice.

Green light: The person will ask if you would like to hear their advice or perspective and respects your wishes if you say, "No, thanks."

Red light: The person always has to be "right" and is unwilling to apologize or take responsibility after their missteps.

Green light: The person is willing to be vulnerable and make repairs when needed.

Red light: The person tends to dismiss or diminish their own feelings or other people's feelings. ("Stop being so dramatic/ emotional/irrational/negative").

Green light: The person can acknowledge and validate what you're going through.

Red light: The person has flimsy boundaries and tends to get enmeshed or personally tangled up in other people's stories.

Green light: The person has established some baseline sense of self and boundaries, and can speak up if something is too intense or triggering for them.

Red light: The person is displaying body posture that indicates they are closed off at the moment, such as arms folded across their chest, turning away from you, looking away, or becoming rigid.

Green light: The person's body posture indicates some comfort with the interaction, such as intermittent eye contact, facing you, and nodding "yes" occasionally.

Red light: The person is going through something difficult or stressful in their life and is nervous, anxious, on edge, or shut down.

Green light: The person may have some stressors ('cause that is part of being human), but they have a baseline of resilience and stability that give them the bandwidth to be a compassionate listener right now.

Keeping an eye out for these red lights and green lights can help you assess the likelihood of having a positive experience when you speak authentically and vulnerably, and help you see areas of growth for you to hold space for others. When working with a professional therapist or coach, it's reasonable to expect them to be in the green light category all the time. When sharing with a friend or family member who is usually in the green, use your intuition to help you determine if it's a good time and situation for you to share what's in your heart. Notice that the last two "red light" and "green light" behaviors are not necessarily habits but temporary states that might change. Finding an appropriate time can work wonders for encouraging a positive interaction of being seen and heard.

Another great way to practice the art of being seen and heard is to specify ahead of time what kind of feedback or reaction you are hoping to receive. You may start a conversation by telling the person you have something vulnerable you are thinking of sharing and asking if it's a good time for a deep exchange. Then you can let them know what kind of response you would like, such as just being witnessed, wanting reassurance or a pep talk, acknowledgment of what you are going through, wanting to be celebrated, or receiving suggestions, advice, or intuitive hits that may be helpful. Here are some phrases to help get your wheels turning on ways to intentionally ask for feedback.

- "Right now, I'm still processing this and what would be most helpful is if you just listen and witness me without saying anything in return. Is that doable for you?"

- "I am experiencing a lot of self-doubt and would love to receive some reassurance after I share what I'm going through."

- "After I share, it would be really helpful if you just acknowledge what I'm going through and reflect my words back to me."

- "I am proud of the resilience I'm developing and would love to be celebrated for that."

- "If any advice, suggestions, or intuitive messages come to you, I am open to ideas on how to move forward."

When someone shares a personal experience or a creative project with me, I like to be proactive and ask them what kind of feedback they wish to receive after they share. I have used this approach in the group coaching circles I have run, and the results have been AMAZING. People feel deeply empowered when they get to specify what they would like to receive in return.

Healing Our Assumptions and Overgeneralizations

When I began to talk with others about some of my sexual trauma, at first I stuck to confiding in females. Women just felt like safer confidants. Beyond the trauma I experienced from male perpetrators, I had some experiences of my voice being dismissed by males in the past. The thing is, these select experiences led me to overgeneralize that being vulnerable and authentic with ALL males was not safe.

Soon after I got engaged to Paco, I subconsciously felt like I had gathered enough evidence to determine he would not react harshly if I spoke my truth to him about my history of sexual trauma. He may not have all the perfect words to say, but I trusted he could respond with compassion. I felt the upwelling of emotion and desire for being seen one night when we were curled up on a motel bed in California. The air conditioner whirred loudly in the background, my tears wetting the scratchy white sheets. The words tumbled out as I told Paco that I was raped at the age of fifteen.

It was the first time I spoke those words aloud to a man. I felt like damaged goods, a person too broken to be worthy of love. Yet he loved me still, and held me, and told me it was okay. The next day, I would have to paint on a smile and zip up my pink bridesmaid's dress for my friend's wedding. But that night, I was flooded with relief as my true, messy self found her voice.

There is power and pain in speaking the truth. There was nowhere to hide anymore, so I had to let myself experience the hurt and the tears. I let myself be vulnerable. I let myself be seen. And in doing so, I let in the possibility that I was worthy of love in my wholeness and complexity.

As we deepen our capacity for being seen and heard, we can look for the places where we might be making assumptions about how people will react based on past experiences that are not tied to the relationship in question. Rather than going into the knee-jerk reaction, we can evaluate each situation based on recent evidence from THIS relationship. For example, if you ever had a relationship with a therapist, coach, or healer that didn't end well, you might be reluctant to ever trust one of these professionals again. However, when considering working with someone new, you can look for the red light or green light behaviors and start to test the waters to gauge if they are likely to be a safe person. They might have the same profession, but they are a totally different individual who may have the capacity to help you feel that deep human need for acknowledgment by others.

This idea of moving beyond overgeneralization applies to sharing your voice more publicly as well. If you've been criticized, spurned, or ignored when sharing a message publicly in the past, you don't have to assume everyone in the future is going to react like those naysayers of the past. As you increase your sense of worth, it becomes easier to find the people who are grateful to hear your world-changing wisdom. When you respect yourself more deeply, you are much more likely to be treated with respect. This is not a guarantee that mean-spirited criticism won't come up, but a reassurance that you will have the resilience to handle those experiences. By incrementally increasing your comfort with being seen and heard on deeper levels, trust in your own voice and validity emerges.

Creating Boundaries that Garner Respect

Setting boundaries in our relationships is the art of making our needs heard and respected. But it can feel really freakin' hard. What I have found is that setting a boundary with your voice or your body is a lot more powerful and easier to do when it's backed up by the energy of your innate divine power. It's pretty common to say "no" to something because we're making an effort to set boundaries, yet inside we feel unworthy and unsure that it's okay to say no. We worry about what the other person will think or do if we stand up for ourselves. Here, the energy doesn't match the words. We wonder if our need is as important as their need.

So let me share what I now know to be true: we all deserve to have our needs met.

I'm not talking about the bare necessities, scraping by, Slim-Fast Shake version of just barely receiving what we need to survive. We all deserve to feel nourished inside and out, physically, mentally, and spiritually. Past incidents of being mistreated, overlooked, or undernourished are not evidence of being undeserving. They are opportunities for us to look within, see how we can set clear boundaries, state our needs, and give ourselves what we need from the inside out.

I used to think it was virtuous and self-reliant not to ask to have my needs met and respected. There were times when I said, "Sure, I can do that task," even though it would have been wise for me to rest and pace myself instead. There were days when I said, "okay honey, you take the last banana," even if my body was craving those particular nutrients. I made it through with something else rather than suggesting we split it.

Sacrificing ourselves can feel like an inescapable pattern, but the Inner Flame of worthiness can help us here. The more you connect to your inner worth and confidence, the more your energy of sovereignty will emerge. I have seen firsthand that when a woman can stand in her power energetically, her boundaries are less likely to be questioned. When she says clearly, "This is what's okay with me, and this is what is not okay with me," she is more likely to be heard. In addition to meditating on the Inner Flame at your third chakra, it's powerful to deliberately practice articulating your boundaries.

It can actually be super fun to create some nonthreatening role-plays with a friend or coach. Practice speaking clearly about what ways of interacting with you are unacceptable and have your practice buddy celebrate your declaration.

A key thing to remember when voicing boundaries is to keep the focus on yourself and your needs. If you say, "You keep interrupting me and you need to stop," this word choice is likely to provoke defensiveness in the other person. To keep the focus on yourself, you might say, "In order to feel respected, I need to be listened to. Please let me finish my thoughts before jumping in or interrupting." If this initial statement is not enough to change the person's behavior, you can introduce the action you will take if your boundary is crossed. You can say, "I feel disrespected when my voice is interrupted. If I notice you interrupting me during a conversation, I will need to leave the room."

In addition to considering word choice, you can also notice that the tone of your voice has the right amount of firmness for the situation. If you are in a personal or professional relationship where there is a baseline of trust, then a kind, clear and confident voice will likely be effective. However, if your first "no" or boundary is not heard, it's time to bring in more firmness and power as you speak. And if someone is ever threatening you or someone you love, you may find that loud, ferocious, mama-bear firmness is called for right off the bat.

Embodying these levels of firmness in your vocal inflection becomes easier when you tune into the energetic side of setting boundaries. To that end, I will walk you through a practice I share with my clients. It is inspired by the Gatekeeper archetype that was taught to me by Rachael Maddox.

Meditation: Energetic Boundaries

First, use your imagination to create an energetic door that you can easily open and close. You can visualize this door in front of you with a doorknob and a latch, and any other details that help it come alive. You are fully in charge of when this door will open to let something in, and when it will close to keep something out.

Then you can imagine something mild that would feel like a "no" in your body- perhaps a food that you don't like, or a type of social situation that doesn't nourish and fill you, or a request for help that would be too draining for you to fulfill. Once you have pulled it up in your mind, imagine closing the energetic door. Then you get to practice saying "no" out loud lots and lots of times, experimenting with different volumes and vocal inflections. It's also great to let your body get in the game, practicing what a stance of a fully embodied "no" feels like.

When the time feels right, switch to the practice of saying "yes." Start by imagining an invitation to do something that sounds and feels fully enjoyable. It may be really small, such as a friend offering to lend you a novel they loved. Practice opening the door of your energy field to let in that deliciousness as you repeat the word, "yes!"

From Being Seen Only in Intimate Settings to Sharing Publicly

How are you feeling, goddesses? Are you starting to get an idea of how to feel even safer with setting boundaries and being seen and heard? Once you have gone a good distance on the path of being witnessed in intimate relationships, at some point you may (or may not) feel the tug in your heart to share your voice more publicly. This may look like joining rallies, sharing your story at support groups, or speaking at events. It might look like trying karaoke or open mic nights or scheduling concerts for yourself. Sharing your voice more publicly might also look like speaking up and setting boundaries at work. Or you might feel a soul calling to share and promote your writing, creative projects, or business more widely by speaking on podcasts, creating events, posting on social media, or collaborating with others who can help you expand your reach.

Whatever form your empowered self-expression may take, don't be alarmed if some internal resistance pops up before you speak up. There is nothing wrong with you! Almost everyone will pay the occasional tax after they have hopped on the self-expression train, and here's the thing: not everyone pays the same amount. The more marginalized your identity, the higher the tax that the outside culture imposes on you. I call this the "role-busting tax" because anytime you are growing beyond the historical roles and stereotypes for your gender, race, or socioeconomic class some people may react in ways that try to "keep you in your place." The culture of domination is maintained not just by people with tons of power but also by folks you meet in your everyday life who are scared of what transformation your liberation might spark in them. When you see women taking other women down, this fear of transformation is often at the root.

The role-busting tax usually takes the form of people giving unconstructive criticism, rejection, shaming, ignoring your work, or questioning your right to speak. Even if we haven't received much personally in terms of unkind feedback, we still pay the tax in the form of emotional energy if we've seen those who look and think like us be criticized for stepping out of line. Watching others be taken down publicly creates a buried fear of what will happen to us when we show up authentically and unapologetically. For women, anytime we leave the obscurity of running the home to speak up or put work into the world, there are still going to be people of all genders who bristle. Our act of making ourselves heard is a threat to the old world order of patriarchy, which feels familiar, and hence comfortable, for a lot of folks. Men may also pay the role-busting tax anytime they display so-called "unmasculine" qualities like sensitivity, uncertainty, or weakness. And gender expansive people pay the tax because their very willingness to be themselves breaks down all the old roles and stereotypes.

When I was a newly married 23-year-old, seeing other women pay the role-busting tax kept me in paralysis. Having seen female musicians objectified, mocked, and gossiped about for everything from their looks to their sanity to their decision-making capacity, I was subconsciously scared of putting myself out there. I remember one winter evening, Paco and I went into a cozy local coffee shop to order some overly hot herbal tea. An open mic event happened to be going on, and a white guy with dark hair sat on a stool at the end of the room strumming his guitar and singing a mellow song. Gripping their steaming drinks, everyone in the coffee shop was turned to watch. I asked the barista about how to get on the list of performers and I thought about coming back to sing one of my original songs for the next open mic. Later that night, I even wrote it on my calendar. And yet, as that first Saturday of the month rolled around, I was filled with a sense of dread. I told myself I was too tired to practice and perform. Even though I have awesome pitch without accompaniment, I told myself it wasn't "good enough" to sing a capella since there was no piano at the venue. I told myself a whole bunch of stories to cover up the fear of being seen and possibly rejected. Underneath it all, I was scared I didn't have the emotional capacity to handle anything other than a perfect reception of my voice. I was scared that paying the role-busting tax would break me.

Looking back on this experience of repressed silence, I see how I wanted to wait until the outside world felt safe enough for me to share my heartfelt songs. I wanted a guarantee that I wouldn't have to pay the role-busting tax, but the only way to do that was to stay silent and never try. Over the years I have come to see that we don't have to live in fear of how we might be penalized for speaking up. What we need is to build our emotional resilience and external support systems so that we have the capacity to handle whatever feedback may come our way. By building up our dependent, independent, and unconditional self-esteem we can sort out those rare pieces of constructive criticism from all the mean-spirited stuff out there. We can fill our reserves so we have the means to pay the role-busting tax if someone feels subconsciously threatened by our blossoming Goddess Voice.

While the role-busting tax is real and all of us may have to pay it here and there, by and large we can expect our voices to be celebrated and honored. When we want to share our message on a larger scale, we will see the impact of our voices being received positively when we focus on speaking to our ideal audience. When you are an empathic person and feel other people's emotions in your body, it's really common to want to express yourself in a way that pleases everybody. You don't want to feel the discomfort that may come from somebody disliking what you share. Yet this often leads us to create watered-down, non-provocative art or messages that aim to appeal to everyone. But in truth, they appeal to no one. When you test out sharing with different people and audiences to see who really relates to your offerings, you can get a sense of the personality traits, interests, beliefs, struggles, and desires of your ideal audience. These are the people that will listen to your voice and say, "Hell yes! I want to hear more!" They will be transformed by your voice and message, which creates ripples that are felt by all of humanity (including the naysayers whom you gave up trying to convert into supporters.)

If you are still feeling stymied by the role-busting tax, consider that we pay a higher price for staying in repressed silence and repressed self-expression. When we recognize that we have the means to pay the role-busting tax, we can reap the abundant rewards that come from empowered silence and empowered self-expression. We can feel the much-needed heart connection that comes from being seen, heard, and known. We can feel proud of ourselves for living, breathing, and speaking authentically. And we can shine as the goddesses we are meant to become.

Unleash Your Goddess Voice Practice No. 6: Empowered Silence and Empowered Self-Expression

Now we get to experiment with following your inner impulses to make sound or rest in silence.

For a recording of this practice, visit saragiita.com/free

1. Rub your hands together vigorously, inviting warmth and love to gather in your palms.

2. Gently place your hands on your neck, throat, or jaw in any way that feels good. *(Continued on next page.)*

3. When you feel ready, ask your throat chakra if it would like to rest in empowered silence or make sounds as empowered self-expression.

4. Give yourself a few minutes to meet that desire for silence or sound.

CHAPTER 7

Harmonize Your Nervous System

I'm not waiting for the world to change.
Safety lies within.
I don't need someone to save me.
Safety lies within.
My grounded resilience is born of
my power that lies within;
My rumbling voice emerges from
my power that lies within.

Creating the Safety to Speak Up

When you want to amplify your Goddess Voice, finding more easeful self-expression starts with creating a felt sense of safety within. Since the nervous system includes an unconscious biological mechanism for sensing and reacting to perceived threats, tuning in with what's happening in your nervous system helps to create the foundation of feeling safe to speak up and be heard.

It took me a while to figure this out. When I felt like I was done with my many years of doing trauma resolution therapy, I pressured myself to jump right into shining big as a musician: big stages, big energy, and big media outreach. Yet my body kept calling me back into a gentler and more integrated pace. Any time I was pushing myself too hard, my body would respond with a fluttering heart, tense muscles, and a sense of unease. Looking back, I see that my system instinctively knew I still needed to apply the principles of trauma healing as I transitioned into a bigger, more visible, more fulfilling life of creative purpose.

In this chapter, I will guide you through some trauma-informed tools so that you can apply them to your path of speaking up and letting your creative voice shine. Why trauma-informed tools? Because almost all of us have experienced voice ruptures, or past moments when our voices were dismissed, disrespected, or devalued. And when criticism, backlash, rejection, or being ignored resurface again when we speak up and put ourselves out there, it can trigger the feeling of that original wound (even if it was a hard-to-pinpoint, slow-drip wound over many years). By learning to work with the waves of activation and relaxation in our nervous system, we can create new patterns of being steady and confident in ourselves even in the face of criticism and rejection. This is what I call harmonizing the nervous system.

In chapter two we touched upon our embodied emergency responses like fight, flight, and freeze, which are common biological reactions to shocking traumatic events. Pete Walker also identified a lesser-known trauma response called "fawning." Repeated stressors like ongoing prejudice, living with narcissists, or growing up with emotionally immature caretakers can trigger this "please and appease" mode. We become hyperaware of other people's emotions, moods, and needs and do our best to make their life easier so that we can feel safer. Many women have been socialized to become people-pleasers; I believe it is the primary trauma response to living with constant, unacknowledged patriarchal oppression. Our bodies are still collectively unlearning the habit of smiling at dismissive behavior and saying, "Would you like some sugar with that?"

Remember that trauma is any overwhelming experience where you don't have the support you need, so you don't have the resources you need to cope. When this happens, the emotion connected to this painful event gets stored in your body until a later time when it might be safe to release it. When emotion is stuck, we often go numb, and being disconnected from our emotions is what makes it more difficult to connect with our sacred Inner Flame.

While the form and the severity vary, trauma is a part of life. And after overwhelming stressful events, we may already have enough health or support on board for our nervous systems to come back to a regulated state, or one in which we can respond to situations calmly and effectively. Coming back to regulation may involve our bodies going through a process of shaking, movement, speaking, sounding, or completing any fight or flight responses that got interrupted or repressed. But very often, we don't get a chance to discharge the pent-up energy that was needed to mobilize us into responding to the stressful event. Then your nervous system may get stuck, still responding to life through the lens of fight, flight, freeze, or fawn mode. We start to go through life feeling disconnected from our inner sense of safety that comes from our divine Inner Flame.

Here's the key thing I want you to understand about the nervous system: just as our bodies have an innate mechanism for responding to perceived threats, our bodies also have an innate mechanism for returning to a state of CALM. Our intelligent, life-preserving nervous systems have the capacity to regulate themselves and return to health. The ability to return to balance is already within us. In several modalities, including the work of trauma educator Rachael Maddox, I have come across this idea of a natural blueprint of health. No matter how deep our traumas, we can gradually return to our innate design of health, wholeness, and stability. For me, this experience of the natural blueprint of health is deeply intertwined with our Inner Flame. Even when stressful life events make us feel disconnected from this innate power, it is always glowing within, ready to come back online as we gradually increase our sense of safety.

When Trauma Resolution is Needed

These trauma-informed tools are designed to be used on your own if you are already in a neutral or good state most of the time, and want to learn how to thrive more gloriously in your self-expression. Buuuuuuut…, if you have intense traumas that frequently get triggered and have not yet been reprocessed in a safe container, you might be at a stage of the journey where one-on-one trauma resolution work with a trained professional is more helpful. Since traumas most often happen in our relationships with other people, they can most effectively heal in the presence of another loving human. I recommend working with a therapist or a well-trained healer or coach who specializes in healing trauma. Your nervous system will attune to the stability and grounded states that your guide embodies, helping protect you from severe overwhelm and distress that may come with disturbing memories. Guiding you to build resilience, a skilled healing professional can gently invite you into relaxation and balance.

Sometimes, people close to us are better equipped to see that our raw reactions to triggers are not "just the way we are" and can be helped with therapy. When I was newly married to Paco as a 23-year-old, he was the one who encouraged me to start trauma resolution therapy. Even though life was good, at any moment I was prone to falling into a dark, anxious hole. Then I'd find myself clawing at the crumbling earth, trying to get out. It seemed like anything could trigger me: a news headline, a suspenseful movie, an unexpected touch. When my new husband and I got into fights, I would cry for an hour, feeling victimized. After one such fight, I spent the evening with my back leaning against the wall, staring into the bathroom. I went through a box of recycled-paper tissues as I cried and cried and could not pull myself out of my misery.

When Paco printed out a list of local therapists who specialized in overcoming the trauma of sexual assault, I protested. I had so many excuses as to why it was an inconvenient time to face my pain: I was stressed from my work teaching 30 music lessons a week, I was too busy, and, furthermore, we were too tight on money. Still, he convinced me that I was worth it. He insisted we could make the money work, because in the end what could be more important than investing in my own happiness? What was the point of replacing our worn-out clothes if I was miserable?

I am grateful for him encouraging me to get help because the years I spent doing Somatic Experiencing and

Eye Movement Desensitization and Reprocessing (EMDR) therapies were absolutely foundational to my process of discovering my Goddess Voice and stepping into my life's work. Without dedicating all that time to healing, I would not have gotten to the place where my nervous system could let me know I felt safe and ready to put myself out there to be seen, heard, and help others. So all of this is to say, if you are frequently overwhelmed and triggered, you can heal and you deserve support!

Building Our Resources

To share our voices in bigger ways, we need to build a resilient foundation of stability in our bodies. Healing is not all about facing the pain; it is essential that we expand our capacity for feeling peaceful, centered, and joyful. In many therapeutic modalities, this is called building our resources.

A resource is anything that helps you feel safe and stable. It can be internal, meaning you increase your own feelings of calmness and strength. Internal resources could be practices like deep breathing, martial arts, visualization, meditation, prayer, yoga, or journaling. Exercise and sports can also be resources, as long as you are not beating yourself to the ground through an overly critical attitude or harsh pace. Hobbies and passions can also be internal resources if they promote our well-being. Reading, gardening, knitting, creative endeavors, fixing things, or playing games are just a few of the possibilities for centering activities. Internal resources can also be intangible, like recalling fond memories or connecting to spirit guides.

External resources are people or support systems we can call upon for help. Any service that helps you relax, such as receiving a massage, facial, pedicure, or energy work could be a resource. Loving pets or animals can be a calming presence for many people. Intimate relationships are also important external resources, as we know how helpful it can be to confide in a good friend. When we are sick or in crisis, we may have friends, partners, or family members that provide a safety net to catch us. When they are absent or unequipped to help, we may call upon external resources such as crisis support lines, shelters, support groups, or charitable programs. Professional counselors, coaches, and healers are also external resources, and they can help you build your own internal resources.

As we explore how to build resilience in this chapter, you may wish to write down a list of resources you already have in place as well as resources you wish to explore or strengthen in your life. Bringing your Goddess Voice into the light will usually include a few dark passages and difficult days, and you can better navigate the challenges when you have a collection of supportive practices, habits, activities, and people on board.

Especially if you are actively healing trauma, it's easy to get pulled into fear and negativity, like a riptide that carries us farther from the shore of our Inner Flame. That's why I want to emphasize building a life raft of positive resources before, during, and after the courageous work of reprocessing and embracing any trauma. In my 20's, one of my struggles with keeping my life raft full came from highly undervaluing rest, fun, creativity, and laughter. I discounted the importance of staying abundantly resourced. Yet sacred rest and joyous play often bring the greatest healing. Our life rafts will naturally stay buoyant when we honor the natural pace of what feels right in the moment for how to invest our time.

When it comes to healing trauma, valuing rest is especially important. Our nervous system needs time to find a restful pace after being activated. If you engage in trauma therapy, I highly recommend scheduling time to lie down and rest after appointments. Throughout the week, remember that building your resources is an essential part of healing. If you ever feel guilty for doing nothing or something that feels like a "waste of time," remind yourself that's probably just from growing up in a culture that passes judgment on activities that don't produce marketable results.

Some of you might say, "But I don't have time to build all these resources and rest and revisit my trauma." I hear you. When you objectively look at your current responsibilities and feel overwhelmed, it may be a signal that it is time to focus just on building positive resources at the pace that feels right to you. As I learned the hard way, there's no need to rush into the trauma territory or push through it. If you are meant to dive in, you will know when the time is right. You can trust that the circumstances will arise for you to move at a restful, embodied pace, with a joyous life raft to carry you through.

Finding Just the Right Amount

Alright, goddesses, let's dive into one of these trauma-informed tools! Dr. Peter A. Levine, creator of Somatic Experiencing, adopted the term "titration" as a tool for healing trauma. In scientific terms, when chemists don't know the concentration of a certain solution, they will slowly add a reactant drop by drop. By seeing how many drops it takes to make a change, they can determine the concentration of the first solution. In terms of trauma healing, titration means moving slowly to find just the right amount to create a change. In my life, I experience titration as taking small, doable steps in the direction of my creative purpose. It's the opposite of flooding yourself with big expectations, deadlines, or comparisons to others. Titration is asking yourself: what amount of speaking up or putting myself out there would feel just right for my nervous system? By tracking physical symptoms like a racing heart, sweaty palms, or numbness, we can assess the intensity of our feelings and ask ourselves: what would feel like a manageable, safe step outside of my comfort zone? This is very closely related to the idea of Compassionate Pacing from Chapter One, with the added concept of finding just the right effective dose to create a change.

Here's how this process looked for my student Ronda. She wanted to sing but started with piano first because it felt less vulnerable. When she was ready, she asked me to extend her lesson so we could integrate singing lessons into her time each week. After several months, she joined a group-sharing circle I hosted and sang in front of people for the first time in decades. This was an effective dose to help her feel the excitement and nervousness of performing without getting overwhelmed.

After that experience of stepping outside of her comfort zone in a safe way, Ronda and I took time to process and integrate the experience. I reminded her to look for the bravery and things that went well rather than dwelling on the nervousness and the mistakes that she experienced. About eight months later, she courageously performed at an in-person recital among other students. She gradually began to play piano and sing with more ease and confidence at subsequent performances. It was beautiful to witness how she grew her capacity to shine by inviting more people to come to her performances and witness her beautiful, resonant voice in its loving glory. Through these incremental experiences, she discovered how to safely open herself energetically to receive attention and be witnessed.

Since I was born as one of those unique individuals who is an introvert but loves to be on stage, I did not have to go through too much titration to be comfortable sharing my singing voice on stage. However, this concept of taking small, doable steps has been immensely important for me in sharing my story of overcoming sexual trauma.

When I first was uncovering repressed memories from my childhood trauma, it was really hard to even voice things out loud to my therapist. That shame really wanted to stay buried. But with her loving support, acceptance, and celebration of my triumphs, I gradually built up the strength to share my story with my husband and immediate family members. I wanted to be known, and though their reactions were often filled with their own shocked emotions rather than support for me, I am glad I went through the process of speaking my truth. In 2017, I began to feel the inner call to start sharing my story more publicly (the #metoo movement definitely helped me feel safe doing so.) I began by first describing myself as a sexual assault survivor without sharing any details. I stayed with that small, doable chunk for a while as my nervous system got used to this new level of vulnerability and sharing. Then I talked about the experience with my therapist before putting myself out there again.

To be clear, I am in no way advocating that everybody rush right out and share their stories of past or current traumas! I felt the call in my heart to share this aspect of my story, but that will not be the case for everyone. Even so, I hope this example shows how titration can help you share your voice and be heard in a way that doesn't overwhelm your nervous system.

Recognizing Activation and Relaxation

As we bravely share our voices with the people we feel called to communicate with, it's helpful to get in touch with the nervous system's waves of activation and relaxation. Activation is like climbing a hill and anticipating the view. Our heart beats a little faster, blood flows to our limbs and we become more alert and focused. Relaxation or down-regulation is like coming down the hill and enjoying the view. Our heart rate slows a little bit and we feel more relaxed and at ease. We are constantly riding these waves, as each inhale brings a subtle activation, and each exhale brings a subtle relaxation. If you like to get technical, what I am calling activation and relaxation is a function of the autonomic nervous system, which has two notable subdivisions. The subdivision called the sympathetic nervous system (or the "get-up-and-go" system) brings activation, while the parasympathetic nervous system (or the "rest and digest" system) brings relaxation.

By the way, we may experience activation as positive or negative. While the fight or flight emergency responses are extreme forms of activation, there are lots of subtle gradations of activation in our everyday life. When we are riding a roller coaster or feeling excitement about an upcoming event, we may enjoy the alive, alert feeling of activation. But when we are under threat, are feeling stressed, or are going through an experience that brings up a painful memory, activation may feel unpleasant at best, and terrifying at worst.

When you speak publicly, perform, or share your work more widely, this will likely bring activation, and depending on your history the activation could be really exciting or really terrifying for you! Here is where sharing on a small, doable scale can help you get to know the cycles of activation and relaxation. With practice, you can reframe the sensations of activation as excitement rather than nervousness. You can be present with the expansiveness that comes from channeling creative energy on a physical or metaphorical stage. You can notice the rapid heartbeat, the sweaty palms, or the sensations of butterflies in your stomach as your body's healthy response that keeps you alert and present.

If you are worried the activation may pull you into overwhelm or shut down, you can connect with one of your resources or do some movement like shaking, tapping, or stretching to stay within your capacity for resilience rather than overwhelm. Practices that help you feel calm in your everyday life are super useful when you are about to get on stage or share your voice publicly. I remember one of my piano students found it really calming to listen to music with binaural beats. Before every concert, she would come early, put on her headphones, and plant her feet on the ground. Amid the bustle of people arriving and chatting throughout the auditorium, I could see the serenity on her face as she closed her eyes and looked within.

I have used the excitement reframe combined with resourcing for years while helping hundreds of clients to get on stage. In the weeks before an upcoming performance or speech, I typically ask clients to rate how nervous they feel about performing on a scale of one to ten, with one being totally relaxed and ten being terrified. Most of my clients will give a number between five and eight, while a small percentage will say three or four. If you are ever at a nine or ten that is a sign to slow down. If possible, find ways to do smaller, more incremental experiences of being in front of others before attempting an event of this size or scale. If you can't reschedule your speech or performance, at the very least consider doing some warm-up performances in front of small groups of people you trust.

When the nervousness ratings are below eight, I let folks know that their rating is a sign that they care about doing well. When the time comes for your performance or speech, your rapidly beating heart will help you to be alert and focused. All of this is to say that it's normal to feel nervousness, and you can reframe the physical symptoms of activation as positive. Looking back on those times when I've been quivering in my shiny silver flats, I've learned that it's a lot easier to enjoy the butterflies when you are well-prepared for a performance, speech, or event. So plan your goddess outfit, practice your craft, and give yourself the confidence that comes from preparation.

If you're ever at a one or two on the nervousness scale, this can mean you are super confident sharing your voice in this type of context. Or it might mean that you don't care much about this event. My wish is for you to find the places where sharing your voice gives a spark of enthusiasm. Give yourself time to reflect on what lights you up and motivates you to show up as your best self.

Another key aspect of reframing activation as positive is to become practiced at riding the waves until they crest and trusting that our systems know how to bring us down and back to homeostasis once again. When you spend enough time watching ocean waves, your body will understand this intuitively. Energetically, riding the waves can be smoothed and mastered by allowing your awareness and your energy field to expand with activation and contract with relaxation. Try this powerful visualization leading up to any event where you will be sharing your voice on a larger scale.

Meditation: Riding the Waves of Activation and Relaxation

Think of a color that would be soothing right now. Visualize this color surrounding you like a bubble. As you inhale, imagine your bubble growing bigger and notice any slight feelings of activation or alertness. As you exhale, visualize your bubble contracting as your system enjoys a slight relaxation.

Playing with Time and Space

Our nervous systems generally prefer incremental change over time, rather than sudden, shocking shifts. This is not to say humans can only move slowly; we absolutely have the capacity to move quickly and stay regulated and calm. It just means that if things move so quickly that they feel overwhelming, we may feel the urge to later repair those experiences by playing with slowing or stopping time in our imagination, bringing in resources, and/or changing the ending of the story. We can play with space by keeping one foot in the energy of the past memory, and one foot in our present space. This is really helpful if the idea of sharing your voice with others brings up the sensations, memories, or fears of past voice ruptures even after you have already done some work to heal those experiences. Oh, the cycles of healing!

I found pausing time to be immensely helpful when revisiting the memory of when I first received criticism for one of the songs I wrote. I was 23, one year into my songwriting journey and I was collaborating with another musician as part of a yogi band. I really wanted us all to perform my song, "I Will Thrive," which was the first song I wrote for myself and not for the occasional music theory assignment. I was practicing the song while my collaborator was taking a break outside. Then he walked in with his guitar and sat down awkwardly. I knew something felt off right away. He said in a falsely cheerful voice, "I was just outside playing this other song and realized that the chord progression could work for 'I Will Thrive.' Here, let's try it—just start singing at the chorus." So I sang along awkwardly, but it all felt off with his new chords. With a shaky voice, I thanked him for the idea and said I wanted to keep the song in its original form. He let out an exasperated sigh. "But you just use the same four chords the entire time. It's so basic and boring."

There it was—the truth of his opinion. I was right in sensing he was not being genuine in the beginning, and I lost the fight to hold back my tears as overwhelm took over.

In retrospect, I can feel some gratitude that he was trying to find a way to be tactful about suggesting new chords. Asking for permission to make a suggestion would have been more helpful, but I can see that he was trying to find a way to do it without hurting my feelings. The thing is, the whole ruse sent me into a shame spiral. I felt like the underlying message was that he didn't believe I could handle a suggestion, and he needed to make it seem like a chance discovery. As if I were a little child. I was thrown into a triggered state, remembering all of the times I had felt embarrassed about crying and wished I could just "hold it together" like other people. My insecurities about the songs I wrote were raging. And my body remembered the sticky-glue freeze state of being treated as unworthy by males during the sexual assaults, and this tiny incident of criticism took on immense proportions in my emotional landscape.

When looking back to heal my shame many years later, the essential first step was to really truly believe I could heal this memory by stopping time, bringing in a resource, and changing the ending. Then I went into the story, using a tool I learned from my Somatic Experiencing therapist, Maggie Kerrigan. She taught me I could give myself a remote control and imagine the incident on a TV screen. This gives me complete control to pause the story for as long as I wish. So I put a pause on that baby from the first moment when he walked into the room. I took a few breaths and pulled in visualization as a resource to help me feel safe and stable. I called in the divine support of my spirit guides, and also imagined my college piano teacher, Carol, was there because she was always such a champion of my musical instincts. I imagined Carol asking me what I was feeling, and I responded by telling her I felt trepidation. She assured me that everything I was feeling was okay and reminded me that I am just right, just as I am.

After taking a few more deep breaths and feeling all of the support and encouragement around me, I felt ready to hit the play button again on the memory. In this retelling, I felt more empowered when singing along with the experimental chords he played. I spoke with more confidence when saying I wanted to keep the song in its original form. Then, at the moment when I started falling into the shame spiral, I hit the pause button again. I let myself feel that shame and practiced dual awareness to also sense all of the love and support surrounding me from the resources I was visualizing. I felt my body want to move and shift a little bit and fell into a minute or so of rhythmically circling my shoulders and neck. I heard the voice of my wise Self reassuring me, "You are worthy. You deserve to trust yourself. You deserve respect. What you create has value."

When I felt ready, I allowed the story to continue. This time I imagined him leaving the room so I could cry in peace. I envisioned my nurturing inner Self holding the 23-year-old Sara, rocking her as she cried. I felt my body start to sway and receive her love. I heard the nurturing voice again, "Crying is healthy. You deserve time and space to feel your feelings. It's okay to feel upset after someone calls your chords boring and basic. Just remember that his comments have nothing to do with your worth or the worth of your songs." With this, I felt myself sitting up straighter. As I tapped into the energy of my Inner Flame, I was able to give the memory a new energy. Rather than coming out of the conversation feeling ashamed and dejected, I felt empowered and steady in myself. I was able to infuse my current-day confidence and worthiness into the memory, and the painful associations melted away.

After the visualization, I gave myself time and space to relax into the feeling.

Playing with time and space can also be used proactively if you're feeling nervous about an upcoming conversation, speech, or launch. Notice any places where your mind keeps looping into fears of what may go wrong and imagine the future scenario on the TV screen. Imagine a remote control and notice the details of how the remote looks and feels in your hands. Then, pause the future event and give yourself all the time, energetic space, and resources you need to feel empowered. Breathe in the feeling of trusting that things will unfold in just the right way for your highest good and the highest good of all. Imagine an outcome that would feel really good, and don't worry if you still experience moments of fear, nervousness, or negative thoughts. Through a willingness to love and accept yourself in the fullness of your emotions and experiences, you can practice dual awareness and gradually come to believe that a nourishing future outcome is possible for you.

Rhythms of Release and Integration

When reading this story of how I healed the stuck emotions around receiving criticism, you may notice a rhythm of pausing, focusing on a resource, sensing what emotions or urges are emerging, and allowing the body to move until the cycle of activation is complete. Sound or visualization may also come with the movement.

After feeling activation or emotional charge, we may find our body naturally comes into periods of rest and integration as part of the rhythms of release. Our nervous system propels us up the hill, and then we can coast on down. In the context of a therapy appointment or playing with time and space at home, you may find yourself zoning out, staring at the wall, or your mind getting carried off on a tangent. This can actually mean your system was ready for a break from the intensity of excavating buried feelings. When you bring awareness to your body, you may also experience natural urges to yawn, sigh, stretch out, change position, or make rhythmic movements such as tapping your toes or hands. Let these periods of integrating body and mind last for as long as your body wants. Healing is happening in this stage just as much as when we are experiencing activation and uncomfortable emotions.

When our body takes time to rest, we can trust that the sensations and urges that arise are healthy ways to integrate the memories or experiences that used to cause distress. From our conscious trips into the Zone of Growth, we remember that the stressful memories are in the past. We learn that we can handle looking at them. We learn that they are not a beast who is constantly trying to attack us. We can integrate the memories of shame or fear into the narrative of our life story. Instead of seeming like scary monsters, the memories get filed along with our recollections of joy, boredom, love, frustration, and excitement. This is a major part of how we heal. The rhythms of release propel us through the dark shadows of what was buried and carry us back to the place of presence.

We also experience these cycles of growth and rest in a larger context in our lives, as cycles within a day, or over the course of weeks, months, or years. When I find myself in a period of stepping outside my comfort zone, I may feel motivated to work more, learn more, or try new things. I also am drawn to reading books that challenge my old ways of being and encourage me to grow. When I am able to tune into my body's natural impulses, it doesn't feel like I have to push myself. The right actions arise spontaneously.

When a period of rest emerges, I need to consciously draw upon my resources of self-acceptance and compassionate self-talk. I will still notice old patterns of feeling I am less worthy if I am not pushing and achieving. I also have to bring compassion to the thoughts that encourage pushing, such as, "If you are not living the life of your dreams, if you don't have a million followers, or you haven't reached all your goals yet, it is because you have the wrong vibration, or haven't been waking up early enough to start working, or haven't followed the right system."

Rest and play are essential parts of the rhythms of release. If judgments emerge about resting and playing, we can reframe our thoughts by understanding the value of integrating what we have learned, stocking up on our bodies' reserves of health and well-being, and enjoying ourselves. In my periods of more rest and not quite so much work, I find myself wanting to stretch and do gentle yoga, read, watch light-hearted entertainment, take naps, and go to the park. I still fulfill my responsibilities, but I also make a conscious effort to honor and value all the life-giving activities that are comfortable and don't seem productive in the outward sense. Self-acceptance goes hand-in-hand with listening to our bodies' natural rhythms of healing.

Choosing Your Own Story

So how are you feeling, goddesses? Are you starting to get a felt sense of how your nervous system expands and contracts when you are speaking up and living your juicy life? Up until now, we have been looking at "bottom-up" strategies for soothing your nervous system that start at the level of body, sensation, and energy. At the same time, it can also be helpful to bring in "top-down" cognitive strategies to increase your resilience and reduce your triggers.

Let's look at a great cognitive strategy to help you heal voice ruptures: changing your story. Stories are malleable and changeable, so we can choose to define our experiences in ways that support our empowerment. I call this Owning the Narrative. It is a process of gradually removing our focus from the hurt feelings, the cruelty, or the injustice of what we experienced, and bringing into view the wisdom and strength we have gained through healing these difficult life experiences. It's about framing ourselves as the heroine rather than the victim.

Before you go all gung-ho on listing your heroic qualities, I want to mention that acknowledging your own wounding is an essential prerequisite for Owning the Narrative. Otherwise, the suggestion that you appreciate the lessons that you're learning can seem like a glossed-over form of dismissing that bucket 'o pain. It's a bit like a child being hurt and a parent yelling, "Just get over it because the pain is going to make you stronger." Let's agree to not be like that parent, okay? We need to first be present with the pain and validate the ways we have been affected.

When fear lingers after an incident, we may also need to go through the reprocessing stage or nervous system repair. Then we will be free to choose an empowering narrative that views the past conditioning, traumas, or experiences as meaningful in the context of our lives.

When we own our narrative, we are strengthening the neuropathways connected to our empowerment. Instead of repeatedly going down the old pathways of pain and powerlessness, we are intentionally widening the neuropathways of feeling safe, supported, and strong. Let's peek at how this works. Our brains are composed of neurons, which are like tiny threads. When we take in new information or have a particular thought, our brains look for patterns. Out of efficiency, our brain will try to fit the new information into a pre-existing pathway. The more time we spend thinking certain thoughts, the wider and stronger the associated pathway becomes.

After facing my childhood trauma in therapy, I had a bigtime need to tell myself a more empowering story. My anxious neuropathways were like multi-lane highways, whereas my peaceful trails were starting to get overgrown with weeds. I had neglected my internal resources and self-love tools that kept my Inner Flame present. As a result, I was still frequently triggered.

Let's look at how my brain might have behaved when I was triggered by a disturbing piece of national news. When I had thoughts such as "the world is such a mess and I am too fragile to cope," they fit in with my well-worn pathway of associating external conflict with being unsafe in my body. Day after day, I reinforced the trails that led me to anxiety. Once I felt unsafe, my amygdala would start firing. These regions of the brain are like "smoke detectors," sounding the alarm to activate the emergency responses. We need the amygdala to assess risk and mobilize us in the face of a true threat. After trauma, though, our "smoke detectors" can fire in situations where we are not in serious danger. This was certainly the case when I was safe in my home and had a panic attack from hearing violent news. Even though I was not in danger, my brain and body were taking me into the helplessness of the freeze state. I began to see these triggers differently once I decided I wanted more joy in my life. My anxious thoughts had become my main road, but I could cut a new trail through the brush. Each time I made the effort to think positively and remind myself I was safe, I strengthened the new pathway.

As I tried out a new story, I discovered that feeling happy and joyous did not feel safe. I could experience the pleasant sensations for a little while, before falling into worries that something horrible would happen, like my husband getting killed in a car crash. I was bringing myself back down to my accustomed levels of mediocrity, limiting my ability to feel happiness in all areas of my life. Through awareness of my thoughts, I found I could increase my capacity for feeling good so that my new, positive thoughts could take hold. Keeping in mind how my brain could build new neuropathways, I turned to journaling to create a new internal storyline with myself as the resilient heroine. Writing and creative expression are some of my favorite ways to Own the Narrative. By transforming our pain into self-expression, we can begin to see ourselves in a new light.

Feeling the Feelings

Here comes the "F-bomb:" Feelings. They are going to arise when you speak up, sing out, and share your creative wisdom with the world. Especially on those occasions when your voice is met with silence, rejection, dismissal, or criticism, feelings will emerge. I have tried every desperate way to cut around it, and the truth is there is no way to avoid the feelings. You just gotta feel them. The only way out is through.

I spent so many years in the tempting territory of trying to avoid all "negative" emotions. But if we suppress disappointment, sadness, grief, anger, or resentment, it doesn't go away. Buried emotions are prone to bubbling up at unexpected times and landing on whoever is near. The solution is to let ourselves feel the emotions in a safe way. If we repress the strong emotions we are likely to turn them against someone else or take it out on ourselves, but if we can create a conscious ritual to release the emotion, it can become an act of self-love and self-care.

Through the process of release, we can bring awareness and intention to avoid staying stuck in the painful feelings. So it's not about walking around angry at everyone for the rest of your life. We are consciously moving through the emotions to create more space. It is similar to how we can remove unwanted items from our closets to make more room for what we love. When we let go of the old anger, fear, and sadness we free up energy for enjoyment, creativity, and inspiration. But here's the thing: the mind can't create a magic wand to make the emotions disappear (sigh). Often, even talking about them with someone you trust will not fully liberate what is trapped inside. We have to let the emotions be felt. When we consciously turn toward what we have been pushing away, our bodies can guide us to feel the sensations in an empowering ritual.

Unleash Your Goddess Voice Practice No. 7: Rituals of Emotional Release

Let's look at a safe way to start feeling your feelings more consciously. We're going to work with leaving the Comfort Zone and entering the Zone of Growth to feel little drops of any difficult emotions that may be stored inside. Pay attention to what feels like a manageable amount of discomfort, and what is approaching your Edge into the Zone of Overwhelm. Anytime the emotions you are releasing feel like "too much," you will bring yourself back to a feeling of comfort and curiosity. Here is the Compassionate Pacing model again to refresh us on regrounding in the comfort zone:

Compassionate Pacing

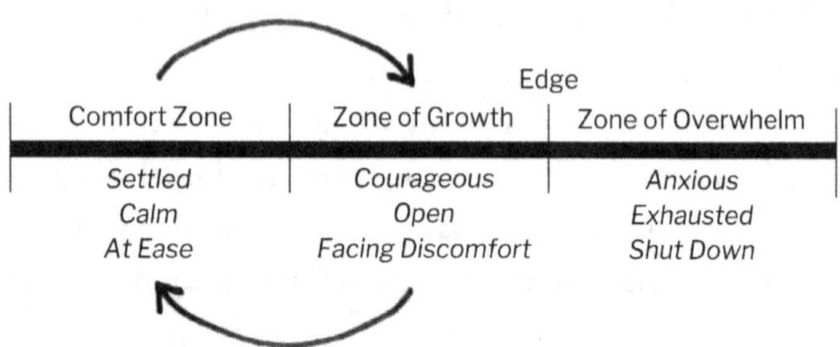

Reground in your comfort zone to create a sustainable cycle.

If you feel hesitant or scared by the idea of releasing your rage, grief, or resentment, there is no need to rush into the ritual or even try anything at all. Your fear or trepidation may be a sign that the professional support of a therapist could help to move through the stuck emotions. As you have heard me say before, one-on-one support from a compassionate professional brings a sense of safety and manageability to healing our voices.

For a recording of this practice, visit saragiita.com/free

1. Gather a pen and paper and find a comfortable place to sit. Allow at least 25 minutes for this exercise, and an additional 10 minutes for the closing ritual that follows.

2. Begin by connecting to a helpful resource – anything that helps you feel safe and stable. This may be focusing on an area of your body that feels comfortable or imagining a place where you feel safe. You could also focus on a beautiful sight, sound, or smell in your environment. Anchor your awareness in this resource and write down a description before moving on. This doesn't mean you have to feel blissful or be completely free from stressful

thoughts. The goal is to feel grounded and aware of something in the present moment that can help you feel calm.

3. When you are ready, bring to mind an emotion you wish to move through and release. Write a few words down to express that emotion. They may be angry words directed at another person, or they may be expressions of sadness, grief, guilt, resentment, or confusion. Let the words come onto the page without self-judgment. After thirty seconds or a minute, pause your writing.

4. Bring your attention back to the same resource you established at the beginning of the practice. You are swinging out of the distressing emotion and grounding back in the sensory experience of something calming.

5. If you wish to stop here, you may skip ahead to the Closing Ritual.

6. If you wish to continue expressing your emotions, return again to writing. This time, notice your Edge and how much is comfortable to feel right now. You may find yourself writing for just thirty seconds again, and then moving back into the resource to feel grounded. Or you may find you wish to go for longer. Find your sweet spot of enough discomfort to grow outside your Comfort Zone, without going into the Zone of Overwhelm.

7. Notice if any movements or sounds want to happen in your body to release the emotions that are coming through. If you feel comfortable, you may wish to speak out loud and follow your body's promptings to move. Or you may prefer to continue writing. In either case, remember to pull yourself back to the resource any time your own system feels like it is approaching too much discomfort.

8. When you feel ready, come back to the sensations of your resource. Notice any sights, sounds, colors, or scents that bring a feeling of calmness.

9. You may wish to continue oscillating between expressing your emotions and noticing your resource, or you may finish your practice with the Closing Ritual.

How to Practice the Closing Ritual:

1. Prepare your space to welcome in a new mood. You may wish to light a candle, put a few drops of essential oil into a diffuser, open a window, or put on music you enjoy.

2. From a standing position, begin to shake your hands, and then your whole body. Your shaking may be gentle or vigorous according to what feels right in the moment.

3. Imagine that any tension or imprints of the emotion in your body can ripple off and fall to the floor.

4. Sweep your hands over your entire body, either touching your skin and clothes or moving them in the air a few inches away from your body. Allow your hands to cleanse any residue of the emotions that were felt and expressed in your emotional release session.

5. Bend down to use your hands to gather up the invisible energy you have released. Form it into a ball.

6. Throw the imaginary ball out the window. Then you can imagine the energy disintegrating or being blown away by the wind. You can even imagine you are throwing it all the way to the sun to be burned up!

7. Bring your focus back into your body as you breathe deeply. Set the intention of what you would like to invite in to fill the void of the released emotion. This may be a feeling of love, calmness, strength, or acceptance.

8. Sweep your hands over your body once more, this time imagining they fill you with the energy of your peaceful intention.

9. Tear up the paper you have written on, and give thanks to the feelings expressed. However unpleasant the emotions seemed, they have been a part of your journey.

10. If your space permits, burn the scraps in a fireplace or a metal or ceramic container outdoors. (Be sure to keep a bucket of water nearby in case the flames should spread.) If you are unable to burn the paper, don't worry. The intention of transforming long-held emotions is what matters the most.

11. Choose what to do with your torn scraps or ashes (be sure to put out the flame). You may bury the ashes, throw them in the trash, or find your own way to let them go. I like to hold the intention of saying, "This no longer belongs to me."

12. Finish by drinking a glass of water to nourish your body. As you sip, remember your peaceful intention that you wish to establish as your new default.

When you become skilled at finding your Zone of Growth and moving from discomfort back into comfort, you may feel drawn to other methods of releasing emotions. One way is through rhythmic movements: stomping your feet to music with a good beat, drumming on a drum or yoga ball, punching a bed, or throwing pillows. You may also like to feel your inner power with animal sounds such as growling, howling, hissing, cackling, or anything in between. Additionally, many people find relief from destroying items such as old dishes, water balloons that have been frozen, or old pictures or letters that remind them of a distressing person. (If you are destroying anything, be sure to wear eye protection and find a safe place to break the items.) With any of these methods, I recommend the same process of grounding in a resource, then expressing your pent-up emotions for a short time, and moving back to the resource.

Some feelings may be freed into the wind with just one short emotional release session. That is beautiful! But don't worry if you sense there is a whole reservoir of anger, grief, or shame left inside still. A longer ritual can help. I heard about doing 21 days of writing your angry thoughts and burning them from author Tosha Silver. Three weeks felt overwhelming, so I committed myself to seven days. When those seven were up I was in the groove and starting to have fun, so I continued for the full 21 days. By the end, I had a full ritual of writing all my "F***-you" feelings toward the person in question, and then using a long hot pack as a whip against my bed while I shouted anything that wanted to come out. My intention was to release the rage from my body. Sometimes I mixed in punching or stomping. When I felt that the adrenaline-assisted loud part was complete, I performed the Closing Ritual. Every few days I took the ripped pages (and sometimes photographs) outside to an old ceramic flower pot to burn them up. I buried the ashes.

CHAPTER 8

Reveal Your
Authentic Wholeness

Gather the scattered
parts hidden inside of me
that have been denied by me
So my Soul
Can be Whole
And Complete.

How to Be Authentic

Once you build the resilience in your body and nervous system to be seen and heard, your self-expression will be most fulfilling when it feels authentic. Authenticity is a nice-sounding buzzword, but what does it really mean? The Merriam-Webster online dictionary defines authenticity as being "true to one's own personality, spirit, or character." So now it's time for me to spout a lot of motivational phrases like: Be yourself! Be true to who you are! There is only one you! These poster clichés persist because they hold some value, but they don't really give us any clues about how to show up more authentically.

The missing key is this: to increase our sense of expressing our true selves, we need to embrace our wholeness.

While we are already whole beings just as we are, many of us are uncomfortable with certain aspects of ourselves and our experiences. We push away the stuff we don't like. These repressed aspects and experiences could be called the shadow, your exiled parts, your darkness, or simply what you resist. You will hear me call it the shadow in this chapter. To embrace our wholeness, we need to be willing to see, accept, and *maybe even love* all of our emotions, all of our characteristics, all of our fears, all of our mistakes, and all of our experiences. We need to allow ourselves to embody darkness as well as light. Bit by bit, as we extend our love wide enough to encompass every last shameful part of ourselves, we can't help but show up more authentically.

When we adopt the stance of welcoming all parts of ourselves to be expressed, it naturally follows that we welcome all people on Earth to live in their radiance. We are all an intrinsic and important part of the collective. When we stop judging ourselves, we outgrow the tendency to scapegoat others based on their bodies, skin color, gender, sexual orientation, age, beliefs, economic status, national origin, political views, past mistakes, or any other characteristic. Inner embrace and release of self-judgment is the process that allows us to release harshness and prejudice against ourselves, but also toward others. **Reclaiming our wholeness is the foundation for healing the world.**

Lofty, right? But I promise that stepping more deeply into your wholeness can be a practical process. In this chapter, we are going to look at four signs that we are pushing parts of ourselves away: filters, all-or-nothing thinking, projections, and control. Then we will explore some tools to help you embrace every last radiant part of yourself so you can speak your truth with ease.

Filters Affect What We Show the World

If we have a lot of inner aspects that we keep pushing into the shadows, it causes us to subconsciously limit what we express through our voices. This kind of repression is like clipping the wings of a bird so its mobility will be drastically reduced. But I know from having a pet bird as a kid that *wing feathers always grow back.* As we learn to embrace and love our exiled parts, our full self-expression will flourish. Our beautiful voices can float on the wind as nature intended.

One way we might subconsciously repress our voices is through filters. A filter is a type of paradigm or worldview that allows you to keep pushing parts of yourself out of sight. Whether conscious or unconscious, it affects what you show to the world. Have you ever used a photo filter on your camera or an app like Instagram? With the tap of the button, all the hues change ever so slightly. The entire feel of the photo can be shifted. In the same way, voice filters affect the tone of our voices and what we allow ourselves to say. The image we present to the world becomes curated. For example, growing up in my family, the "cheerfulness" filter was really big. We learned not to complain too much and to focus on staying positive. While there are a lot of benefits of positive thinking, this filter can cause people to minimize their suffering and the suffering of others by pushing it into the shadows.

There are probably as many types of voice filters as there are people, but let's look at a few common ways folks alter the tone of what they express. You may come to realize you have a "composed and level-headed" filter that highlights the ways you are creating order and success in your life and hides away all the messiness. You may have a filter that says, "Showing emotions makes you weak," which encourages you to tamp down your feelings but causes you to feel shame or isolation when those natural human emotions do emerge. The "politeness" voice filter is especially drilled into girls but may be present for all genders. It encourages you to speak in a way that will be perceived as pleasing and polite to others. While thoughtfulness to other people's feelings is valuable, the politeness filter can cause us to override our inner needs and feel uncomfortable setting boundaries. It can cause us to display a meek, accommodating version of ourselves to the world. Likewise, a "blending in" filter creates a habit of not drawing attention to ourselves. We mute our bright colors, our eccentricities, and our divergent opinions so we can fit in and feel safe. Or we may go the opposite route and take on a "defiant" filter in which our appearance, words, and actions are all dictated by staying in opposition to cultural norms.

No matter if they emerged from inherited familial patterns, cultural norms, or personal experiences, voice filters are a form of protection. They are not bad. But they can definitely feel confining. When we don't have empowered choice around how we show up, voice filters can keep us in the realms of repressed silence and repressed self-expression.

They ensure we keep parts of ourselves tucked away and out of sight (until we get triggered, anyway). When we start to notice and acknowledge our unconscious filters, we may see that we have been showing a grayscale version of ourselves to the world. Embracing the inner aspects that we previously judged and dismissed helps us to display our vibrant, authentic colors.

When you have empowered choice, you can become more nuanced about what you show to the world and when. Authenticity is not about constantly over-sharing or having to tell your whole life story to the grocery clerk. You can be thoughtful about what you want to share and when, rather than feeling compelled to hide parts of yourself in all situations. For example, one of my coaching clients felt comfortable speaking up and telling me about a childhood trauma that she had experienced. Having looked at it already in therapy, she did not need to go into detail but just wanted to have this previously locked away part of herself be witnessed and honored. From sharing in a safe environment, she was able to embody more of her authenticity and wholeness. However, she did not wish to talk about her trauma with her coworkers. She decided it felt right to show the closer-to-the-surface aspects of her true self in that context, and I supported her thoughtful expression of empowered silence.

All-or-Nothing Thinking

If we find ourselves in loops of black-and-white, either/or thinking, there is often a part of our personality or experience underneath that we are unwilling to face. We create rigid, all-or-nothing paradigms to wall off the parts we are subconsciously hoping to hide. When I was 24, I got quite rigidly fixed into the mentality of "I am completely healed now!" I had just completed six months of Somatic Experiencing therapy and faced the pain of the sexual assault I experienced at age 15, and I began to feel a new sense of empowerment in my life. I no longer felt like a prisoner of my past. With this fresh energy, I began the singer/songwriter career I had dreamed about and released a full album called *Take the Leap.*

When we heal past traumas and wounds, we free ourselves up for new possibilities and greater ease. I now see this beautiful expansion of healing and integration as a joyous gift. It's like a spontaneous dance party, or a set of giggles with a friend, or a feeling of receiving grace. The joyous side of healing cannot be forced or manipulated. It is meant to be free-flowing and effervescent. Yet I tried to solidify the momentary relief and joy into a permanent guarantee of happiness. This grasping only ended up causing me more suffering (doesn't it always?) I felt like a failure when life's struggles inevitably emerged. I felt like if I were more evolved, I could make happiness last for every single moment. Attempting to seal off the remaining trauma, pain, and shadow in my life, I was very hard on myself anytime I felt something other than exuberant happiness. This is what happens when we exile certain emotions or experiences. We keep them locked away through inner harshness.

Looking back, I see that my soul took me back to a place of healing and integration. I was not the failure I imagined myself to be when I crashed down from my expansive high! As I plunged into my dark night of the soul, I received an initiation into the rich forested territory of uncovering my wholeness. While it was difficult, I began learning how to accept all parts of myself with love and compassion. With time I found that opening up to the darkness as well as the light creates a more embodied, deeper self-expression from feeling whole. When we take a both/and approach rather than turning everything into either/or, we also loosen the grip on needing our healing process to have a defined endpoint. Healing becomes an everyday, in-the-moment, ongoing process of nourishing and loving ourselves. Now don't get me wrong: when you are in a dark place, it is only natural to want it to be over as soon as possible. I don't wish for anyone to be stuck in a dark place! What we're going for is bringing light into the darkness, day by day, until little darkness remains. Instead of an attempt to fix or brush away the difficulties, healing becomes a process of inner union and deep acceptance.

I was thrown into the journey of allowing conflicting emotions to coexist when I got pregnant for the first time. I never imagined I would find myself pregnant at age 24, a year into my marriage. Even though my ego was scared and overwhelmed, my intuition knew it was my destiny to have this child. I started to notice the split, too. One part of me knew the timing was perfect, and another part was brooding and saying my life was over and I'd never get to be a successful musician or have any fun or have any *me* left at all. As the shock and first-trimester vomiting wore off, the side of my intuition and acceptance became stronger. Instead of being in the rigid mentality of this experience being good or bad, I saw how it was both insanely challenging and cosmically perfect. *I'm going to be a mom,* I repeated to myself as I rubbed my blossoming belly. I was nervous and excited and terrified as I moved away from my habits of all-or-nothing thinking.

Learning to Trust Your Voice in the Face of Projections

Like filters and all-or-nothing thinking, projections are another signpost pointing us to shadowy places that need to be healed and embraced. A projection happens when somebody's exiled inner aspects overlay a story onto someone else. Rather than accepting the other person as they are, the projector criticizes or judges in others what they have judged in themselves. Let me give an example based on my work of helping several clients repair boundaries. Let's imagine two women who become roommates, Lori and Margaret. Lori felt like she was never allowed to have boundaries as a kid, and her few attempts at speaking up for her needs as an adult have received pushback. All of these boundary ruptures plus a lack of emotional resources have led Lori to hide away the immense pain of having her voice and body disregarded. Yet the pain gets triggered anytime she witnesses another woman speaking up for her needs and setting boundaries. Rather than listening to the vulnerable voice within that says, "How come she gets to set boundaries and I don't?" Lori creates a story that speaking up for yourself is rude and selfish.

When Margaret moves in, Lori frequently opens Margaret's bedroom door and wanders in as she pleases. At first, wanting to create connection, Margaret doesn't say anything. But she soon realizes that she needs her own space to be respected. While a part of her says she should just suck it up and "be nice," Margaret recognizes the need to speak up. She approaches Lori and says, "I'm someone who finds it really important to have my own space to recharge without interruption. I need you to always knock before coming into my room and to please only enter with my permission." Unwilling to tend to the vulnerable emotions inside, Lori gets rocketed into projection mode. She overlays the story of boundaries being selfish onto her new roommate. And, sensing the place of self-doubt within Margaret, she starts to push back. "This is my house, and you should be grateful I'm renting this room to you. How dare you try to shut me out." What's happening here is Lori is projecting her own pain onto Margaret.

For these unconscious projections to be made manifest, there has to be both a projector and a receiver. (And pretty much everyone has been on either end at some point.) While the projector is sending their disowned stories and pain outward, there needs to be a place for them to land within the receiver. There has to be some matching puzzle-piece-like opening of self-doubt or discomfort that allows the projection to fit into place. This is not to say it's your fault if you receive someone's projections, but that it can indicate a place within yourself that could benefit from more healing and inner embrace. Each time someone projects their unprocessed baggage onto you, it is an invitation to trust your own voice, intuition, and sense of self-worth. By filling up on the inside with this radiant trust, other people's projections will no longer have a place to land. And if you notice yourself doing the projection, you can gently take that energy and pull it back. Rather than unconsciously replaying your story of wounding with another person or group, shine the compassionate light of your awareness on the parts inside that have been triggered.

The Painful Invitation to Claim My Power (Trigger Warning)

In my twenties, I struggled to heal the pockets of self-doubt in myself that were susceptible to projections, and this struggle clearly emerged as I went into labor with my first child. Do you remember how I described my rediscovery of instinctual sound way back at the beginning of the book? My raw sounding was celebrated, witnessed, and honored by my therapist, Maggie. My tender shoot of truth was nurtured. Yet what followed was not more celebration, but a painful invitation to claim my power. It felt like my little seedling of a voice had to endure a torrential hailstorm the night that I went into labor. What emerged was a lesson in trusting myself. When we speak up from a place of confidence and self-assurance, people are a lot more likely to listen.

After several hours of timing contractions at home, my mom and husband took me to the birthing center where we were planning to give birth. I found myself coping with the pain of the contractions by making loud moaning sounds. From being supported so lovingly by Maggie, I had learned how sounding moved me through the feeling of being trapped in my pain. Those guttural sounds were my life raft. Yet my sounding was shamed and shut down by the midwife who was on rotation at the birthing center. Let's call her Stacy. Stacy told me my moans were "too dramatic." She said I needed to conserve my energy and even suggested that I was just seeking attention because I got louder when more people were in the room. She never hooked me up to a monitor to measure the actual strength and length of the contractions, but just assumed that I was in very early labor by the fact that my contractions happened at irregular intervals and my moans lasted 45 seconds instead of a full minute. She shamed my impulses instead of meeting me with compassion and support.

Unfortunately, things spiraled out of control after she suggested I tone down my voice. Stacy had the intern check my cervix again, and since it was still only at one centimeter after four hours, they sent me home. I was given no choice or comfort in the matter. I screamed, "I'm not going home, I'm going to the HOSPITAL so they can CUT this baby out of me!" Yet no one paid attention to this plea. We were all under the spell of believing the midwife's story that I was being dramatic and I would have the baby in another 12 or 16 hours. And since I didn't really have conviction or confidence behind my plea, people were less likely to listen. So, home we went. I asked my mom to pull over so I could vomit on the curb. There. At least someone listened to one of my requests!

Once we were home, I told my husband and mom to get some sleep downstairs, believing Stacy's projections that I needed to stop the attention-seeking and let my support people rest for when it got "really bad."

I now understand intuitively that I was the recipient of Stacy's projections. Piecing together things she told me in the long conversations we had after the birth, I see how she was uncomfortable with my expression of my intense emotions. She told me that she had predicted it would be a difficult birth because I cried in all of my prenatal appointments. I sense that my messy, big emotions and wild expression triggered something repressed in her well-controlled, ordered life. Her contempt for my loudness was thinly veiled underneath professional platitudes of wanting me to conserve my energy. I wish that my 25-year-old self had the internal worthiness and trust to say, "Fuck this. She doesn't know what is best for me. My moaning is healthy and needed and right. My voice is right, and I deserve support!" But, alas, my vocal trust was such a tiny whisper, far from growing into a mighty roar. I internalized her punitive projections and felt completely defeated when we arrived at home. I believed I had to follow Stacy's suggestion to be alone. After all, she was the "expert," and I was drowning in fear.

So I spent the most painful four hours of my labor alone. In repressed silence. Tossing and turning on my new queen-sized bed. Many times, I thought of screaming out for my mom and husband to come upstairs to support me, but I reasoned myself out of it. I thought that it was more important for them to get their rest, which was just a backward way of saying that their needs were much more important than mine. Finally, at 5:30 AM I vomited again, and this brought home to me the urgency of my situation. I felt so dehydrated that I knew I could not keep going like this. I screamed, "HELP!" No response. I screamed again.

After the third scream, I heard some stirring downstairs. The groggy figures of my mom and husband entered the room. Through panic and tears I pleaded, "Take me to the hospital, I need an IV. I am dehydrated I vomited I'm not okay it hurts."

Disoriented, they said they couldn't understand me. I would be okay, they said, I would have the baby in the afternoon like Stacy said. Have you ever had this happen to you? That you waited so long to voice a need that you became desperate and discombobulated, and it was hard for others to understand and respond? By delaying and reasoning myself out of speaking up sooner, I allowed my situation to become even more dire. Instead of taking me to the hospital right away, they decided to have my husband call the midwife. Meanwhile, my mom helped me into the bathroom between contractions. I thought I might try getting in the bathtub to take the edge off of the excruciating sensations ripping through my pelvis. As soon as I was in the bath, I felt the urge to push. Worried, my mom told me not to push because she thought it could be dangerous if I wasn't fully dilated. But my body knew what to do. As soon as that contraction and urge to bear down had passed, I got out of the bathtub and instinctively put my fingers inside my vagina. I could feel my baby's head just an inch or two away from crowning.

"I can feel the baby's head!" I yelled. My husband came over and took a look for himself. He told the midwife on the phone, "I can see the baby's head!" Do you know what she said in response? "That's impossible." Yet this time, I had the clarity to understand that she was completely out of touch with what was going on. She was dead wrong. I felt a return to trusting myself as the next contraction came on. I knew I was birthing my baby right here in the bathroom. I knew that it didn't matter what Stacy said, and told my husband to hang up with her and call 911. Speaking with certainty and self-trust, my voice was finally heard. I stood in a squatting monkey position, leaning against the wall. On the fourth push, my mom caught our slippery baby. We heard his loud cry, and my mom had the good instincts to place him in my arms. I sat down on the closed toilet seat, my feet resting on the fuzzy bath mats I had purchased a month earlier. How had I known to get the red ones which would not show any stains from the birth? As the paramedics arrived, I started singing softly to my baby, wanting to create calm amid the chaos. The paramedics stormed around my buck-naked body and my baby, taking blood pressures and asking questions. It was all a blur. Yet there was a tremendous relief when they said the baby seemed healthy, but we still needed to get to the hospital. I rode in the ambulance as the sun rose, still singing, in a surreal state. My son has always shown himself to be a thriver with a loud, strong voice, despite the fearful circumstances of his birth.

Here's what I learned from this ordeal: that midwives are bad. No, just kidding! I still have respect for midwifery and know many people who have had lovely births that were supported by professional midwives. I learned that I was very susceptible to giving my power to other people who positioned themselves as authority figures. In that powerless state, I was vulnerable to the projections of that person's shadow. I let their viewpoints seep in, drowning out my own voice. I let the projections corroborate my feelings of unworthiness. This tendency to give my power away was especially sticky with men and women who displayed traditionally masculine traits. Stacy fit the bill here, as a woman focused on rationality and having control over emotions. My own capacity to lovingly embrace my emotions was not yet deeply rooted. I still felt like I would be a "better" person if I could avoid the big, intense, "dramatic" emotions.

This whole experience of shutting down my voice under the spell of projections was a catalyst. It set me on the course of reclaiming my power. As I healed from the trauma, I wrote songs around the themes of standing on my own and discovering my strength. I saw the need for trusting my own voice. I saw the need to commit to myself, rather than abandon my knowing when faced with people who push back. I learned that I am incredibly strong and I can trust my own instincts.

I have since circled back to this lesson many times, finding deeper layers to heal. Life has brought me situations with a similar dynamic of an authority figure trying to impose their viewpoints that clash with my inner knowing. Luckily, these other conflicts have been much milder and less painful. Though the projections of a coach or healer are not fun to receive, I frame them as opportunities for me to speak up and claim my power. With each cycle, I learn how to deepen my energetic sovereignty and own my powerful lioness nature.

Now do you see how projections work in action? Unconscious projections cause pain. They cause judgments of other people's voices. They cause fractures where we allow other people's criticisms to tone down our self-expression. They keep unseen parts of ourselves in feelings of abandonment. And sometimes, projections cause babies to be born in bathrooms with conveniently colored floor mats!

Control vs. Vulnerability

When we find ourselves trying to control every little thing, it can be another sign that we are trying to push away parts of our personalities or experiences. An unconscious mentality runs the show, whispering "If I can just make sure everything works out according to plan then I will never have to feel the way I did back then. I will never have to see the part of me that is splintered off and wounded." Control as a means to wall off our shadow parts can take many forms. You could try to control other people's behaviors through judgment or micromanagement. Or you could try to control outcomes in your life through perfectionism. Both show resistance to the wholeness and flow of life. Both are attempts at keeping vulnerability to a minimum.

Another flavor of control that has popped up for myself and some of the clients I have worked with is called hyper self-reliance. Imagining yourself as an island, hyper self-reliance is when you try to do everything yourself. Asking for help is vulnerable. It requires trust. You could end up disappointed. But vulnerability is a medicine that also brings benefits. Vulnerability fosters connection and meaning. It helps you feel supported rather than carrying all your burdens on your shoulders. It is an essential component of experiencing your wholeness.

My son taught me how to ask for help. Between my traumatic stress, postpartum depression, and exhaustion from our baby's frequent night-waking, I relied on my husband a lot. At first, I had to ask Paco to change a diaper, calm him down, or put him down for a nap. Neither of us grew up with fathers who were involved in those day-to-day caregiving tasks, so it felt like we were in new gender-role territory. Soon it became a habit, though, and he became the expert at helping our son fall asleep. He developed an amazing rocking technique that calmed the baby's crying so well. Each night after I nursed our little one, my husband would swaddle him and cradle him in his arms, shushing him to sleep as he gently danced back and forth. We have an amazing photo in a cheap plastic frame on our bookshelf that shows Dad holding our one-month-old baby against his chest. Apparently, we were not used to judging baby sizes yet, because the blue cotton onesie with rolled-up sleeves hung loosely off our son's long, slim body. But my husband was oblivious and enraptured, with a serene glow to his face as he inhaled the baby scent of our little one's dark hair. Looking back, if I had been thriving and energetic in the transition into parenthood, I probably would've kept going with my habits of trying to do it all myself. I wouldn't have left the house so often for solo walks, exercise classes, and shopping trips. Though I felt bonded to my baby, my exhaustion brought me to my knees. I desperately needed help. The vulnerable act of asking my husband to step in gave him a beautiful opportunity to bond more deeply with our son. And, yes. I had to let some of my desire to control fall by the wayside. Because he didn't always do things how I thought he should. He did them in his own, just right way.

I had to get comfortable with another new level of relinquishing control and asking for help when it came to inviting babysitters into our home. My husband was easy to trust, but he was back at his office full-time after two weeks of parental leave. With no family in town, I needed to find a babysitter so I could resume teaching music lessons part-time. I worked up the courage to ask my neighbor, Mary, a lively retiree who adored babies. I was nervous to ask and worried about what I would do if I didn't like her style with kids. Once I asked her, though, she was delighted and insisted she would do it for free. The first time she came over, I saw how both she and my son lit up with smiles and laughter. She often told me that babysitting was the highlight of her week! And here I was, worried I was imposing. Look, it's easy to think empowerment means being independent and not needing the support of others. It's easy to think depending on others is a sign of weakness. There are times to stand on our own two feet. But there are times when refusing help is more of a coping mechanism to prevent being hurt where others have betrayed our trust in the past.

Perhaps hyper-self-reliance is not an issue for you. Yet you may find other areas of your life where embracing vulnerability will create more space for your whole self to show up. You may feel an inner pull to bring a vulnerable experience into the light so it can be witnessed by your therapist, coach, partner, or trusted friend. You may feel called to start giving talks or guest lectures or speeches. This might feel really vulnerable if you're scared you'll open your mouth and be at a loss for words, just like what happened when giving a presentation on Mozambique back in seventh grade. Or you may find yourself in the brave position of initiating intimacy with your partner after a long period of disconnection. No matter the context, putting yourself out there again is a vulnerable act. It carries risk. There may be disappointment or rejection. But by taking this step toward embracing the wholeness of your experience, you open up so many new possibilities. We know from the research of Brené Brown that vulnerability fosters connection. It creates room for fulfillment. It allows you to show up as your true self.

Mother Earth as Teacher

Now that we see some of the signs of inner fragmentation, let's look at some metaphors and tools to help you embrace your authentic wholeness. In true goddess form, I find that the cycles and wisdom of Mother Earth are a perfect teacher for how to embrace both shadow and light. Reclaiming the parts of ourselves that we have judged or pushed away is a process of patient, loving attention, much like tending a garden.

Amid my early motherhood days of being a sleep-deprived mess, I was focused on just getting through each day. Thank goodness I made a new friend to help me rediscover the beauty of nature as healer. Melia was another first-time mom I met in birthing class. She could always help me see the bright side of parenting as we piled up our nursing pillows and settled in on the couch, or took thirty minutes just to get ready for a short walk with the babies. Most importantly, Melia helped me start to feel the rhythms of the Earth through gardening. As a child, I had watched my mother garden, but I was never particularly interested in helping her. I preferred to wander the yard, humming to myself, collecting leaves, stones, soil, and hidden treasures to turn into a mud pie. Gardening had always seemed boring to me, what with all the weed-pulling and hose-dragging to keep up with. With Melia, though, gardening became magic. We marveled at the quiet beauty of planting a seed and watching it grow and flourish. We let our babies crawl and explore as we turned a bare patch of ground into a vegetable garden and turned a long-forgotten bed of thistles into a blaze of wildflowers. When the frosty change of seasons eventually killed off our summer plants, we philosophized about life's wonder and fragility.

Melia taught me to look deeply for beauty. Where others saw only an overgrown backyard of weeds, she looked harder. She reveled in the soft soil and abundant earthworms. She smiled in awe at our magnificent old tree. Her ability to see the merits of what others judged as ugly helped me soften my own habits of self-judgment. I learned to tend to a vulnerable seedling as I learned to tend to my emotions with care. Each little shoot of possibility within me stretched its green leaves upward, ready for a chance at new life.

Some of our plants died, bringing me face to face with the wholeness of life and the inevitability of death. I learned to see the potential for something new to grow in its place and ask how I can nourish the soil and try things differently next time. We planted a cherry tree the spring when my son was two years old, and that same summer it gave us five delicious cherries. Yet the tree did not survive the harsh winter. I mourned its death. The experience taught me that we must still take the risk of raising our voices, putting ourselves out there, and trying new things. The tree's short life was worth it for the memory of a small child reaching up to grasp a cherry, pulling it toward his mouth.

I am amazed by the persistence of some plants. I planted purple kale seeds, expecting the plants to die when winter came. Much to my surprise, the plants reemerged from the roots the following spring. They grew tall with slender leaves, and in late summer I realized the strange, skinny capsules that had formed were seed pods. Just one plant gave a legacy of hundreds of tiny black seeds. Year after year, the kale lived on, through tiny seedlings that become bountiful plants. In the same way, I began to realize that my creative voice needed a new life. I was wrong to think I needed to end my singing career because I was a mom. I did not want to be a parched seedling, living a stunted and small life. I wanted to bask in the creative flow, growing big, bushy leaves. I wanted to thrive.

Grief Begets Wholeness

When we feel alone, broken, splintered, or unlovable somewhere inside, grief is a natural process to restore us to wholeness. Whether we are grieving the loss of a loved one, grieving our unmet needs, grieving the dreams we didn't get to live, or grieving our failures, life is asking us to be present with our feeling of loss. And it's not easy. But if we follow the cultural injunctions to stick a Band-Aid on the pain and move on as quickly as possible, this comes with a cost. If we bury our grief, we have to create a psychological dam to keep all that emotion at bay. Not only does this make it hard to speak authentically, but we will likely be scared that the dam could break at any point. The only way out of this predicament is to willingly dismantle that crumbling old dam and allow ourselves to grieve.

When my son was three, I began to explore my own relationship with grief. I had always wanted two children. After my first birth experience, though, I was scared to go through it again. I didn't want the pain and fear of going into labor. Nor did I want the sleepless nights or spit-up or the overflowing diaper pail that come with those first months. I didn't want to fearfully wonder if my baby was okay. I wasn't too keen on the hormone-induced mood swings either. When your child reaches age two, strangers, neighbors, friends, and colleagues start to ask if you are "going to have another one." Some asked conversationally, while others proclaimed their opinion that children without siblings develop poor social skills and lead sad, lonely lives. I did my best to ignore their comments, knowing I was not ready to make a decision.

My son began preschool just before he turned three, and I reveled in my newfound freedom. I devoted more time to songwriting and contemplated scheduling more concerts. I also began to think that perhaps my son would be an only child. I gave away a lot of our baby things. Generosity can be liberating. The act of letting go helped me make a decision based on what my husband and I truly wanted, instead of what others thought. Some part of me wanted a life with just one child, but the longing for another baby kept surfacing. I felt like there was someone else out there, waiting patiently, ready to complete our family. I wanted a daughter, and I wanted another person to love and cuddle with. I sat with the decision for several months. I was expanding my capacity to feel the conflicting emotions: the fear, the hope. The dread, the excitement. In the end, hope and excitement won out, as they often do. I came to feel joy as we attempted to get pregnant again. We didn't have to wait long. I soon got that positive test and began resting my hands on my belly, sending love to the beautiful life inside of me. When the morning sickness hit, I began eating copious amounts of hash brown potatoes and doing my best not to vomit on the kitchen floor as I prepared peanut butter and jelly sandwiches for my three-year-old.

Our children are always a gift on loan, they are never truly ours. At twelve weeks I discovered my baby's tiny heart had stopped beating. Five days later, I finally was able to say goodbye and began to bleed. I lost so much blood that I fainted and was taken to the hospital. I felt light-headed and weak for days afterward.

What I was unprepared for, though, was the grief. I had grieved my grandparents, though their deaths felt easier to accept after their long, happy lives. Grieving my unborn child, I had to let go of all my hopes and dreams for our future together. I had to let go of the love and connection I felt with her. When all I could feel was absence, I reminded myself that we are all connected, we are all young and old and alive and dead and here and across the galaxy. We are all one in a way that my mind cannot prove or disprove, but that my soul feels is true. We planted a lilac bush for our tiny baby, letting her go back to the earth and nourish new life. I sang for her as I clawed at the dirt.

I learned the importance of giving myself time and space to grieve. The urge to numb our sadness is just like the urge to run away from our past. When we find the courage to sit with our pain, when we can embrace it lovingly and appreciate its presence, we give it space to melt away. I did my share of numbing, watching sitcoms to turn down the intensity of my feelings for a little while. But then I would turn it off, and often found myself with my right hand on my belly and my left hand on my heart. I did Qi-gong practices to let in more love and nourishment. The experience of facing my trauma prepared me to feel my feelings of grief as they arose. I came to appreciate that everything living must die; when I go, I will leave space for the young to flourish, and my remains will nourish the soil. We are meant to embrace the dark and difficult emotions as part of the fullness of life's design. Grief, death, and despair are the destructive forces that are intrinsically part of Mother Nature's creation. They are a part of how the Goddess expresses her wholeness through our lives.

As I learned to grieve as part of showing up authentically, I saw other places in my life where I had stuffed down my feelings of loss and disappointment. This was especially the case with the music album I recorded while I was pregnant with my first child. Knowing nothing about marketing back then, I imagined that I would release my heartfelt creation into the world, tell a few friends, and it would magically spread like wildfire. And that definitely did not happen. A handful of people bought copies, and several of them gave me compliments. And that was that. I had dreamed that releasing an album of my own compositions was the only effort needed to get hundreds or even thousands of downloads and CD sales. Like so many artistic newbies, I was let down by the "build it and they will come" myth. Feeling tremendous disappointment, I took it all personally. I wondered if the project was a soul calling after all. I told myself all kinds of stories about nobody liking my music or my lyrics or *me*. I felt like a failure. But once I learned how to let myself grieve, it was time to mourn my lost hopes and dreams. I had to let myself feel the sadness because holding onto it kept me paralyzed. Only through embracing the grieving process could I open up space for something new to be created and expressed in the future.

Looking back, I see the album that I birthed into the world not as a failure but as an important "stepping stone" project. It opened the doorway to sharing my story of overcoming trauma and speaking my truth. The project gave me skills, capacities, and lessons that have helped in later projects that furthered my evolution. And the process of grieving and recovering from my disappointment built the foundation of resilience I needed to step into leadership and share my soulful message on a wider scale.

Facing What We Have Pushed Away

Just as we allow ourselves to grieve, part of embracing our authentic wholeness comes from facing what we dislike in small, doable chunks. Therapy sessions have created a safe container for me to learn this art. Four years after my son's birth, I realized I still had unresolved fears and emotions from that trauma. Yet as I went down those neuropathways of feeling powerless, another memory kept arising. It was an image of myself as a child being sexually assaulted. My therapist reassured me that repressed memories are a common coping mechanism for childhood trauma. I was not crazy. But was I strong enough? Could I handle the weight of remembering? I had been running from this trauma since age five, working hard to push it back into the recesses of my mind. On some level, I always knew, but it was time to fully acknowledge that I was sexually assaulted by my friend's dad. It was time for me to look my pain in the eye, to let it be seen and felt instead of denied.

So I began my descent into the dark night of the soul, the archetypal journey of facing my darkest demons so that I could emerge in my courageous wholeness. I did not face my pain bravely, with my shoulders squared. I went in kicking and screaming, still wishing to avoid the pain of my past. It felt like I was being dragged into the haunted forest of memories, and I could not turn back. The only way out was to go through it, to experience the fear and march onward, trusting I would break through to the sunlight of an empowered life.

Cloudy memories surfaced one by one. Thankfully, my innate sense of pacing made sure I would not get overwhelmed by seeing everything at once. The images and sensations that arose did not come in any chronological order. My logical mind certainly strung them together in order, but I now understand this is my "trauma story." As trauma researchers have seen, the brain often encodes traumatic memories in fragments. Most survivors make sense of this mess by creating a story that explains the sensations and feelings associated with the fragments. This is called the "trauma story." Some people absolutely remember with clarity and detail what happened, even if they were young. All ranges of experience are valid. Everyone has their own truth to bring into the light. Our bodies know what happened to us.

With each memory that came up, there was always the doubting self that fought to keep the truth buried. It fought **hard.** I kept hearing things like, *It's impossible that you could have been molested, you had such a nice family,* or *Things like that don't happen to good people,* or *That is too horrific to be real, you must be making it up.* Yet deep down I knew the truth. I always knew. I was sexually assaulted when I was just five years old. And once I began the very essential first step of acknowledging the wound, I began to see the glimmering light of my wholeness that led me through the tangled forest of memory.

I share this story to give a picture of how we can face even the heavy and scary things that we have pushed away when we have the right support. However, facing the parts of ourselves that we have pushed away does not always involve things like traumas or repressed memories. If you dislike your thighs, you can start to embrace your wholeness by giving yourself a short period of looking in the mirror and consciously observing rather than judging. Just as an artist would look at the curves, shadows, textures, and shapes, you can witness this part of your being from a place of neutrality. Or, if you tend to feel some shame around the fact that you grew up in poverty and are afraid of your roots being revealed when you speak, you can find safe places where you can begin to talk about this valid part of your experience. Anytime we shine a light on part of ourselves and allow it to be seen, we can experience the fulfillment of showing up authentically.

Embracing Polarities

Authentic wholeness requires us to accept our own contradictions. Every quality has a shadow and a light side, and they are two sides of the same coin. Good and bad, mystery and certainty, sadness and joy are all part of our human experience. Loving kindness is not separate from cruelty; they are polarities that naturally coexist like night and day. As a society, we use shame to keep people from expressing their cruel side. Yet this is like building a dam to separate the loving-kindness from the cruelty. Instead of being one free-flowing body of water, half gets closed off into the realm of shadow and repression. Yet we have to remember that the mean energy does not go away. It still lurks in the subconscious realm. When our shame gets triggered, we are thrown over the dam and flail about in habitual reactions and patterns of harm.

By the way, I am not denying that there are times when people consciously act out of meanness or cruel intentions. This is also part of the current human reality. Yet I do believe most of us have positive intentions and do not wish to inflict harm, even when we lash out at others and repeat the stories of our own wounding. I also believe every person who seeks redemption, rectification, and healing deserves forgiveness. No matter what our intentions were in the past, we are all worthy of love. No exceptions. This metaphorical dam of shame is the reason we cannot always be our "best selves" and speak up with love, patience, kindness, and equanimity in all situations. When we begin to dismantle the wall and slowly embrace our polarities, we find we have the gift of choice. When we are not hating ourselves for having the capacity for meanness, then our hurtful, unconscious reactions will gradually loosen.

Embracing our seemingly opposite qualities is related to the practice of simultaneous awareness that we touched upon in chapter three. Our amazing minds can become aware of more than one emotion at the same time. If, for example, you feel embarrassed about how you tend to giggle, self-deprecate, or feel inadequate when speaking in front of other people, you can also become aware of your natural blueprint of worthiness inside. You could feel the power and confidence of your Inner Flame even when those feelings of inadequacy surface. We can hold both at once. We can allow ourselves to contain multitudes. We can also maintain simultaneous awareness when we are going through polarized emotions in a certain period of our lives. During my dark night of the soul, I experienced both torment and joy. I spent my days feeling good, carrying on with life. I gardened and sang and went on walks and made paintings with my preschooler. I took naps and cooked tasty meals. I maintained a small but steady roster of voice and piano students.

Perhaps I was dancing with the werewolf archetype because as the sun set, I would descend into the territory of painful memories. I spun into anxiety, fear, irritability, and panic. Most evenings, I was easily triggered and had to fight to stay present and even to function. I had so many sleepless nights of desperately turning away from an unacknowledged memory. Yet, again and again, the fear and pain was so much greater when I avoided it. By turning toward the memory, by welcoming in the sensations, my anxiety dissolved. It still hurt, but I was able to move through it. I was able to breathe again. This is what happens when we stop running away from the parts of ourselves that have been pushed into the shadows: they stop chasing us. With compassion we can say, "I see you. What you feel matters. You are a valued part of my being."

Learning to embrace the shadow rather than eradicate it took time. I first became stuck in the "trauma loop" where I stayed mired in the feelings of the trauma. I kept revisiting and revisiting the memories, believing I had to get it all out and make the pain go away once and for all. I kept scheduling more and more appointments, and even started doing Eye Movement Desensitization and Reprocessing (EMDR) videos on YouTube in between (which I don't recommend doing on your own). My brain got more and more stuck in the feeling of terror. While the reprocessing and revisiting of traumatic memories was an important first step in my healing, wholeness came from accepting my exiled parts. Feeling fully at peace came through embracing the paradox that we can be two seemingly contradictory things at the same time. I could feel broken inside, yet wake up to the sunshine and know I was whole. I could be both, on different levels, at different times.

My dark night of the soul ended four years into this round of therapy. It all shifted one morning when I plopped down on my therapist's yellow couch and said, "I'm tired of sifting through the past." I was waiting and waiting for the magical day when the trauma would become so insignificant that I would never get triggered. I was waiting for the magical day when I could be 100% healed so I could be happy again. And the waiting was not working. That morning my therapist suggested we begin the EMDR "future template." We looked at situations that frequently brought up my anxiety and worked on feeling safe when I experienced them in the future. This brought about a profound shift in my life.

The biggest change, however, came from allowing a new belief: I didn't have to wait until I was completely healed to begin feeling happy. The realization washed over me as I stared into the colorful painting on my therapist's wall. I stared at the rough brush strokes of those moonlit tables at an outdoor café, thinking they looked more like timpani drums than tables. And then suddenly I saw my own healing in a new light. I saw the past four years, filled with nightly trembling, and realized I was keeping myself stuck in the same pain. I was trying to get through the pain as fast as possible, so I could one day escape pain entirely. Except that fabled pain-free day was never going to come. I was keeping myself fragmented by denying life's polarities. I still had moments of feeling weak, so I didn't believe I could be empowered. I still had moments of despair, so I didn't believe I could be happy.

As I looked back on my all-or-nothing attitude toward healing, I realized that perhaps healing my childhood trauma would never reach an endpoint. Perhaps healing would look like loving myself, and living an amazing, empowered life, and occasionally experiencing triggers of my past helplessness. The key, though, is that when I am rapidly pulled into the past, I can recognize what is happening. I also have a plan in place for how I can calm down and time-travel back to the present. I decided I could feel happy and bold and beautiful right where I was. I could accept that life will inevitably include both the painful lows and the joyful highs. By choosing a both/and approach, we become expressions of the perfect polarities that make up the Universe.

A Second Chance to Use My Voice

As I embraced life's opposites, I started to see how beauty and joy could coexist with pain. I saw the amazing possibility of healing when my second live birth felt meaningful and peaceful, despite my fears of repeating my traumas. While I still felt like I was in my dark night of the soul from the surfacing of childhood trauma, I learned that we are not doomed to reenact the pain of our past wounds and patterns. We can move forward, letting the present unfold beautifully.

It was a clear June night in 2014. I gave birth to my daughter in the comfort of a large, private birthing room in a local hospital. While there was physical pain, I felt supported and safe. I was calm and centered. This time around, I felt empowered to use my voice. I let sound carry me through the contractions, moaning unapologetically. I also used my voice to assert my needs. I no longer believed everyone else's needs and opinions were more important than mine. I asked my husband and doula for exactly what felt right, be it a backrub, a bath, words of encouragement, or a change of position. I screamed at the nurse to get her hand out of me when she tried checking my cervix during a contraction. She respectfully responded. Then I pushed out my baby.

For an impossibly long moment, our daughter did not breathe. Then the nurse cleared the fluid out of her mouth, and she gave her first cry. Instead of a rush of sirens and questions, we got the blissful, quiet time to soak up our baby in our arms. With the lights turned low, I held her to my breast. She didn't want to suckle yet, so we gazed into each other's eyes. I had learned to turn toward my fear, and I was rewarded with joy and growth. I was rewarded with deep chocolate eyes, peaceful and trusting, filled with the infinite knowing that shines through when we are fresh out of the womb.

Reflecting on the two birth experiences I had, I see a metaphor for how life's struggles feel from a disempowered, unhealed stance compared to what it feels like when we are willing to embrace our wholeness and trust our voices. When we have a lot of buried pain or disowned selves lurking in the splintered-off corners of our psyche, life's challenges can spiral into darkness really quickly. Our unconscious reactions and fears take the wheel. We may be overwhelmed as we spin into fight, flight, or freeze mode. In my first birth experience, fight did not work when I yelled at the midwife and my husband that they couldn't send me home because I was going to the hospital. But no one took me seriously. Flight would just not work, because there is no way to run away from physical pain. (I was too triggered to think of pain meds, and furthermore I was very judgmental about how "bad" they were.) The only option left was to go into freeze mode, keeping myself trapped in silent terror for hours. My buried shadows dictated how I experienced the birth and made me wait to ask for help until it was extremely dire. I don't say this to blame myself—that kind of self-harshness is never helpful. I did the best I could with the inner resources I had, which were not very robust.

Four and a half years later, I had started to embrace life's struggles and feel like I could handle hard things. I could speak up for myself in a clear way, knowing I deserved to have my needs met. While the circumstances of the second birth were admittedly easier, my experience of the contractions was completely different. I didn't feel victimized by the pain. I didn't feel anxious. I knew I could get through them, focusing on making sounds with my vocal cords instead of the intense pressure. I laughed at the nurse's jokes and stories between contractions. I smiled.

This shows how we can experience the challenges of life when we are on the path of healing. It's not about creating the mythical land of pain-free, blissful living that I used to long for. The pressure comes, the struggles come, because that is how we grow. Yet we can approach them with embodied confidence, knowing it is safe to face the darkness and bring it into union with the light. We find moments of joy and meaning even when life is really hard. We trust our bodies' innate pacing, knowing the joy can outweigh the pain, just as the breaks between contractions are longer than the contractions themselves. Going through the birth canal creates pressure, whether we are babies being born, mothers feeling them come through, or human beings in the midst of a fiery rebirth. We find freedom by embracing it all, welcoming the shadow, the light, the pain, and the joy. Then we can raise our mighty roar!

Unleash Your Goddess Voice Practice No. 8: Playing with Instinctual Sound

Making sounds that are not considered "normal" is a fun and powerful way to embrace your wholeness. By seeing what judgments arise as you use your voice, you get to practice bringing more compassion to the parts of yourself that have been deemed "unacceptable." In this practice, you are invited to make any kind of sounds with your breath and vocal cords—sighs, grunts, growls, speaking, singing, or anything in between. This kind of free-flowing vocal improvisation can be really vulnerable, and that's where the self-compassion piece comes in. It's okay if your sounds are weird or unpleasant.

For a recording of this practice, visit saragiita.com/free

1. Begin by practicing Open Channel Breathing, noticing how your diaphragm descends and your ribs expand outward as you breathe in. Allow your throat to be soft and open as you breathe.

2. When you feel ready, try making some humming noises, sighs, growls, or singing tones.

3. Feel into your heart and notice what sounds wish to emerge next.

4. If you feel any self-judgments creeping in, that's a great time to vocalize some kind reassurances. You can say, "My voice is just right. There is no right or wrong way to make these sounds. It's okay to sound strange or wacky."

5. Continue playing with sound for as long as you wish

CHAPTER 9

Embracing Your Expressive Inner Child

I journeyed through the forest,
I journeyed deep,
And found a hungry soul-child,
hidden among the leaves.
How strongly she had held on
when loving sustenance was spare
How warmly she welcomed me
when I embraced her there.

It Took Me Years to Embrace My Inner Child

Working with my inner child has been the most potent practice for building my confidence to speak up and be heard. But it took me a long time to get on board with the idea. I used to roll my eyes when I heard people talking about their inner child. The first time I had a conversation about someone's inner child, I was sitting at the small kitchen table in the third-floor apartment of my host family in Ecuador. With her face glowing and peaceful, my host mom told me all about a retreat she just attended to get to know her "niño interior," (inner child). I smiled and nodded as she told me about it, secretly thinking that it was stupid. She was an adult, for goodness' sake. How could there be a child hidden inside? And if by chance she and this crazy retreat leader were right about the inner child, I definitely did not want to meet mine.

Yet as I went through therapy years later, I kept seeing an image of myself as a small, scared child huddled in the corner. I called her Little Sara. She yearned to be held, soothed, reassured. She was so scared that she was bad or unlovable. She had held on bravely for years, staying buried with my trauma. But a soul needs nourishment, and she was so hungry for a loving embrace. Through experimentation, I developed a visualization practice that I call "Embracing Your Younger Self."

Still, I felt squeamish about the term "inner child." In 2018, I went so far as to lead a visualization of "Embracing Your Younger Self" during a keynote speech for 500 audience members, without ever acknowledging that this was inner child work. After the speech, a middle-aged straight couple who were both therapists came up to my table to chat. I asked them how the visualization went, and the man told me, "It was great. I saw my inner child and he told me to keep on loving him." I thought to myself, *did I just lead an inner child practice? Have I become like the retreat leader that helped my host mom in Ecuador find her inner child?*

Yes. Yes, I did. And thank goodness I got on board the inner child boat, because after that speech in which I shared my story of overcoming sexual trauma, I needed to give my inner child some serious love. Even though the speech went well, my Little Sara was feeling super vulnerable from speaking her truth to so many strangers and never wanted to share her voice again. It was only through learning techniques to allow my inner child to write and speak to me that I was able to heal and feel safe speaking publicly once again after that big expansion and the subsequent vulnerability hangover.

Once I had seen the transformative power of giving love to this tender aspect of my psyche, I was able to embrace not only the vulnerable child within, but to enjoy the silly, playful, and creative aspects of my childlike energy as well. When we can heal and care for the inner child, it doesn't mean they go away. We can approach most of our lives from the standpoint of the responsible, caring adult. Then when we are ready to be creative and have fun, we can turn on the inner child's playfulness. Freeing the child within brings unbounded joy and flow. We can access the rapture of a small child to play and laugh without judgment or worry.

If, like me, you don't relate to the idea of an inner child, you can still open up a compassionate dialogue with the vulnerable parts of your psyche. You may simply notice where in your body you feel fear, anxiety, or tenderness, and ask gentle questions as you focus there. You may find an image, phrase, color, or sensation that represents your deep vulnerability. And working this way, you can bring love to that wounded part and restore it to wholeness, safety, and abundant self-expression.

Embodying Your Self as Caregiver

You can think of the inner child as a subpersonality or part of the ego—but remember that the ego is not bad! The ego evolved to help us survive, and it deserves love because it, too, is a tender, important part of us. Yet if your awareness lies solely at the level of the ego, a lot of fearful patterns probably run the show.

If we are ready to expand our awareness beyond the fearful patterns of the ego, we can soothe and reassure every last tender part by embodying the Self. As we have touched on before, your capital-S Self is the overarching part of your being that is connected to your Inner Flame and the wisdom of the Universe. In Chapter 5 we looked at the Self as a detached witness to the parts that are scared of playing big with your voice, creativity, message, and life. Now, we get to take it a step further and cultivate the presence of our Self as a loving caregiver, protector, provider, and supporter of the inner child and other aspects of the ego. The Self can offer love through words, loving energy, presence, and guiding us into supportive rituals and practices. Anytime a vulnerable, childlike part feels scared of speaking up or creating something new, your Self can step in to offer reassurance and guidance.

The trick to cultivating the voice of our Self is to personalize the ways we envision it. We take what is formless and imagine it in a way our human psyche can grab onto, through a relationship with an inner entity that offers us love. I call this an inner caregiver. It is an aspect of the Self that we have given a form and a voice. We imagine, hear, feel, sense, or even smell a person, a magical being, an animal, and/or an archetypal spirit that we can call upon and ask to speak to us at any time. At first, relating to the inner caregivers may feel really fuzzy, deliberate, or awkward. If that's the case, you can consciously choose a form and test it out. Maybe you're a dog lover, so imagining petting a golden retriever with silky fur would be a good place to start. Or you may feel curious about a Goddess form such as Brigid, Kali, or Quan Yin. You could pull up an image or devotional music online and then close your eyes and see what arises.

Over time, you will get used to the process of working with inner caregivers and protectors, and the fuzzy initial connections will grow into long-lasting relationships. At some point you will shift from saying, "Is this even working?" to noticing your Self freely and consistently offering love and wisdom through the form you have imagined. Then we go from being identified solely with the young, scared, combative, vulnerable, wounded, or abandoned parts of our ego and shift into a dual awareness that we are also the loving inner caregiver who offers compassion and guidance. Bringing in awareness of your inner caregivers feels like a warm blanket and a soothing hug. They bring gentleness and an undying belief in your worth.

If you are starting to squirm and think you might just go watch TV right now because you will not be able to receive such loving attention, know that you are not alone. When we have not received the open-hearted love and unconditional acceptance we deserved in the past, it might seem safer to not even try to receive that nurturing. If we keep our expectations really low, then we will not be let down. However, we can feel compassion for ourselves and this protective coping mechanism at the same time. There may also be work of unlearning your conditioning to deconstruct the beliefs you absorbed about how safe it is to receive nourishment. Remember you can connect to your Inner Flame even if you still have unhealed patterns. Your worth shines on, even when you can't feel it. To receive more nourishment, you can start with questions. Could I receive a tiny drop of love from my Self? Could I feel safe enough to embody inner softness for a brief moment?

Many people who feel resistant to receiving nurturance from humans may be more open to connecting with an animal. That brings us to the first way we may imagine our inner caregivers, as a trusty inner support animal. We feel the support animal through its calm presence. It offers affection and acknowledgment of our feelings. It can be any animal you choose, and since we are in the realm of imagination, don't shy away from unicorns, purple rabbits, or talking animals. If they are presenting themselves and wanting to offer you love, go with it! Bring in some lightness and fun, knowing that the way you relate to the inner caregivers can evolve and change at any time. You are not committing yourself to a lifetime of a singing fairy on your shoulder if she happens to pop into your mind one day. Just trust that the experiences that arrive have something beautiful to offer in this moment.

In addition to welcoming a nurturing animal, a lot of folks are drawn to receiving nurturance from spiritual masters, angels, spirit guides, gurus, deities, and archetypes. These may or may not be entities that you grew up with. If you feel a divine connection to one of these forms, remember that they are not solely "out there" in the Universe. They are also within you. And you get to feel this loving, divine presence as a voice that speaks from your own soul. You don't have to do anything at all to grow more deserving of this inner nurturance. Nor do you need to overanalyze who shows up to nurture you. In my 20s I threw myself into the yoga-based spiritual path that I grew up with, and developed a deeper relationship inside with Baba, the guru. And I found it nourishing. But as I crossed into my 30s and started to grow beyond the gender boxes and spiritual rules that I picked up from the group, for a while I thought I had to distance myself from Baba too. After all, I had always felt like having a guru made me weird. Yet despite my intentions to drop it all, Baba's presence has kept popping up inside, wanting to offer me love. Who am I to say no? Likewise, bestselling author Sue Monk Kidd went through a period of feeling like connecting to Mother Mary was incongruent with being an empowered woman ('cause Mary's been stripped down to a one-sided image of a gentle mother over millennia). Sue felt like a formless divine presence was simpler. Yet her heart taught her it was possible to receive Mary's loving presence and still cultivate not just the stereotypically feminine qualities of gentleness and nurturance within herself, but also to embody strength, determination, creativity, and wildness.

Hallelujah, these Parents are Free!

Just as we can imagine inner animals or divine forms as inner caregivers, I am a big fan of finding/creating/connecting to our inner parents. Now take a breath if the word "parents" brings up a whole wheelbarrow full of manure-like feelings. Because our inner parents are NOT the same as our outer, real-life parents. Even if we are super grateful for all that our parents gave us, they could not be there for us in every moment of difficulty in our lives. There will be at least a few times when they have let us down or been absent. Furthermore, we are all messy and imperfect humans as we parent our outer children (which my two kids could tell you all about!). The imperfections in the parenting you received are the invitation to meet your inner parents, who exist independently of all past familial patterns. Your inner parents are free from the limitations, beliefs, and habits of your real-life parental figures. They can look different, speak differently, and celebrate you in ideal ways. They can re-parent you and give you what you wish you had received as a child.

The marvelous thing about having parents on the inside is that they are with us wherever we go, every moment of our lives! Our tender parts can learn to trust the inner parents with the knowledge that they will never be going away. Take a minute and breathe that in. You have inner aspects that want to shower you with love in every moment. They will be offering this unconditional love, every time you invite them in, until the day you leave this body. You deserve your own infinite embrace.

Though I support our culture moving toward greater gender fluidity and celebration of all gender expressions, I still believe we all have a mix of masculine and feminine energies within us (regardless of gender). And I find it super helpful to cultivate the presence of an inner father and an inner mother to cheer us on as we share our Goddess Voice. There are times when I crave the fatherly voice within who keeps me motivated, telling me I can summon the strength to get through this hard spot in my life. And there are times when I crave the flowing wisdom of my inner mother, who reminds me I am whole and complete as I am without having to achieve anything at all. You can also imagine gender-less parental figures if you find that more nourishing.

My friend and client Maria experienced profound healing through connecting to both motherly and fatherly nurturing aspects within herself. Like so many of us, Maria has long considered herself an empowered woman who has parts inside which she embraces and feels proud to show the world openly. She shares,

> "I also have those fearful parts which I push away and hide, even from myself, because they are so very uncomfortable to experience. Yet, what I have found through Sara's guidance is that befriending, not ignoring

these lonely, scared parts, leads to deep healing and more confidence. I have been able to do this because I feel safe being vulnerable with her. During a coaching session with Sara, she asked if I would like to receive the healing energy of metta meditation. I noticed my head gently nodding 'Yes.' We closed our eyes for three minutes as I opened up to receive healing, and Sara actively channeled light toward my being. Here is what spontaneously happened so vividly in my mind's eye during those three minutes:

My six-year-old self is embraced by a Spirit Mama, immersed in white healing light within and without. A friend playfully picks me up and twirls me around, making me feel joyful abandon and freedom. Then Daddy gives me a piggyback ride up to bed, where he and Mommy tuck me in, one on either side. My parents tell me they want me to explore and be creative and the only time they would slow me down was if I was doing something dangerous. They said they would be with me in spirit through my dreams to offer more healing.

I shared what I experienced with Sara, as cleansing tears flowed freely from my eyes. Growing up, I was not encouraged to be creative and explore but to follow the way I was told to do things. Experiencing myself as a six-year-old child who was embraced and encouraged to be creative by my parents brought deep healing to this part of me which has felt disempowered for many years. Now, when I think of my dad, who has passed, and spend time with my mom, there is a felt sense of greater ease and love between us."

Rather than imagining inner parents who are independent from her real-life parents, Maria was able to envision receiving a deeper level of support, understanding, and encouragement from inner aspects that looked like her real parents. This goes back to the practice of Playing with Time and Space where we can revisit memories and imagine ourselves receiving what we needed during a tough time. Through this inner child work, we can time travel and rewrite the stories to help our childlike aspects feel whole and complete.

The process of caring for our inner child can be pretty magical and fun if we are open. Learning to embody the inner caregivers is the ultimate empowerment, because we can give ourselves what we need emotionally. By becoming self-nurturing and self-filling, we cultivate the resilience to speak up and navigate the consequences and reactions that come from sharing our truth. Loving embrace leads us to feel whole and complete on the inside so we can express ourselves outwardly.

Your Inner Warrior

Yi-yi-yi-yi-yi-yi-yi-yi-YA! (Did that sound like an ancient battle cry in your mind? 'Cause that's what I was going for.) In order for your inner child to feel safe, they need to know there is a strong, rooted adult presence within that can step up as protection in the face of any perceived threats. I call this the "inner warrior." She is strong, wise, brave, and resilient. She can erect effective boundaries in the blink of an eye. When needed, she will instinctively growl and stand tall and let others know you are not going to be taken advantage of. This is different from being in fight mode all the time. The warrior's power lies not in reacting harshly every time she is triggered, but in embodying the confidence that she has great skills and the energetic gravitas to keep herself safe. Many martial arts traditions teach complex forms of fighting while making it clear that the goal is NOT to fight. The goal of the master is to be so centered and self-assured that people would be out of their minds to try to mess with them. Whether or not we learn a tradition like martial arts, this energetic power is available to all of us when we connect with our inner warrior over time.

What warrior archetype would feel strong and protective to you? Your warrior may take the form of an animal, a person, a superhero, a giant, a goddess, a god, or another divine form. They may carry weapons or they may have magical superpowers. You can have fun with the details. The key is that they are a part of your own internal strength that exists to accept and protect you.

My client Sandra found that twinges of powerlessness from past mockery seeped into her present-day experiences of singing in front of others. I suggested we experiment with contacting her inner warrior, and she heartily agreed. I asked her, "Is there an animal that represents strength and power to you?" She furrowed her brow and looked out the window at the blazing red leaves of the maple tree in my front yard. Then she got a playful look in her eye. A smile that was almost a snarl started to emerge as she stood up straighter. "I could get on board with imagining a tiger." Together, we played with sounds, movements, and visualization to embody that tiger energy. We invited in the strength of the warrior's presence. Then, when she sang her song again, I witnessed that same glowing, strong posture in her movements and self-expression. Her inner child, who was scared of being mocked, now had a fierce and confident protector on board to greatly reduce her chances of being thrown into that old, powerless state.

If you are working on your own, you can get to know your inner warrior and inner caregivers through writing or visualization.

Begin by speaking out loud an invitation, such as, "I am ready to meet you. I trust that you want only my highest good." Remember that the inner caregivers and inner warrior can be human, animal, or mythical. As you write or visualize, notice where in space you feel each protector. Are they in front of you? Behind you? Standing by your side? Above or below you? Inside your heart?

One at a time, ask your inner aspects of the Self to tell you about themselves. What are their strengths? What are their commitments to the vulnerable parts of your psyche? List the messages you heard from your inner caregiver(s) or warrior(s). You may find it helpful to draw a picture or make a recording to help bring you back to the feeling of protection in the future. Before you reenter your daily life, imagine that your inner caregivers can come with you. Their strength and courage will help you draw firm boundaries, speak compassionately to yourself, and stay firmly rooted in your own confident energy.

Critical Protectors Need Compassion Too

For many people, it can initially be difficult to hear their inner warriors or inner caregivers over the blaring noise of a different protector energy: that of the inner critics. That's why we are going to revisit how to work with critical thought patterns. Simply put, an inner critic is a voice in your head that says mean things to you. When you start asking a critical voice the right questions, they often reveal their positive intentions. The inner critics are actually protectors that want to help you. It just turns out that their methods of protection (criticism, fear, judgment, and self-blame) are extremely ineffective.

In the face of pain, an inner child part may get sent into hiding or exile. An aspect of your authentic voice gets tucked away for safekeeping. As Internal Family Systems therapy outlines, there is often a Critical Protector part guarding the exiled child. It tries to keep you safe by avoiding pain, rejection, or criticism from others. For example, a kid may naturally be talkative, energetic, creative, or loud. If their parents are unable to handle the child's natural, healthy energy, they may be constantly telling the child to be quiet. Then the child learns that their natural desire to be heard is somehow wrong, bad, or "too much." Their critic would start telling them to hush up so they can hopefully avoid the pain of being scorned by others. Very often, our psyches splinter off into wounded childlike parts due to messages from peers as well. We get laughed at for the way our body looks. Or the way we talk. Or for being different. When some part of us gets rejected, we feel the pain of that rejection as a threat to our safety. Our human evolution has made us very sensitive to being accepted by the tribe. And long ago, abandonment did make us much more vulnerable to predators. There is a biological reason why rejection feels like being thrown to the lions.

Tasked with keeping our inner childlike parts hidden, our critical protectors can get really loud. They are kind of like the giant Wizard of Oz head who doesn't want you to notice the small person behind the curtain. I experienced this noisy distraction when I was contemplating sharing my story of overcoming sexual trauma in my first-ever podcast interview in 2018. My inner critic kept shouting, "No one wants to hear your story, it's too much. Too intense. Too self-involved." When I listened a little harder, my inner critic was saying "It's not safe to speak about this trauma." This protector energy had been working since I was five to keep me from sharing this part of my truth. And initially, the critical protector was saving the life of my splintered-off, vulnerable child. Before I had the resources to process the trauma and step into my power, staying silent was an adaptive function. Yet for me, the time came when my critic pushing me away from speaking up caused more pain than the risk that comes with being vulnerable. Repressed silence was taking its toll on my inner fulfillment. I was ready to reclaim the energy that had long been hidden behind the curtain so I could go beyond surviving and begin to express myself more fully. My inner voice of unworthiness had a positive intention, but it was no longer serving me.

I was ready to work with the Critical Protectors rather than be squashed by their inner noise. And the best way to start transforming a critical voice is by offering acknowledgment from the standpoint of your wise inner Self. The critics really really, really want to be heard! So let them know you appreciate their efforts to protect you from future pain. Once your inner critics feel heard, you can get curious and ask 'em some questions. Here are some examples to get the dialogue started:

- How are you trying to help me?

- What message do you have for me?

- Why are you scared?

- What are you worried will happen if I take the next steps?

- What do you need?

Then, ask if the critical part is willing to let you speak to the exiled child they are trying to protect. When you approach with love and gentleness, the childlike, vulnerable parts may feel ready to be heard and healed. You can ask the inner child what they need and find ways to meet those needs consistently over time. If they need you to say 'hi' during meditation every day for two years, do your best to show up from the stance of an inner caregiver. If they need to hide in a sleeping bag for a while, let them know you support them and are here if needed. If they say they need a hug, give them a hug. If your dear child needs to scream, find a safe place to let that holy scream loose. If they want to play dress-up, why not give it a try?

What ends up happening to the critical parts? With love and patience, the inner critic parts will likely agree to take on a more positive role as an inner cheerleader, warrior, nurturing protector, or other form of helper. Their frantic condemnations can transform into supportive voices who see the value of tapping your authentic, whole Goddess Voice.

The Healing Power of Commitment

The idea of becoming your own loving caregiver can feel really empowering. But for some people, it might come with a sinking feeling in their stomach. Taking on this responsibility can seem disappointing if you really hoped you could find the right romantic partner or people-pleasing friend or long-term healer to take care of your inner child. It's natural that a child will look outside to find someone else to give her security.

But if you leave the caregiving job up to anyone else, they are going to let you down. I say this with certainty, because they can't be there for you all the time to do a job that was never theirs to begin with. You must become the caregiver you need.

That's why the path of safe, confident authentic self-expression requires an inner commitment to caring for your vulnerable parts. It's usually not enough to show up once and then expect your inner child to be on board with speaking her truth again and again. Like a glorious emerging tree, sharing your Goddess Voice with the world can best emerge from the well-tended soil of an unwavering commitment to your inner child.

Even a year into my practice of visualizing and embracing my younger self, Little Sara doubted if I was committed to caregiving. She was perpetually insecure because for so many years my goal had been to banish her and all her painful, messy feelings. It didn't help that I used to think she would go away when I reached the mythical endpoint of being 100% healed. I finally discovered that Little Sara didn't have to be eliminated, silenced, or pushed away. She just wanted to step into the light and receive my love. She wanted to be an active partner in my life, as the truth-teller and artist. So I made a vow of love, which I do my best to renew every day:

Little Sara, my shadow self, I am here. I am here, and I am not going anywhere. You have been afraid of abandonment. But I will never abandon you. I vow to keep you by my side, always. I vow to love you even when you feel ashamed. I vow to listen to you, support you, encourage you. I vow to let you speak the truth, even when I am tempted to wear a mask and cover up our darkness. I vow to fulfill your needs, Little Sara, even when other people and responsibilities threaten to crowd you out. They will not stand in the way of my love for you. They will not take away from the nourishment and attention you deserve. You are my deepest self, my truth. And I vow to love you always.

The key to healing is giving ourselves this kind of unconditional love and compassion. Whether or not we feel support from the people in our lives, we can learn to let in a little bit more self-love and self-acceptance each day. We can become a loving, parental figures for the parts of ourselves that feel small and scared. We can learn to reassure and comfort ourselves on the path of finding our voices.

Playful Self-Expression

By committing to healing and celebrating your inner child, your delightful capacity for childlike play, creativity, and self-expression will start to emerge. You might find yourself twirling, singing, scribbling, or running through sprinklers with spontaneous glee. Or you might find your inner kiddo needs you to gradually and thoughtfully step back into the world of play and creativity. A good place to start is by making a list of activities you used to enjoy as a kid. And I'm not talking solely about the formal ones like playing an instrument or sport. Talking to yourself in the mirror, playing dress-up, riding a bike, or making mud pies all count as activities too! From your list, choose an activity that has been forgotten amidst all your "adulting," and see if your inner child wants to try it out again.

Your list might also have some playful pastimes that you never completely abandoned which your inner child would love to do more frequently. My friend Catherine remembers feeling most alive and free when spending time outdoors as a child, picking dandelions and gathering herbs for magic potions. Now her inner child loves tending her garden and calls her outdoors when she is getting too immersed in office work.

I find it easiest to let Little Sara out to play while making visual art. While writing and music are creative modalities I have honed professionally, I intentionally keep my visual art as something just for me. That way it's easier to release the pressure of it being "good" and go for messy and fun instead. My inner child enjoys making collages, abstract pastel scribbles, and paintings. She got especially excited one day a few years ago when I spontaneously started fingerpainting. My daughter, who was around five years old at the time, asked if we could paint one Saturday morning after breakfast. Still in my PJs, I got out the box of painting supplies and laid the spotted purple plastic tablecloth down on our kitchen table. I grabbed the green tempera paint, but instead of pouring it on the palette, I found myself pouring it straight onto my hands instead. I had a heyday with making handprints on a giant paper and started swirling the colors. When I felt like it was time to let that dry, I dove right into the next piece and had fun ripping up some old abstract art and gluing and layering it on paper. I felt such a deep satisfaction in my body from ripping the thick paper. Every cell in my body felt alive and lit up. I was in an ecstatic flow as I moved on to more fingerpainting and finished with a cloud of gold glitter.

Even my daughter, who can easily step into a creative flow state, was moved by my ear-to-ear grin. She said with admiration, "You look like you're having a lot of fun, Mom!" Little Sara felt seen and heard, and she was delighted to have a safe space to fuel our creative fire. I experienced the power of our inner children to provide the playful spark for our authentic self-expression.

Creating Containers for the Inner Child

As you start to unleash the playful self-expression of your inner child, you may have a hidden fear that the childlike energy will just take over and it will be hard to fulfill your adult responsibilities. I get it. We don't want to lose ourselves in a puddle of ice cream or drop all our commitments in favor of smearing glitter glue on the walls. That's why I recommend creating safe times and places for your inner child to come out, while your inner caregivers are still present to step in if needed. Creating a metaphorical fence around the playground is not squelching your inner child, and it can actually help her to feel more safety when she knows there are healthy limits in place.

Just as growing kids will thrive when they know there is a competent adult in charge, your inner child needs to know she is not the one running the show. At first, I thought my job was to give my inner child whatever she wanted. After all, I wanted her to be seen, heard, and honored after having huddled in hiding for so many years.

The thing is, our inner children don't have the big picture of our life's trajectory (especially when they are still being healed). Their fears can stop us in our tracks if our goal is to just give the inner child whatever they want. I noticed this happening after I wrote the first draft of this book several years ago. Feeling an intense creative flow, I wrote it all by hand in a journal over the course of several months. In my heart, I knew the book was meant to be shared. But once I stepped out of the creative flow and thought about other people reading my most vulnerable stories, Little Sara got super scared. She did not want to publish the book, or even take steps to work on editing. And for at least a year, I felt like it was important to honor her wishes. I shoved the book onto the back shelf of my life.

As much as I love my inner child, she is not my whole identity. Another part of me recognized the task of finishing the book was about more than feeling safe or unsafe. It was about fulfilling a calling. So how could I reconcile my inner child's fears with the adult longing to create and share something deeply meaningful? I eventually found the answer in connecting more frequently with my inner caregivers. I let Little Sara know that I would be with her every scary and delightful step of the way. I acknowledged that she was right in saying there are no guarantees about how something we create will be received by others. Negative feedback or other disappointing responses are a possibility any time we put heartfelt work into the world. But the key is knowing we have the tools and resilience to care for ourselves through those rough spots. If my inner child feels heartbroken, I will love and witness her through the process of mending. Once we trust our ability to recover from emotional setbacks, the joy of expressing ourselves authentically is worth the risk.

Realizing my inner caregivers and warrior needed to take the lead, I spoke to my inner child. "Just because it's scary doesn't mean we won't finish and publish the book. We need to release this book in order to feel fulfilled and serve the people who are meant to read it and share it. And I promise to make it as easy and fun as possible by letting your playful voice be heard. Since we don't know the future outcomes, I promise to be here to support any feelings that come up from the process." I created a boundary, acknowledging a desire she had that emerged from fears, while not letting that desire steer the course of our life. Have you ever had it happen that your inner adult aspects see a mountain ahead and know it needs to be climbed, but meanwhile your inner child is throwing a tantrum at the trailhead? You can help her get on board by offering piggy-back rides, silly songs, motivational speeches, and tangible rewards along the way. She can be soothed, reassured, and cared for as you make the journey together.

Unleash Your Goddess Voice Practice No. 9: Embracing Your Younger Self

Alright, let's give ourselves some love! While this practice leans on visualization, you can also adapt it by incorporating writing and drawing, or by choosing a large huggable stuffed animal that represents your inner child. For clarity's sake, I will call the inner caregiver "you," while "your younger self" refers to an image of yourself at a younger age.

For a recording of this practice, visit saragiita.com/free

1. Keep a pen and blank journal or paper nearby in case you wish to write during the practice.

2. Sit or lie down in a comfortable place where you will be free from distractions.

3. Begin by grounding yourself with four deep, diaphragmatic breaths. If it feels good, let yourself sigh loudly on the exhale.

4. State your intention of getting to know your wounded younger self and any protector parts that may be keeping them in hiding.

5. Allow an image of your wounded younger self to appear in front of you in the present moment. Feel her presence. Let your eyes radiate complete love and acceptance as you sit across from her.

6. Ask your younger self how you can support her. Would she like a hug? If she is not ready for an embrace, perhaps she might accept a gift such as a beautiful flower, a song, a poem, or a comfortable place to curl up. You may wish to speak out loud, hear the words in your head, or write them down.

7. From the standpoint of your inner caregivers, speak or write to your younger self reassuringly. Let her know that she is good, and safe, and that you love and accept her. Let her know that she is free from blame. Remind her that she can grow, and heal, and move past this pain. Let

your embrace melt away her fright. Let her feel worthy and whole and beautiful in her imperfection. And let her know you will support her unconditionally. Your love and acceptance come in an infinite flow, always available.

CHAPTER 10

Aligning Your Energy to Make Your Voice Heard

Like a deeply rooted tree,
I will not be toppled.
Like a swimmer in the waves,
I will not be stifled.

My sovereign core,
My unshakable power,
Grows outward into song.

The Energy of Making Yourself Heard

All along in this journey of freeing our voices, we have been building the resilience to create, speak up, and sing out. To deepen that confidence, next we will explore how to work with our energetic body to stand in our truth and make ourselves heard. I think of the energetic body as how we experience our intangible life force, *prana,* or *chi.*

Even when our minds are aligned with empowerment, our energy may be muted under the layers of protection we may have built up to prevent others from seeing our true, vulnerable insides. It's kind of like walking around with many layers of jackets, sweaters, and coats that are not made of fabric, but old stories, beliefs, karmas, and patterns of wounding. To safely soften and unpeel these shells or walls, we will explore the energy of four archetypes: the tortoise, the ladybug, the lioness, and the Goddess. I call these the "voice archetypes."

Before diving deep into each energy pattern in this chapter, I want to give you a quick overview. We will start with the trusty tortoise. The primary feature of tortoise energy is carrying our sturdy, heavy, energetic shell around with us everywhere so we can tuck those soft, vulnerable parts inside the protective shell anytime we need. And our most tender underbelly never even has to be exposed! I want to be clear that this is not negative. Having energetic layers of protection around yourself can be helpful in the right context. There are times when our systems need the medicine of the tortoise, especially if you make the conscious choice to contract, pull in, and conserve energy. But if you are constantly hanging out in tortoise energy because hiding seems like the only safe option, at some point all those layers of protection may start to feel like a super heavy burden. You may grow tired of carrying the shell/story that no one wants to hear what you have to say. You may be constantly retreating into your shell to avoid the people outside. During those times when your soft tortoise head, arms, and feet are showing to the world, you might feel like a defenseless energetic sponge, picking up on every nuanced emotion and judgment that people around you are projecting.

It can be a relief to intentionally crawl out from under that heavy shell and relate to a new energetic archetype such as the ladybug. Like the tortoise, the ladybug also has a protective shell. The super cute red, orange, or yellow spotted wing cases on top of the ladybug are called the "elytra." When you see the ladybug munching on aphids on top of a green leaf, it doesn't look like the insect has wings. Yet the nimble and light protective shell can swing open and these gloriously thin but strong black wings unfold. Then the ladybug can take off and go wherever she wants to go (this is fascinating to watch in slow-motion; thank you, YouTube!) Like the ladybug, we can imagine ourselves with a nimble protective energetic shell that we can open up at a moment's notice. Then our voice/wings can unfurl and soar as we taste the freedom of authentic self-expression, before coming back to rest inside our protective casing. We can imagine our many layers of protection having a clean vertical break in front of our body where we can choose to swing open the doors when the conditions feel safe enough. Ladybug energy is bursting onto the stage and saying, "Here I am, world!" knowing you will go back into your shell and close up your energetic doors after the final bow.

I love this ladybug energy. But it can feel tender because those wings are so delicate. At times we want our energy to feel more rooted, and that's where the lioness archetype comes in. Like the inner warrior, the lioness embodies fierce, unwavering confidence. She doesn't feel the need to carry shells, walls, or layers of protection because she feels so strong and steady in herself. This sovereign energy pattern is defined by filling yourself up with confidence on the inside and providing the protection you need. Working with your Inner Flame and the energy of your third chakra at your solar plexus can help you step more into the lioness energy. By embodying light on the inside, you can walk and roar with confidence and free yourself from energetic shells, cords, and karmic agreements.

In recent years, I have come to experience a fourth archetype for the energy of self-expression: the Goddess. She carries the steady fierceness and confidence of the lioness. Yet there is also an all-knowing, all-reaching benevolence that comes with stepping into alignment with your Goddess energy. Standing tall and proud, your inner Goddess is connected to the earth and the sky. She is simultaneously confident and humble, opening herself up to be a conduit for the highest will to be expressed through her voice and actions. This capacity to open yourself as a vessel for infinite divine energy is what defines a moment of sharing your voice from the standpoint of the Goddess archetype. As you offer your voice in service, the infinite love in your heart can be shared in ever-expanding circles of influence and impact.

Thank You, Tortoise!

In order to embrace the tortoise energy, we need to understand the cyclical nature of the voice archetypes. While it might seem like these four self-expression archetypes offer a clear progression or evolution, in reality, we embody them in nuanced and cyclical timing. Because we're talking about releasing the energetic layers of protection that keep us from being seen and heard, just like all healing, it's going to happen in cycles and gradations. For example, I spent a lot of my younger years in ladybug energy, feeling like I could unfurl my wings when singing other people's songs or acting in a play. Through the shell of a character, I could hear my own voice. I was loud. I was confident. Pretending to be someone else, I spoke up, and people listened. Since I didn't yet feel safe sharing my whole authentic self, I would fold my wings underneath my protective casing once the performance was complete.

Crossing into my early 20s, I started to have moments of experiencing the lioness archetype as my authentic self-expression began to expand. But when I became hyper-focused on healing my sexual trauma during my dark night of the soul, the fear and vulnerability of facing those memories made me need the tortoise medicine. I was not moving backward, but simply needed a safe place to hide without being seen or heard. I would frequently tuck myself away in my bedroom when feeling triggered or vulnerable.

When I felt ready to peek my head and arms and legs out from my shell to express something that could no longer stay trapped inside, composing music became a lifeline. I was able to express myself as an act of healing, without feeling the urge to share my voice publicly that often comes with the other archetypes. I explored my desire to peek out from my shell of heavy burdens through a song I wrote called "I Rise." It became an anthem I sang to myself during anxious nights. As I sang, I pounded the rhythm on my thighs and felt soothed by the tapping. The song found a new evolution one summer night when we were visiting my parents in the mountains of Colorado. I put my kids to bed and then snuck out into the fresh night air. As the sun went behind the mountains, I hid away on a tiny patio my mom had created in a grove of scrub oak trees. Solar-powered garden lights lit my path as I descended the stone steps set into the hillside. The smell of sage permeated the air.

I was ready for some howling, as trying to be quiet in a house full of people was making me more anxious. But what came out were new parts to "I Rise." I realized it needed to become a song for choir, with many parts and voices. Over the next few days, I joyously imagined the interlocking parts. I had never composed for a choir, but acapella women's voices seemed like the perfect incarnation for my song of healing.

Initially, the process of composing was intimidating, and learning to use the music notation software was slow. But once I found my rhythm, the artistic outlet became a blessing. I used to dread the evenings, full of anxiety and trembling and feeling unable to cope with anything other than hiding in my shell. Once I had a joyful purpose, though, I couldn't wait for night to fall. I would help my husband put the kids to bed, and then race downstairs to my digital piano and computer, ready to birth a new part or tweak an old one. I did my best to let the creative energy flow through me. When I would get hung up on trying to get it perfect or worrying that a part wasn't good enough, I reminded myself that the goal was not to attain perfection. The goal was to peek out from my shell and express the pain and joy of personal transformation.

As I completed the song, I began to live these lyrics:
I'm on the cusp
Of waking
From the hundred-year slumber
My deepest self is taking
I'm on the verge
Of tapping
The fiery power
My past is dampening

The eggshell
Is cracking;
Birthing
A new me.
And then I Rise,
Rise
Rise
From my slumber.

It was time for me to leave my heavy shell behind and grow into a new voice archetype. However, I still briefly revisit the tortoise energy from time to time after experiences that feel particularly vulnerable. It goes hand-in-hand with tending to my inner child when she is upset. And I have found that while I initially experienced the tortoise energy during a life period with intense anxiety, now I can come into that feeling of being protected by a sturdy shell with a sense of calmness and ease. When I intentionally curl up, there's not anxiety from feeling confined but a grounded trust that my need to hide won't last for long. Rather than coming into tortoise energy because my voice is in fear and repression, I can now choose to come into a shell as an expression of empowered silence. I believe we all crave the comforting confinement of having protective walls at times because it reminds us of our mother's womb. Even if your experience of being in the womb came with stressors, your energy body still remembers the warmth of being safely tucked away from the world so you could incubate and grow.

Unfurl Those Ladybug Wings!

The invitation to regrow my wings and start sharing my voice publicly once more came in December of 2016. I had invited my friend Melia to the historic Women's March on Denver, and she sent me a link and a message: "They are looking for people to sing inspiring songs! You should apply." *She's right,* I thought. *I should!* But part of me really wanted to stay in hiding, which is why I found myself trembling on the kitchen floor, sitting against the wall for support. I looked up at the dingy white ceiling, watching the steam rise from the minestrone soup that I cooked every three weeks on a Wednesday night. I glanced down at my phone again as doubts and self-criticism took over. *I am too much of a mess. There is no way I could put myself out there in front of so many people, what if I had a panic attack? And they probably won't want me to sing anyway, I am no one…*

Deep down, I knew it felt right to be on that stage sharing my music in a big and meaningful way. Yet the very idea of sending the email filled me with anxiety. I felt paralyzed. Terrified. I was drowning in self-doubt, fearing my post-traumatic stress syndrome was too debilitating at this point for me to take such a big risk. Through all the noise, I heard the quiet voice of my intuition. *Send the email,* it said. Don't worry about all the other stuff. You have to try.

So I pulled myself off the floor. I stood, phone in hand. I sent the email explaining what I could offer as an empowerment-focused singer-songwriter. At that moment I came out from my tortoise shell. I acknowledged that my fear and self-doubt are real, but that I wasn't going to let them stop me from putting myself out there, being heard, and being seen. Even if I still needed protection at times, I was not going to forget that my voice is made to fly.

A little over a month later, I raised my voice with the crowd of 100,000 people as we marched between skyscrapers. We were done being silent. We were done tolerating the misogyny that society repeatedly ignored. When we circled back to Civic Center Park, I saw the huge stone amphitheater and the twenty-foot-tall towers of speakers. Thousands of people of all genders were gathered, displaying their colorful signs and pink hats. I went backstage along with the other speakers and performers, strong women of many backgrounds with a message to share. My nerves rattled. But I kept breathing. Finally, the stage manager ushered my guitarist and I onto the stage, and we led a few thousand people to sing along to the chorus of my song. The sound echoed through the stone pavilion, as we sang, "I Claim My Power." Together, we voiced our power. I felt tender but also aligned as I unfurled my ladybug voice/wings for the first time in years.

In the months after the march, "I Claim My Power" became my anthem as I sensed my habit of hiding was shifting. Creating by myself, within the safety of four walls had guided me through my trauma. But I dreamt of not just creating, but sharing. I wanted to be a professional musician. I wanted to make myself heard. My self-doubts created deep shadows. *I'll probably fail anyway. No one wants to listen to my music. I should just write songs for myself and forget about everyone else.* But my intuition knew I needed more opportunities to split open my protective shell and let myself be seen in my authentic glory. I discovered that sharing my voice was a process of allowing all the doubts to be present, and continually returning to my inner alignment. When I tap into my Inner Flame and sense of worthiness, I can share my voice with the world from a place of purpose and trust.

With this burgeoning sense of expansion, I began to seek out more opportunities to perform. I joined a group coaching program where aspiring musicians learned how to book gigs, build an audience, and get featured by media outlets. I also realized I did not have to make this journey alone. I found a soul sister to create music with named Anastasia Rose, and we helped each other build confidence. Putting ourselves out there became a healing act, a willingness to be seen and heard. Opening and closing my energetic shell became easier and easier with practice. As I let my voice soar on more stages, I began to feel like I was living my purpose of expressing myself deeply and inviting others to do the same.

Like me, you may sense that your ladybug energy involves showing up bravely on physical or online stages. But there are so many other ways to express yourself authentically. If you are not someone who feels called to share your voice on stage, embodying the ladybug energy may happen through conversations and creative expression. In moments when it feels safe, you may naturally find yourself swinging open the doors of energetic protection so you can be seen and heard in your authenticity.

Another personal experience emerged from embodying the ladybug archetype: for the first time in a decade and a half, I found that I could play piano for more than five minutes a day without pain. The heavy stories I had carried around the tendinitis that hit me at age 19 began to soften as I came to enjoy playing piano once again. The dance with this pain is not completely over in my life's learning, as I still get flare-ups of pain from time to time. These episodes are a reminder to step away from any pushing energy that may have crept in and to care for my inner child who feels like she is not a "good enough" pianist because of this pain pattern. By taking breaks, stretching, practicing Alexander Technique, and using massage tools on my trigger points, I can manage the flare-ups. As I'm learning to embrace these opportunities to recharge, I reframe the periods of rest away from the piano as times of folding my wings back underneath their protective casings.

Let Us Dance, Lioness!

I feel really comfortable in ladybug energy, and I have observed quite a lot of women who feel the same. Ladybugs, like tortoises, are amazing creatures and valuable archetypes. But the downside is that they are easy to overlook. Their underpraised beauty is easy to ignore. That's why at certain times we may feel the urge to embody the commanding energy of the lioness. The lioness represents your sovereignty, or your ability to be in the driver's seat of your life, free from external control. When you embody this confidence, you can make yourself heard. When you find the people who are meant to receive your voice and message, they will naturally perk up their ears and feel interested in what you have to say or share.

To start embodying this archetype, we have to let go of some of our energetic layers of protection. We have to shed our shells, metaphorically speaking. And this can feel quite vulnerable, especially if you are an empath who easily feels other people's emotions and energies. The good news is that once you get the feel for the lioness energy, your tender tortoise underbelly or delicate ladybug wings transform into something much stronger. By filling up with the blazing light of your Inner Flame, your energetic body doesn't have space to take on other people's baggage or projections. While you are still energetically interconnected with others through Unity Consciousness, with the confidence of the lioness you are clear on what is not coming into your field. Your light sets the energetic tone of each interaction so you're no longer on a roller coaster of matching other people's energy. With deep self-trust, you can start to have more moments of feeling that you don't need all those invisible sweaters and coats that stand between your authentic self and the rest of the world. You can express yourself, and people are more likely to respond with respect.

I have experienced my lioness voice garnering more respect from a person in my life who used to frequently criticize my decisions. He was quite out of tune with how his comments came off, and anytime I called him out on being critical, he would defensively say he was just making conversation and that I was overreacting. Over the past two years as I have been tapping my sovereignty, I have intentionally paid attention to sending the energy of his comments away from me rather than letting it rest in my body. I imagine the criticisms as a ball that I toss into a compost bin full of happy worms, and this practice helps me to take our interactions less personally. I have also been setting clear verbal boundaries with him, and amazingly his criticisms have greatly diminished. Looking at the equation of our relationship, I see the factor that has changed is my lioness energy coming more online. I have aligned more parts of my being to know I deserve respect, and he has unconsciously reflected it back to me.

Similarly, my singing student Julie has received more respect for her voice in her corporate career. She shares, "I experience an intangible increase in people's reception of my benevolent power and respect of my leadership. Rather than needing to speak up, people seek me out for advice and to elicit my perspective on tough questions."

Stepping into your lioness power happens in degrees, and is not an all-or-nothing endeavor. During the period of my life when I was embodying ladybug energy by singing on stage, I spontaneously tasted that lioness power and confidence during one particular performance. I was singing with a local women's choir led by Dr. Tina Lynn-Craig, and she invited me to choose a solo song by Mexican composer Consuelo Velázquez, who is best known for her classic composition, "Bésame Mucho." I was drawn to performing the piece, "Amar y Vivir," which is a passionate song about refusing to hide your love from others. Since I always like to attach personal meaning and stories to songs I perform, I experienced it as a song of empowerment, ferocity, and embracing my drama queen side. As I practiced in front of the full-length mirror in my music room, I had fun taking on a strong posture and letting the song's feeling of certainty move through my body. I tended to perform my own compositions, which often expressed my lighthearted ladybug energy at that time. But this song called for an energy that said, "I will show up bravely and authentically and stop worrying about being judged."

As the performance approached, Tina and I both agreed I needed a fiery accessory to throw on before the song, since I would be wearing the basic black choir uniform along with everybody else. A red scarf would be ideal, but hard to find in April. So I opened my linen closet and found a shiny red thrift store tablecloth that usually adorns our table on Christmas Eve. Using safety pins, I fashioned it into a wrap or stole of sorts to encircle my shoulders. I felt a bit self-conscious beforehand about wearing a tablecloth. Yet when I stepped onto the stage it all melted away. While I didn't yet have the language to describe the lioness archetype, those hours of practicing with a fierce body posture helped me naturally show up boldly. Rather than embodying the false bravado that often gets mistaken for confidence, I was filled with trust in my worth that felt grounded and authentic. I was completely enthralled with the moment as the cascading lines of my voice carried us all through waves of emotions. The packed auditorium had the house lights turned up slightly so I could see everyone's faces in rapt attention. My natural lioness energy invited everyone to perk up their ears and be carried along for the ride.

After this empowering performance, I sensed there was more energetic work to be done to be able to embody this self-assuredness when singing my own songs and speaking my truth. As my cyclical journey of healing unfolded, I learned that we can dance with the lioness energy and fill up completely during times when it is accessible, and it's natural to also have times when that power feels out of reach.

One challenge that comes with the lioness archetype is that the energy can feel isolating. Sovereignty is essential to confident self-expression, as being the queen of your own domain allows you to show up without worrying excessively about what others think or how they will react. Yet at the same time, we need to balance sovereignty with interconnectedness. There are times when we want to fill up with the light of our Inner Flame, yet leave a little space open in our hearts to feel what others are going through. Rather than focusing just on the strength of the lioness, we can practice simultaneous awareness to embody her confident power while also leaving space for tenderness and empathy.

Speak Through Me, Glorious Goddess!

We have explored the tortoise, ladybug, and lioness energy as models for how you can actively choose to show up and speak up. While these focus on getting behind the steering wheel and making empowered choices around how you manage your energy, the Goddess archetype hands the control back to your own soul and the Goddess within you. The primary energetic feature of this archetype is opening yourself up as a humble yet empowered vessel for the Divine to be expressed through your voice. You can stand tall and be a bridge between the earth and the sky, sending your love outward and receiving attention and respect in return.

The goddess archetype allows you to become a "small-G-goddess" here on this earthly plane by opening yourself up to be a conduit for Her sanctified expression to come through. When your surrender is sincere, the "big-G Goddess" (who is also in you) will take over and rock the stage with an expansive power and heartfelt authenticity. Some of you may already be shouting "Hell, yes!" to embracing this energy. But I want to take a moment to speak with my sisters who have gotten this far in the book and still don't feel particularly connected to the word, "Goddess." Perhaps that is because you don't relate to any particular goddess forms like Aphrodite, Durga, or Isis. Perhaps you're just a practical, concrete kind of person and don't see yourself in the images of women surrounded by animals, donning flowing dresses and possibly carrying old-fashioned weapons. Well, you are in luck, because there is no wrong way to be a goddess or love the Divine Feminine. She is simply the omnipresent divine energy taking a feminine form, which you can embrace in any way you wish.

So wear your long red dress and walk barefoot through the forest if that is how the Goddess wants to express herself through you, but don't be worried if she asks you to stay home in your sweats and knit cozy scarves instead. When you offer yourself as a vessel for the Divine to be expressed through you, you have to throw out your ego's old stories about what is the "right" way to show up. Whether those stories say you should show up by relentlessly putting yourself out there, or speaking sweetly, or waiting to share your message until it is perfectly polished, the Goddess may have other plans. She may chip away at those old patterns until you can be a clear, open channel for something even more powerful to be expressed through you.

I first witnessed the power of becoming a spiritual conduit back in my early 20s, when I was on the tambourine-shaking, bus-busting, yogi song tour through Mexico. When I wasn't complaining about food or lateness or whatnot, I got to sing alongside a seasoned New Zealander singer named Jyoshna. Through the overflowing love she embodied as she sang, she taught me to sing with a depth no vocal coach had approached. Our band gave concerts to audiences large and small, and no matter the turnout, she gave her all with transcendence and grace. I, the vocal performance major, could point out plenty of mistakes in her technique. Yet her music and way of showing up were not about flawlessness. How could she go so deep, be so vulnerable, and create enough space for that potency of higher love to come through? And how could I become more like her, opening myself as a humble instrument for divine inspiration to be brought into form?

At first, I simply observed and wondered at her devotional practice of becoming a creative conduit. Then, not through effort but through grace, I experienced the expansiveness of being an instrument for the first time. To conclude our five-week concert tour, we did an amazing all-night recording session. We set up our folding chairs in a circle in a white-walled art gallery turned temporary recording studio. Seven female singers and a tabla drum player from India joined Jyoshna and her guitar. By the time we had the equipment set up, the clock neared midnight. Insects buzzed outside the window screen as the humid night air wafted in gently. We recorded the whole album of kiirtan (mantra music) straight through, without stopping. Jyoshna led us through highs and lows, sweetness and pain as we let a string of melodies flow through us. I experienced such a high that I knew there was no turning back from that point. I was grinning from ear to ear, enraptured with the moment, sending the song from my heart out into the ever-expanding Universe.

This glorious experience of my Goddess Voice came from being swept in the current of my fellow singers who were facilitating the energy. Through their contagious devotion to being a conduit for love, I could float along on a river of divine expression coming through my voice. It took me more than a decade of experimentation to open my channel enough to allow that feeling on my own. Through surrender, I have had many experiences of leading and facilitating the collective energy for those who receive my voice or my witnessing presence. While I suspect Jyoshna's capacity to be a collective conduit came from decades of practicing devotion and surrender to a guru, my experience emerged more through energy work and a commitment to unveiling my authentic self-expression. I have learned to live the paradox of the Goddess archetype, which is being humble and empty while simultaneously being confident and full. Truly, both need to be present for you to be a conduit.

Be careful here, as I have seen plenty of people embrace surrender as a spiritual-sounding reason for the ego to cling to unworthiness. They hunch their shoulders and say, "Oh I am just a tiny drop of water with nothing valuable to say. Only my spirit guides know what's best, so I let them take over." If you sometimes fall into wanting to be a vessel from a place of unworthiness, keep yourself grounded in the confidence of your Inner Flame. It might also be helpful to remember that channeling the Goddess is really just allowing your own expansive soul to take over. That massive, holy power is an intrinsic, worthy part of you. Confidence creates the structure needed to bring this intangible divinity into form, while balancing it with humility creates space for the light to move through.

So how do we actually open our energy to become a vessel or cónduit? By balancing your chakras and getting really familiar with how you move energy, you can learn to call in a waterfall of light that moves through your being. Because a waterfall is a steady stream, your intention directs the flow outward. That divine energy gets to interact with the world of form through your voice, body, and/or hands. Yay for creativity! We are all constantly moving energy whether we are aware of it or not. When we walk from the bedroom to the bathroom, our muscles are firing, and we are pushing the air and pushing against the floor. When we say, "hello" to someone, we are moving energy and impacting eardrums through our voice. It's like we are magicians directing the flow of life force in every single moment. Why not start paying attention and delight in the magic?

Meditation: Becoming an Open Channel for Divine Expression

Begin with an intention or prayer asking divine energy to flow through you in service for the highest good of all. Then hold your hands up to the sky and imagine that they are beckoning a waterfall of light that surrounds you. You can also imagine the light coming up from Mother Earth, and add in any movements that help you fill the space around you with divine support.

Breathe in that nourishing white light, letting it feed and fill all of your cells. Once you breathe in the white light, send it out as a stream of love. Try making some sounds and imagine that the sound waves are visible. What would they look like? Where would they go? What unknown corners of humanity would be gently painted with the colorful vibration of your voice? You can imagine a person, plant, or animal receiving your sound and really taking it in with appreciation. What if the recipient of your sound could send gratitude back to join your field of white light? Play around with the energy coming through your voice being something perceivable and observable. Goddess Voice, it's time to meet the world!

Getting to Know Your Energetic Field

Now let's explore some strategies for mastering your energy so you can choose which voice archetype to embody in each situation. It all starts with getting to know what life force energy feels like in your body. Because we're talking about something intangible that we currently don't have any instruments to measure or observe, it helps to find ways to make it feel more tangible in your body. Just as we explored using your dominant learning styles to deepen your bodily awareness back in chapter four, I encourage you to find your own ways to work with your energy.

You may have noticed already that I gravitate towards visualization as a means of working with energy. If you find visualization to be a tool that works for you, you can get to know your energetic field by imagining you are painting a bubble around yourself. You get to choose the combination of colors and how far outward your energy extends. If you are a lover of words, you may enjoy writing or speaking out loud to describe the sensations of the energy moving through your body. Is there a place where you feel density or lightness? Bubbles rising up or water droplets sinking down? Words may help you to get a more concrete experience of your ever flowing energy.

Energy is very much related to sound waves, so if you find hearing to be a strong and important sense then have fun experimenting with instruments, tones, and vocal sounds. See which tones and vibrations help your energy field feel open, relaxed, and trusting. What sounds can you make to help define the edges of your own energy field? Which sounds would help you create an energetic shell of protection, and which would help you open it up? What vibrations would help you embody the strength of the lioness archetype? As you play with the energy of sound, keep in mind that tones heard inside your mind can also have an impact.

If you are a kinesthetic person, you may not find that sound, words, or visualization do much to help you manage and master your energy. It may be all about the sensations and movements for you. You can try moving your arms all around you to define the membrane of your energy field, as if you are creating a clay house and patting down the sides all around you. You can also experiment with movements to release energies you no longer wish to carry, such as shaking and throwing them out the window. When you want to fill up, gathering divine energy could involve creative movements like holding a bucket in front of you, imagining it filling with divine energy, and then moving your hands to pour it over your head.

For those who are most able to integrate experiences through a logical framework, at first it might seem like this is incompatible with the woo-woo world of energy. But I do believe you can conduct your own experiments and gather your own data to help you become familiar with your energetic field. Take some deep breaths and slow down your mind for this work. Then you can start by holding your hand 6 inches away from your belly. Take a few breaths and ask yourself if the air between your body and your hand feels like it is still a part of you. Does this feel like it's part of your space? Can you sense if the electrical impulses from your heart, brain, and neurons are somehow impacting this space between your chest and your hand? Write down your observations. Then try moving your hand a little farther out and ask the same questions. Repeat until you find a place where it feels like you end and the rest of the world begins. Note that this is the boundary of your energetic field!

Releasing Blocks and Energies that are No Longer Needed

Once you become well acquainted with how you experience energy, you may start to notice some energies that feel pleasant and some that don't feel so good. You may also notice that some of the draining energies are actually things you are carrying from the past or other people's projections that you have subconsciously agreed to take on. And you might want to find ways to get those buggers out so there is more space for your Goddess Voice to come through. I am a bit hesitant to call this housecleaning, (because you don't want to see my closet, and I'm only occasionally motivated to scrub down the stove), but the truth is that cleaning your physical space is a good metaphor for how you can clear your energetic space.

If someone has hurt you in the past or present, you may be carrying their energy. You may sense this as a cord or a lump that is tangled up or mushed together with your own energy in one of your chakras, organs, or body parts. During my post-therapy period of starting to manage my energy so I could hear my own voice, I experienced a profound clearing that shows how even intense shame can be released. As I put my kids to bed one night, I started to feel anxiety welling up. From years of getting familiar with my own freak-outs, I could recognize this particular brand of anxiety as coming from an urge to suppress an intense emotion. Once I was able to get some time to myself, I was able to let myself feel a little bit of that feeling. It's interesting how the anxiety melts away once I actually turn toward the emotion I've been trying to avoid. I've seen this pattern in myself again and again. As I started to listen inside, I found the place where I was still holding on to some of the shame of the "bad man." That's the name my inner child uses for my friend's dad who sexually assaulted me.

The energy was on my right side, in the back, just below my lowest ribs. I felt the grip and understood why I was holding onto this. I heard the voice of my wounded child saying, "I have to carry this so he won't tell anyone. So they won't see my shame." Understanding that this wounded child had a reason to hold onto his harmful energy helped me feel deeper compassion. Getting to know the reasons our ego parts continue to grasp is such an essential step to letting go of old patterns. I fell asleep with my hands over this place of holding, offering love and acceptance.

Around midnight, I awoke again feeling intensely awake. My awareness came once again to the imposed energy I was carrying under my right lower ribs. Reassuring my inner child self that it was safe to let go, I commanded the energy to leave. But it felt like an excruciating exorcism. It felt like too much to rip it out all at once. Then I remembered I could unwind the energy, like string coming off of a spool. His energy unwound easily, and I let it gather in a sacred space in front of me. But at the end, it was firmly attached to the spool.

I realized that the stuckness came from a soul contract. I had long ago made a subconscious agreement to carry his shame. I visualized the agreement as a paper and wrote "null and void" in red ink. I tossed the contract in with the string and called in a divine flame to clean out the shame. The string and paper burned to nothing, and I invited the flame to clean out that pocket where his shame had festered for so many years.

Interestingly, I found an additional ball of energy tucked in there. It was shame I had subconsciously agreed to carry for a long-time friend. Though she was not involved in my trauma, somehow her energy was a match for this pocket of shame and holding. Knowing we could still love each other in our hearts, I commanded her energy to leave. Then I commanded the "bad man's" energy to leave my body and energy fields, across all dimensions of space and time. I repeated the command out loud several times, feeling into my authority and power to keep this out for good.

I felt the space in my body and around my body as a powerful core, contained in my sovereignty. Coming back into the now empty pocket, I heard a little voice saying, "I don't know who I am without this." I stepped into the role of the inner caregiver and softly held her tender fear in my arms. I gently reassured her, "It's okay. I got you. With the release of the shame, there is space for something new. It's okay if we don't know what that is yet. I'm here to keep you safe." My inner child part nuzzled into that comfort. Then that space in my body grew a door that opened into my core. I felt the walls dissolving as that place of shame became part of my genuine self, welcomed into the light of love.

After this vision, I curled up like a tortoise and gently drifted back into sleep. I dreamed of being in a public bathroom, flushing the excrement other people had left behind. I see this as symbolic of releasing the shame that was never mine to carry in the first place. I am the one who has the resources to flush out the pattern of pain that has been passed along for centuries.

Just as you would pick trash up off your floor and move it to a waste bin outside, you can clean energy out of your field. If you feel called to release other people's energy that has been stored in your body, it may be the case that a person or group imposed that energy upon you consciously or unconsciously through a boundary rupture. If there was foul play, let yourself feel any anger or helplessness as it arises. But the power to move on is completely yours. Even if someone imposed their will upon you, there is a reason why a scared part of you is allowing the outside energy to continue cluttering up your field. And you have to help that scared, tender part understand it will be safe if you let go of the cord or lump that doesn't belong to you. Since we're getting into the territory of inner child work, it may take more than one meditation session for the part that is clinging to feel safe enough to let go.

Meditation: Clearing Outdated Energy

First, identify an energy pattern or someone else's energy that you wish to release. Then, bring in your nurturing Self energy to compassionately talk to the part of you that is holding on to the outdated pattern. Ask yourself what benefit comes from holding on. Offer the clinging part an alternative for how you can feel safe without holding on to this energy.

Once you sense your parts are ready to release the energy that belongs to someone else, you can use visualization, movements, sound, or writing to send it off. If the energy came from wounding being passed along, imagine throwing it into a compost pile where all that negativity will be transformed into something nourishing for the earth. If the energy still feels stuck to your body, imagine unwinding it like a long cord before gently plucking it off, or separating out the places where your own essence is mixed in with the outside energy you wish to release. When the energy feels particularly big and hard to clear, you can call in a spirit guide and offer the cord or lump of energy into their open hands.

After you send that energy out of your body, it's time to come back to the part of you that was initially scared of letting go. Ask them if there's anything they need to feel safe and grounded in this new freedom. Rub your hands together and place them over the area of your body that has just been cleared out, inviting empowering energy to flow in and take root. Then speak out loud some declarations so your voice can bring these energetic changes into the world of form. You may wish to say, "I declare there is no longer space for this person's energy in my body. I am so filled with light and nourishment that I no longer need to carry it. May all unneeded energies be composted into the Earth. May everything unfold for my highest good and the highest good of all."

As you become practiced at clearing your energy field, you may notice times when it feels appropriate to send the energy back to the person or group to whom it belongs. Sometimes it's not necessarily negative energy from someone else you are carrying, but just a place where you have allowed their influence to take root. Perhaps it's time to hear your own voice, and you can compassionately send their energy back across time and space.

After clearing outdated energies, you can return to the four voice archetypes and sense what has shifted. Does it feel good to call in an energetic tortoise shell right now and curl up in its protection? Do you feel like you want to unveil your ladybug wings and soar with some playful expression or perhaps a wild booty shake? Does your inner lioness want to walk around in her fierce power? Or are you called into a higher surrender to be the vehicle for divine Goddess love to flow through? No matter what medicine you need, give yourself some time to anchor into the new energy being connected to your Inner Flame, free from other people's unwanted energies.

Energetic Boundaries that Feel Good for Everyone Involved

When you are clearing energies from people you are still in relationship with, it is possible they might sense a change. And… they may not be happy about it. (Especially if you have long held the role of taking on their pain or sending them your pity.) People don't usually want to say goodbye to their subconscious energetic crutches, but you can ease this transition into a new way of relating by setting energetic boundaries. What the heck do I mean by energetic boundaries? If you imagine your life-force energy as a bubble all around you, creating energetic boundaries is the capacity to open your energy field to what you want to allow in and close it off to what you want to keep out.

When we looked at speaking boundaries out loud in chapter six, I introduced the practice of imagining a door in front of you that you can open to allow in things that feel good and that you can firmly close to keep out stuff that doesn't support you. Taking this practice a step further, you can pay attention to what happens to the energy of the stuff you keep out. Where does the energy go once it bounces off your field? Can you bring in divine support to transform the pain into something neutral or positive? This awareness helps you keep out unwanted energies in a way that doesn't feel closed off or harsh to others, especially those close to you. And it can be done in meditation, without uttering a word.

A great way to reinforce your energetic boundaries is to call in spirit guides to hold you both as your systems get used to sovereignty rather than enmeshment. Interestingly, when using this practice I sometimes see divine forms that the other person relates to, like Jesus or Mother Mary, rather than those that usually support me. I imagine the person I'm creating an energetic boundary with being hugged by the divine form that shows up. Then I imagine myself being held by my guides, who pour a lot of white light to fill up the space between us. Adios, energetic cords and lumps! There's no space for that unhealthy attachment because we are filled to the brim with light.

While this clearing practice focuses on releasing energies from the past, you can also set energetic boundaries in the present if it doesn't feel healthy for you to allow in someone else's emotions or energies. This is especially helpful when practicing active listening and supporting people who are going through a rough time. Rather than just closing off your energetic field like a wall, you can imagine yourself surrounded by a bubble of Divine Fire that burns up and transmutes any negativity coming your way. The ashes become compassion, love, or something nourishing for you both. Much like the practice of dual awareness, you witness the difficult energy someone is bringing in. But you don't allow it to take over. Because your Inner Flame is shining so bright, it can uplift even the heaviest of emotions and energies. And it's not that you come down a little and they come up a little. Because divine energy is infinite, with practice you can stay in the flow of love without being brought down. It's like when I sing with someone who can't stay in tune when they are singing by themselves, but they can match my pitch if we sing together. I am centered in knowing I'm on the right pitch, and they are able to bring themselves up to match it. When it comes to staying centered in loving energy, it might take a little bit of extra focus and intention on my part. Yet even in the face of wounding, unconsciousness, or heavy energy, we can allow it to be burned up and emerge from the interaction feeling sustained rather than drained.

Physical and Energetic Alignment

Now that we've seen how to define and declutter your energetic field, let's look at another aspect of energy work that can help you make yourself heard. Aligning your energy is closely related to your posture and the alignment of your vocal mechanism. You can start on the physical or energetic side, and one will affect the other. For example, many people practice power poses such as standing with your feet spread and hands on your hips, and this physical posture can unblock and amplify the power of your energy system. If you begin on the other side and first empower your energy body, this can actually make it easier for you to stand tall and proud and train your muscles to make it a habit.

When you want to speak or sing, keeping your torso, neck, and head in a vertical line will improve the quality of your breathing and vocal sound by eliminating unnecessary strain. When you are making sound through your voice, the air and sound waves are affected by the positioning of your resonance spaces, which include your throat, mouth, and sinus cavities. I often tell clients that the throat is like a flute. If you bend that flute by slouching or squeeze it by constricting your muscles, it's going to mess with the sound of your voice when you speak or sing. Likewise, if you tend to keep your jaw locked and your mouth in an almost closed position, the energy of your voice will be trapped inside and the sound will be muffled. Your words come out like, "Mwaa mwaa mwaa," and everyone else says, "What did you say?"

If you can imagine a central channel along the midline of your body, you want all parts from toes to crown organized around this vertical axis. Traditions like Qi-gong work with this idea of a central channel, and I like to imagine mine as a vertical cylinder about four inches in diameter. When you realize that the cylinder is an open energetic space, you can more easily bring energy from the Earth into your body, or allow light from the sky to flow down through your crown. Your vessel becomes a bridge between the Earth and the sky. Organizing your posture, movements, and energy around the central channel also supports your vocal tone. When you are aligned, your breath and sound waves can emerge clearly, and your life force energy can flow powerfully.

When you align your physiology and energetic body, you can also choose the appropriate amount of breath and volume for speaking and singing. When the context calls for a reassuring tone, you are free to create soft, gentle coos. When the context calls for a moderate, conversational volume, you can easily step into that. And when the situation demands a loud, booming declaration of your sovereignty, tapping into your central channel will help you to flip that switch. If you have been acculturated to speak kindly and sweetly, I recommend spending some time aligning your central channel and practicing making loud sounds. At a local open space, I sometimes like to visit a concrete underpass where a small stream trickles through. I stand at the edge of the tunnel and yell into it. The echo makes my loud exclamations extra gratifying. If you want to practice liberating your loud voice, first warm up your voice for a few minutes with some sighing sounds, gentle humming, or singing scales. As you use your voice, notice how the sound originates from your diaphragm, not your throat. Feel the power of your breath, which allows you to create a loud sound with ease. Then you might yell, "I can be loud," or declare in a strong voice, "I deserve to be heard!"

Your volume can easily be amplified when your whole being supports your vocal tone. I took a fun physics class in college where we did a unit on acoustics and sound waves. One day, the professor played tones through stereo speakers on either side of the lecture hall. We were then instructed to move around the space and pause in different locations, observing where the sound was louder and where the sound was quieter. Sound travels as waves that push the air molecules, and waves create patterns. Because of these wave patterns, there will naturally be places where multiple waves joining together will make an even bigger wave (louder sound), and there will also be places where the waves cancel each other out (quieter sound). Even non-musicians could easily identify some of the "dead spots' where the sound was quieter and less vibrant in the room. I see this as a metaphor for aligning your posture and your energy. When they are working together, they create an even more impactful sound. But when your posture says, "Let's be loud," and your energy says, "No, let's hide," it can create an effect like the waves canceling each other out. Your voice and message become less vibrant.

Fine-Tuning Your Resonance Spaces

Classically trained singers often explore another aspect of alignment called vowel resonance or vowel placement. Since this involves fine-tuning the way your voice vibrates, it can be fun for speakers and spiritually-attuned folks as well. When you are singing a particular vowel sound such as "ah" or "ooh," factors like your tongue position, mouth shape, and the degree to which you drop your jaw will create subtle shifts in your sound. The sound waves will reflect differently off the walls of the resonance spaces, which are your throat, mouth, and sinus cavities. By playing with and adjusting the position of your resonance spaces, you can find an arrangement where the sound vibrates in a pleasing way. Have you ever been in a dome-shaped building, tunnel, or canyon where your voice echoes or reverberates? What's happening here is the sound waves of your voice are bouncing off the walls of the space in a way that adds richness to the sound. This is called resonance. Similarly, acoustic engineers and architects design concert halls so that the walls reflect the sound to create an optimal experience for the listener. When you start to observe how to subtly shift the resonance spaces of the throat, mouth, and sinus cavities, you can design and tweak your own mini concert hall for the instrument of your voice to vibrate.

You can start exploring vowel resonance by making some sustained tones on vowel sounds such as, "ah" as in "father," and "oh" as in "open." These two vowels require your jaw to be dropped and your mouth to be comfortably open and wide for the sound waves to resonate in ideal ways. If you're looking in a mirror, you should easily be able to see the front half of your tongue. Other vowels, like "ooh" as in "food," and "ee" as in "feed," have better resonance when your jaw is slightly more closed, with about as much space between your teeth for a pencil eraser to fit. (It will be wedged in between the teeth for "ee," and can pass through for "ooh.") Other vowels, such as "a" as in "chaotic" will require a mouth opening somewhere in between the wide-open vowels and the more closed vowels.

As you start to explore, you may notice that one or two vowels just feel easier and sound better than the others. Almost everyone has favorite vowels, because for whatever reason your resonance spaces naturally align in a way that creates a pleasing sound. You can start by vocalizing this favorite vowel, and then shift back and forth to sing another vowel that feels harder. What do you notice that moves inside as you change vowels? How does your tongue change position? How does your jaw change position? Can you play with adjusting your palate, or the roof of your mouth, to feel more lifted or relaxed? Can you create a ringing feeling in your sinus cavities behind your eyes, especially on high notes? How does your lip shape change between the vowels? Try making slight alterations and observe how this affects your sound. If you want to go deeper, a voice teacher can also give you feedback and suggestions to help you find optimal resonance.

When you hit upon a configuration where everything lines up, you can hear the difference. The acoustics become ideal. I also believe this kind of refined alignment of your posture and vocal mechanism affects the energy that is transmitted through your sound. You become a finely tuned instrument, able to communicate even the most subtle expressions of human longing. Your unique Goddess Voice can swirl and reverberate in ways that uplift your own energy system and the energy bodies of everyone who receives your sound. Acoustic resonance can amplify the possibility of people resonating with and relating to what you share.

Balancing Your Chakras

Another aspect of aligning your energy to make yourself heard is working with your chakras. If you are new to all this energy stuff, let me give you a little basic rundown of our seven main energy centers or chakras. The awareness of these energy centers has been cultivated through meditative practices for thousands of years in India. Each chakra can be experienced along the midline of your body. The lowest chakra at the base of your spine is the most tied to the physical world, relating to the element of Earth. When the energy here is stable, you can progress into awakening each higher chakra, with the energy getting more subtle and expansive as you progress upward into your crown.

I did my yoga teacher training in a system that builds upon the ancient symbols and colors for the chakras, which are different than the New Age rainbow colors that were popularized in the 1970s based on the work of Christopher Hills. Because I embrace a plurality of paths, I don't necessarily think one system is right and the other is wrong. I think they are different ways that we can work with the life force energy that flows through our bodies. The fact that there are differing interpretations of these energy vortexes tells me we need to trust our own inner voice and guidance rather than fixate on rigid external interpretations. This is your own subtle energy, and you get to sense what is most balancing for you. That being said, I will share the ways I work with the seven main chakras and list the names, locations, colors, shapes, and seed syllable mantras here. The descriptions listed are translations of the Sanskrit chakra names, which I learned from an online course on chakras by Kristine Kaoverii Weber. She was one of my teachers for yoga teacher training and I highly recommend her well-researched work.

First Chakra/Root/Muladhara/The Root Support

Location: base of your spine
Symbol/color: yellow square
Element: solid factor/earth
Seed syllable: Lam' (pronounced "Long")

Second Chakra/Sacral/Svadhisthana/In One's Own Abode

Location: approximately 3-4 finger widths below your navel
Symbol/color: white half-moon shape
Element: liquid factor/water
Seed syllable: Vam' (pronounced "Vahng")

Third Chakra/Solar/Manipura/The Jeweled City

Location: at your navel, with the flames fanning up to your diaphragm
Symbol/color: red triangle
Element: fire/luminous factor
Seed syllable: Ram' (pronounced "Rahng")

Fourth Chakra/Heart/Anahata/The Unstuck

Location: in the center of your breastbone, next to your physical heart
Symbol/color: smoky green, round
Element: air
Seed syllable: Yam' (pronounced "Yahng")

Fifth Chakra/Throat/Vishuddha/Purity Center

Location: at the notch that protrudes from your larynx
Symbol/color: many colors, like a mist
Element: ether (space)
Seed syllable: Ham' (pronounced "Hahng")

Sixth Chakra/Third Eye/Ajina/The Command Center

Location: right between the eyebrows
Symbol/color: no color or shape
Element: none
Seed syllable: Om' is commonly used;
some traditions say it has no seed mantra

Seventh Chakra/Crown/Sahasrara/Thousand-Petaled Lotus

Location: the space above the crown of your head
Symbol/color: no color or shape
Element: none
Seed syllable: none

The simplest way to balance your chakras is to attend a yoga class with a variety of poses. The asanas or yoga postures will put gentle pressure on your glands, balancing your endocrine system and your chakra system. For me, practicing yoga pretty much every morning has been super powerful. However, as I started to learn how to manage my energy, I realized that my lower three chakras needed attention throughout the day. When I started to feel ungrounded, I often needed to tune in to my first chakra and visualize the yellow square energy as solid, contained, and stable. At other times I have worked with the image of growing roots down into the earth from my perineum. From this rooted place, it is easier to stay in my confidence and speak authentically.

When I would start to feel anxious, I would often notice that the water energy of my second chakra was completely dispersed, trying to find some sense of security by touching in with how everyone else was feeling. I often still need to engage in the practice of calling all of that energy back in so it can rest in the sacred chalice of my second chakra. By concentrating the energy rather than dispersing it, that metaphorical water can nourish the seeds of my empowered self-expression. While teaching the practice of tuning into the second chakra to one of my students who didn't yet know that it went with the element of water, she naturally visualized her white half-moon as a gently swaying cup full of water. She intuitively sensed that this flowing, expressive energy needed a container in her body.

When I start to feel helpless and get overtaken by the feelings of depression that go with that lack of agency, I know that it's time to tune in with my third chakra. Even if I'm in the middle of cooking dinner, interacting with my family, or going on a walk, I visualize the sun or flame behind my navel. I remind myself that the power of Divine Love is always glowing within me, even when I feel disconnected from it. Taking a few breaths while tuning into my third chakra has become a very powerful practice for establishing my sovereignty and making myself heard.

The heart chakra and throat chakra are also intimately interwoven with the art of creating vocal sound. Your heart chakra is connected to the air and breath, which powers your voice. An open heart allows you to take in a full breath with ease. Its power can then move upward into your throat chakra, which is the center for self-expression. When the throat chakra at the larynx is blocked or partially obstructed, you may find yourself falling into habits of repressed silence and repressed self-expression. In a sense, this whole book is about opening the throat chakra so you can communicate with ease and joy. Removing obstructions and creating space for the energy to flow through this center allows you to bring your intangible Goddess energy into the world of form. Through the ethereal beauty of the throat chakra, you create sound, share ideas, and birth experiences and circumstances into being.

Unleash Your Goddess Voice Practice No. 10: Inner Alignment

In this practice, we are going to tune into the inner alignment with our central energy centers so we can speak and/or sing from a place of balanced, compassionate power. It is a simple practice of merging your physical alignment with your energetic flow.

For a recording of this practice, visit saragiita.com/free

1. Stand with your feet facing forward, keeping your stance as wide as your hips.

2. Begin to focus inward on your central channel in the middle of your body. You can imagine it as a vertical tube that is four or five inches in diameter.

3. Allow your body posture to relax and organize itself around the central channel. Ideally, you want to feel the weight being distributed evenly between the balls of your feet and your heels. Keep your knees slightly bent so they are not locked, and think of your ears being over your shoulders so your head can rest on top of your spine.

4. Tune into your energy centers/chakras that reside within the central channel one by one. You may wish to take

a breath in and out at each center. Here's a recap of the locations:

- Root- base of the spine or perineum
- Sacral- three finger widths below your navel
- Solar plexus-from the navel up to the diaphragm
- Heart-at the height of your physical heart, but in the center of your body
- Throat- inside the larynx
- Third Eye- at the height of your eyebrows, in the center of your brain
- Crown-the space right above the crown of your head

5. Once you feel this inner alignment, imagine you can pull the energy of the Earth up through your central channel and send it outward through your breath and voice.

6. Using this energy alignment, speak or sing out loud a simple phrase such as "I deserve to be heard."

7. Keep repeating your phrase until you feel like your energy matches the meaning of the words. Find the right volume and tone of voice for this moment.

CHAPTER 11

The World Needs Your Voice

You are a lioness,
A dancing priestess,
A steward for the light—
You are the Earth Maiden,
The Song-Filled Mother,
The Wise Crone of All Souls.

Your voice is medicine.
Share it with love
In every place where you feel called—
Each sound a footprint
On grateful Earth,
Made whole through your voice.

A Voice Touches Everything Else

Now that we have savored the many ways your Goddess Voice can come through with more clarity, we get to explore the ways your self-expression will influence and impact the world around you. When you speak up, sing out, or even hum a little, those sound waves and energetic vibrations change the world. Perhaps the change will be pretty darn imperceptible. But there will indeed be an impact on you personally, on other people, and/or on the intangible realms of nature and spirit. These three levels of impact are happening all the time with every act. If I remember something funny and enjoy a giggle, that will leave me forever changed. In addition to these subtle shifts, with intention we can amplify our impact and spread love through our voices.

When you find your voice, clearly there's going to be an effect on your personal life. At first, you might have that raw, broken-open feeling that comes with expressing truth. And eventually, you're going to feel more empowered. I promise! You're going to have more capacity for setting boundaries and advocating for your needs. Creative communion will become more accessible. You will feel more at home in your body as you live your purpose. You may start to genuinely enjoy the sound of your voice when you are speaking or singing. Things like playing, having fun, and feeling joy are also likely to flow when you dedicate yourself to expressing your voice.

If you have a business or creative project to share with the world, unleashing your Goddess Voice will make it easier to promote your work and receive attention and financial resources in return. You may feel the call to start reaching out to others for collaborations, referral partnerships, guest blogging opportunities, speaking on podcasts, or speaking at in-person events. You may put your work out there through networking events, going to tradeshows or conferences, or promoting your work on social media. And most importantly, you will build the resilience to be able to handle the rejections and disappointments that often happen on the pathway to hearing "yes."

Even if there were zero impact on other people and the intangible realms, these positive effects of expressing your voice would be worth it. Because you're worth it! Positively influencing yourself is just as important as impacting others, so take a moment to reflect or journal on why liberating your voice is important for your personal life. When was a time you spoke up in the past, and how did it feel in your body? What emotions emerge from honoring your voice? In what areas do you see the potential to explore your voice for your own personal growth and fulfillment?

Sharing Your Voice as an Act of Generosity

Just as it is important to honor the impact of your self-expression in your personal sphere, your voice will influence others. A whole lot of us have some subconscious stuff lurking around that makes us feel selfish for wanting to speak up or express ourselves creatively. In a culture that considers attention-seeking and having needs as negative, we can get all twisted up and feel that it's not important for us to want to be witnessed and to have our voices received by others. Feeling like your contributions are not important is such a tangled web, and you deserve to be free. When you do speak up and share your voice, you will serve others. When you open yourself as a channel for your Goddess Voice to come through, creative expression is a generous act. Your voice becomes a gift for all people. Why keep your authentically human expression all to yourself?

When I was beginning to build a music career, I feared I was being selfish. My inner critics chanted, *Who am I to deserve joy and fulfillment when so many people in the world are suffering? And, besides, shouldn't I be saving the world in some tangible way, like planting thousands of trees or feeding the hungry?* Yet my passion still pulled me forward, and I began to see the impact of my voice by watching my daughter. As I grew excited about a concert I was organizing, I decided to buy some new shoes (tarnished silver Mary Janes) to go with a turquoise dress I was planning to wear on stage. My daughter, who had recently turned three, called them my "concert shoes." After she saw me on stage, she started digging them out of the closet when we were at home. She would put on a fancy dress or a sparkly scarf. Then, she climbed on a stool with an old, broken microphone in hand. She proclaimed, "Thank you so much, everybody. My next song is called 'I Claim My Power Elsa is the Queen." Then she would sing a medley of songs, blending my own compositions, children's songs, and imaginative words of her own invention.

Whenever I watched her on that yellow stepstool stage, I was reminded that it's not selfish to follow my passion. I am teaching my daughter that what we say matters. I am teaching her that our creative expression matters. Perhaps she will grow up valuing her voice more than I did. And at the same time, I am also teaching my son to feel solid and secure in himself, so he can value his own voice while also celebrating everyone's journeys. I am living by example, modeling how to show up authentically.

As I built my confidence and went after more performance opportunities, I began to have more moments of seeing how the impact of my liberated voice touched others. One moment of presence and power was gifted to me during a summer concert series performance with my duo partner, Anastasia. As I stood on stage sweating in the July heat, I felt the divine sunshine pouring through me and radiating back to me through the faces of my attentive audience. A blessed breeze picked up, carrying a faint scent of flowers through the beautiful park. Anastasia sat down at the piano, pouring her soul into each chord. It was time for me to sing. I shared my story of overcoming sexual trauma through song, weaving power and poetry where there was once pain and helplessness. As my words resonated on the breeze, I met eyes with a woman in the front row. Her face was open. For a moment, I felt as if our souls were touching. We were inhabiting a sacred space, where our true selves shined through. I understood that my willingness to be seen and heard in my truth was equally a gift to myself and to the people listening. We were one and the same, mutually uplifted through the universal Goddess Voice being brought into form.

Both of these stories illuminate a kind of impact that is impossible to measure. And while there are times and places for judging things by the numbers, if your gifts lie on the creative, nurturing, and/or empathic end of the spectrum, trying to quantify your wide-reaching vibrational contributions can foster self-doubt. Let's say you're a writer who currently has just a few readers of your heart-felt blog or books. If you are measuring impact simply by the number of eyeballs that read something you've written, it's easy to assume your impact is negligible. But what if you measure not just width, but also depth? What if you look at the ways the people closest to you have been affected by hearing your voice and reading your words? What if you have helped someone to free themselves from their suffering? What if you look at how you are role-modeling genuine self-expression for others? What if you consider the presence and vibration that you helped anchor for all of humanity during those quiet hours of writing in solitude?

If some vulnerable part of us is looking for proof from the outside that our voice is worthy, loved, and needed by others, there is really no way to feel content and whole on that path. Our work, then, is not to pursue compliments, likes, followers, bigger stages, or bigger material success as measures of our impact. All of these can be fun to receive if they emerge as side effects of living our truth. But the true world-changing impact comes on the level of the love we channel and embody, both in moments of empowered silence and empowered self-expression. This love is boundless and so much bigger than the specific number of people who receive our voice. As we show up to embody our Goddess power, confidence, and radiance, we are offering a gift to the Collective Consciousness.

Together, we need to elevate the role of these unquantifiable gifts. Creative expression, emotional intelligence, heartfelt connection, Divine Grace, and passionate stories give our lives a sense of meaning and purpose that can never be measured. All of these intangible expressions are just as important as the quantifiable possessions and results that our economies value. We need both the qualitative and the quantitative to be whole human beings. We need every single person's creative gifts to be shared to help humanity heal. So please value your impact as you show up as a wise voice-weaver. Sharing your deepest whispers supports the mutual empowerment of all.

Circular Impact

Most of us were trained to think of impacting other people as a linear, one-way street. You give money to a charity. Or you give loving advice to a friend who is suffering. One person gives and the other receives, and then the story is done.

Alongside this linear model is what I call a triangular model of one leader serving many. One chosen person stands at the apex of the triangle and shares their wisdom or viewpoints to influence all the eyes and ears within the triangle. Think of the huge influence of people like Oprah, Brené Brown, and Tony Robbins; fame creates a triangular model of influence. In both the linear and triangular stories of impact, the giver becomes the singular hero just like Wonder Woman or Superman. The culture of domination loves the singular hero because that perpetuates the myth that some people's lives are more important than others. It also deepens our feelings of powerlessness and maintains the status quo if we are waiting for someone to save us.

While linear and triangular influence models are important in shifting culture, I place just as much importance on circular impact. This looks less like elevating a few voices as worthy of attention, and valuing the contributions and leadership capacities of all people within an egalitarian circle. Circular impact gives enough space for reciprocity, sharing, and mutual empowerment. It is not a new model; circular impact is a way to understand the natural influence we have on each other through our families, friendships, teams, and connections. One of the cool things about circles is that they spread. When you toss a pebble into a pond, it creates concentric circles of impact that ripple outward. Each tiny act affects all people in seen and unseen ways. In a culture of mutual empowerment, all people's heroic acts of resilience are celebrated. All voices deserve to speak up and be listened to with love. Small acts of kindness matter deeply along with the wide-reaching acts of change.

In some cases, creating circular impact can come from taking turns with who leads. I experience this in my writers' group, the Divine Author Goddesses. While I started the group and created some initial group agreements to make it a safe space, my intention was always to give and receive as an equal member. At times I am the one guiding the flow and being cognizant of time. And just as often, the other two women naturally step in to lead. There are clear times when I am in a giving role and offering attention and feedback to someone who is sharing their writing. And in true circular fashion, I am in the humble place of receiving when it is my turn. The impact we have created by celebrating each other's wins, realizations, and creative output has been profound. From this model of circular sharing, I have been able to lean into more confidence in my voice and have developed the courage to share my writing more widely. While the three of us are in the center of the circle of impact, the internal shifts we have experienced ripple outward and affect all of those people who we interact with directly, which in turn has a subtle effect on the people they interact with. This one circle of transformation creates concentric circles that ripple outward through the world.

In other places, it makes sense to still have clear leaders while valuing the contributions of everyone in the group. I experienced this flavor of circular impact when I attended a yoga teacher training course with 15 other students from many corners of the globe. We had four teachers who were in clear leadership positions. They had the necessary experience and certifications to ensure we were getting comprehensive training, and not just some fluff about twisting into a pretzel so you could burn off some stress. Yet the leaders also gave opportunities for the students to have moments of leadership. Every morning after we did meditation in the window-filled, wood-floored dome, a different student would have the chance to share their choice of spiritual reading and give a short reflective talk. When it was time for questions and discussions, I had the sense that all of our voices were valued. The goal of the teachers was to empower us as leaders, and toward the end of the training we were given the opportunity to practice leading yoga classes for the rest of the group. We were doing more than standing in tree pose. Through the power of circular leadership, we rooted deeply in our potential as agents of change who couldn't help but influence the people around us in every moment following the course.

Responsibility vs. Rescuing

Impact is happening all the time, whether we realize it or not. But when we wish to broadcast our voices and serve bigger groups of people, this comes with responsibility. We have to be willing to be held accountable and repair things when our positive intentions don't create the results we expected. With every sound, every word, and every action, there is a space between intention and impact. Positive intentions do not guarantee positive outcomes. This is related to the spiritual idea that actions are within our control, but the outcomes of those actions are beyond our control. Not surprisingly, it's the ego that gets clingy and attached to everything turning out a certain way. But when we yield to the universal flow and surrender the outcomes, we can trust the results are unfolding at the right time according to a cosmic plan that is bigger than the ego's habits of clenching.

I want to create art, teach classes, and share stories that promote things like connection, compassion, and authenticity, and I'm assuming you have similarly positive intentions. Even if there are elements that might make people feel difficult emotions, wholeness and healing are still the driving desires. When I speak on a podcast, my intention is absolutely to serve and uplift others. But there's no way I can guarantee that's the actual outcome. One time I wrote a song and shared it with a friend. I hoped it would be inspiring. But afterward she said, "Now I feel really sad all of a sudden." Whoa. That's not what I had in mind. The thing to remember here is that you are not a bad person, and it is not a criticism of your voice if the impact turns out differently than you intended. If we ever have a negative impact or offend someone, part of taking responsibility is to humbly acknowledge the impact rather than defend our good intentions as a way to try to deny the harm. Certainly, I hope you will go into the process of impacting the world through your voice with positive intentions. Most of the time, those joyful results will become a reality. And when the impact turns out to be confusing or negative, stay committed to making repairs if possible.

This kind of responsibility that comes with leading through your voice is different than rescuing. Rescuing or a savior mentality is a kind of conditioning that the traumatic systems of capitalism promote. For those people who don't buy into the whole "material success and acquisition will make you worthy" model, they can hop over to the "saving people will make you worthy" model. Now I'm not saying that helping is a bad thing, but that the whole premise is that you have to prove your worth by "being good" rather than just feeling whole and worthy as you are. I grew up feeling like it was my personal job to save the whole gosh-darned world. It turns out I suck at that job because, well, I'm human. And furthermore, my compulsion to rescue came from my own wounding. After I was abused, I had the ultimate privilege of returning to a safe home. Sure, it wasn't perfect, but I was loved, and my basic needs were met. That privilege made me feel enormously guilty because my friend and her sister were not so lucky. I could not save her, but I could spend the next thirty years of my life with a rescuer complex!

There's no shame in using your guilt or core wounds as motivation to speak up on behalf of others. It's a valid way to show up. But, my oh my, it is such a relief to stop carrying the burden of saving the world. Having to earn our worth by "being good" or "making a difference" is an exhausting road to burnout and paralysis. So let's get clear on one thing: it's not up to us alone to fix every problem in the world. That's way too much rescuing for one hero. We can return to the knowledge that we are already good and whole and enough on the inside without having to earn or prove anything.

You may be saying, "But wait, Sara. I need to feel guilty and be a rescuer to make myself be good. Otherwise, I would be a lazy, uncaring perpetrator of injustice!" This is an inner critic voice that shames us back into believing we have to earn our worth. It leads us to believe we would lose the motivation to be kind, generous, or helpful if we felt okay inside. Does that kind of thinking feel empowered or fearful to you? Listen, there is a profound, Goddess-dripping power in recognizing that your Inner Flame burns no matter how much positive impact you make in the world. It truly frees you up to be a conduit for right-sized, right-timed, loving actions for the good of all.

If you want to help another, start by listening. A good rule of thumb to encourage responsibility rather than rescuing is to always ask people what they need. Unless they are experiencing an emergency, are being abused, or are currently incapable of communicating, don't ever assume you know what's best for someone else. While some people may be in a space of needing you to offer options for how they could move forward, this still allows them to trust themselves rather than being stuck in the role of the helpless victim. Consent is empowering.

If you're not yet sold on letting go of rescuing, consider the fact that it can actually interfere with the potential impact of our voices. In 2017 I decided I should do a free concert at a shelter for women and children escaping domestic violence.

I was fresh out of therapy for healing childhood sexual abuse, and I wanted to make an impact on women's lives so I could prove to myself that music was a worthwhile way to help the world. So I set about organizing this concert that was somehow going to make me feel like my calling mattered to others. I got Anastasia on board and called the shelter. After a fair amount of phone tag, we scheduled a date. When our duo arrived, they had forgotten that we were coming. So we moved the furniture and set things up by ourselves. No biggie. Sometimes rescuing involves heavy lifting. During the concert, a few women and children were engaged while others were going about their business in the common area and listening passively (which was probably just right for them). I shared some stories about my own journey of healing from sexual assault in between songs that Anastasia and I had written. A few people chatted and said, "thank you" afterward and then made their dinner. I left with an all-consuming feeling of disappointment.

Looking back, I realize I placed a lot of pressure on myself and the audience members by hoping I would significantly change someone's life. Rather than trusting the impact of my calling and approaching the opportunity to share songs and stories from a place of mutual empowerment, I hoped that someone's gratitude would help me feel better about their suffering. I was operating from a place of limiting beliefs around my value and impact on the world. This approach actually made it harder for me to connect in an authentic, open-hearted way. I felt a tremendous letdown afterward that I didn't rescue one single woman from her pain! I share this story because it illustrates how trying hard to "be good" and "save people" actually closes us off to deeper, openhearted connections and being a conduit for true service. Furthermore, being a condescending helper placed me in a separate category from those I wished to help, which was just a method to avoid feeling the pain of my sisters in distress.

Luckily, I had a contrasting experience of inspired action some months later when I organized a benefit concert for a children's home in Haiti. The opportunity emerged from collaborating with my friend Kate Donnelly who had spent time volunteering in Haiti and listened to the needs of the school staff to raise funds for a new roof and other building improvements. While I'm sure I still had some surreptitious desire to be a do-gooder, I had learned a lot about my desire to save people from the concert at the women's shelter. I decided to organize and play at the concert because it felt like an exciting, aligned idea, rather than an attempt to prove I was worthwhile.

This time, there was more flow to the process from listening to my intuition. It was easy to set a date and get musicians to participate. I learned how to effectively pitch a story to the media, and several local radio stations and publications featured the concert (and those media features helped our duo land great paying gigs later on). There were still a few headaches with drummers double-booking themselves and whatnot, but for the most part, it was a smooth and life-giving experience. We raised over $4000 to help the children's home get a new roof, and it came from a desire to do something fun and generous. I experienced the power of knowing I am whole and enough no matter who I help. That freed me up to give spontaneously in a way that was sustaining and also brought benefits to my own life.

When I sought to create a positive impact through this concert, following my intuition was an important aspect of staying more in the energy of responsibility and less in rescuing. Once you have listened to the needs of the people you seek to serve, trust that your intuition will guide you to the right actions to take at the right time. When you've tapped into your intuitional flow, you may feel guided to raise your voice and kick some ass. You may feel guided to grab your bullhorn and speak truth in the face of hate. You may feel guided to give to a cause that you love, or feed someone, or help an animal, or plant some trees, or sing a song. You may be called to listen to another's story with an open mind. Our intuition will show us the right steps to take, and the actions will almost always feel *sustaining* rather than *draining*. We may be filled with passion and hope as we follow the promptings of our inner knowing, recognizing that our voices are important no matter how many people we help.

Sound, Nature, and Spirit

In addition to impacting yourself and others, when you tap into your holy Goddess Voice you are creating ripple effects in the natural and spirit realms. I call this "intangible impact." As I plant my feet on the blue carpet in front of my piano and transform the invisible air into a single, ringing note, the energy is felt by the Collective Consciousness in some way, because we are all one. The vibration is felt by the Cooper's Hawk perched in the tree outside my window, who may somehow sense that humans are not just here to terrorize and destroy but also to nurture and create. From my landlocked home near the Rocky Mountains, I can sing with the whales who are swimming in the Great Mother Ocean. Each soundwave from my voice is an offering of love and gratitude given to my spirit guides. I believe that in some subtle way, our Goddess Voice is felt by all of the cosmos.

My singing student Elle has noticed her voice influencing the bees that live in several bee boxes in her yard. When I asked her if she wears protective gear for harvesting honey, she replied that she has not needed it. She just sings a calm song to the bees, and they stay really mellow and non-aggressive. She has only been stung once and attributes it to the power of tones and frequencies. While this kind of presence, calmness, and impact on the natural world is easy to overlook, I see it as vital and essential. Like Elle, when you open your mouth to sing you are spreading peace.

I felt the call to start exploring how my voice interacted with the natural world a few years ago. There's a park near my house where I like to take solitary walks as well as meanderings with my husband and kids. A canal borders the park on one side, and there was a wonderful thicket of cottonwood and willow trees shading the canal. I would often stop and sit for a few minutes at the base of one particular large cottonwood tree that leaned over the trickling water. But one late winter morning my jaw dropped in horror when I saw heavy-duty construction equipment in the canal and piles upon piles of freshly cut trees, including my favorite cottonwood. Feeling as though I had lost a good friend, I stood there and cried.

Then I went home and made phone calls. I learned from the city parks manager that the canal is privately owned and managed. The canal company was not quick to return my phone calls, but I was persistent and determined to speak up on behalf of the trees. When they eventually called me back, I learned that this massive thinning of the trees is considered maintenance. The company's goals are not capturing carbon or creating a beautiful space along the edge of the park. They are focused on their goal of providing water to municipalities and farms in a semi-arid climate where water is a precious necessity. When I suggested that the shade of the trees reduces evaporation during the hot summer, they stood by the reasoning that the trees drank too much water. It was clear that independent citizens did not have a say in how this private land was managed. I also discovered that I consumed some of the water provided by the canal through my city tap system.

At a dead end, I still wished to give a voice to the trees. So I walked down to the park and faced the destruction once more. And I began to hum. I toned, and then I chanted mantras, and I eventually composed a song. I sang my grief and my appreciation for the souls of all these trees that had nourished me and my children and our community with their gentle presence and life-giving oxygen. Through glimpses of Unity Consciousness, I sense that my voice was felt and received by these majestic silent beings whose needs were subverted to the needs of the humans. My tender heart believes that singing to the Earth and the trees is a practice that matters, whether we are showing appreciation for the patch of greenery down the street or grieving and honoring the destruction of massive forests across the globe. Growing right alongside the environmental destruction and fear of impending climate doom, we can cultivate hope, renewal, regeneration, sustainability, and love.

Our voices can become a prayer:

May we allow, create, and contribute to the awakening of human consciousness to restore Mother Earth as the center of our well-being. May we feel reverence and appreciation for her resources that we consume to sustain our lives.

Let the love and hope in our hearts blossom, guiding us to the right individual and collaborative actions to regenerate our planet. May all beings thrive with respectful and equal treatment as we restore balance to our climate and our world. When fear of the future arises, may we be present with the suffering.

Let us grieve together, let us work together,
Let us plant together, let us hope together.
Thank you, Mother Earth.
Thank you, Father Sky.

Thank you, trees and plants and oceans and carbon-capturing soil.

Thank you to all beings for your presence in this opportunity for collective awakening.

I see this kind of prayer as more than a wishful plea or a form of self-soothing. Especially when voiced out loud, our prayers are a way of birthing our truest intentions into life in the collective consciousness. The prayer becomes a vision that now has the possibility of becoming a reality on the physical plane.

Offering song prayers for the trees shows how sound, nature, and spirit are so intertwined. Your voice impacts the energetic presence of Mother Earth and all of the invisible spheres. While I am not connected to the faerie realm, I have no doubt that there is some vibration of faerie love that you can amplify through your voice. While I have no idea what is happening in a concert hall in China right now, through Unity Consciousness, all of our voices are one. So sing to the angels if you feel called. Speak to the souls of your departed loved ones if you long to feel connected once again. Become a diva with a hairbrush microphone in front of your cat. Your intentions and influence are holy in the most subtle, immeasurable ways. Speak up, sing out, and don't hold back, Sister!

While I find it helpful to understand and value the three levels of impact, in the end, they are not so separate. Your personal life, the people you interact with, and the realms of nature and spirit will all be uplifted by your Goddess Voice. We exist on all three levels, interwoven with all the other people and creatures in our unfolding dance of self-expression.

Receiving as Impact

Much of our discussion of impact and influence has focused on giving. But receiving is a form of impact that is just as important! In our human ecosystems, which are part of the wider Earth's ecosystems, we are in a constant, free-flowing dance of giving and receiving. For a cycle to be sustainable, we have to take turns being in the giving and receiving roles. Staying in just one is a road to disempowerment and/or burnout. We need both the yang of giving and the yin of receiving. Supporting causes you care about goes hand-in-hand with receiving financial resources to support your own thriving life. Speaking your truth goes hand-in-hand with listening deeply to others. When you are in receiving mode, with your palms opened, heart softened and ears perked, this means the giver's gift has a place to land. And this is deeply impactful. Receiving someone's voice, support, or love completes a cycle. It's really unsatisfying if you offer a gift and the other person refuses it or ignores it. By opening yourself to receive, you are allowing mutual fulfillment.

As the equal flow of giving and receiving is so essential to our equilibrium, why then do many people struggle with receiving? What's with the pushing away? For one thing, there is a cultural notion that giving is better than receiving. I suppose this was intended to promote generosity rather than mean-spirited selfishness, but we live in an era where we can move past the black-and-white thinking to find ways that both giving and receiving can serve the highest good for all.

Another reason I see for denigrating receiving is that we operate within power structures where the giver is assumed to be more powerful. The one who treats everyone else to dinner is seen as more prosperous and therefore more powerful. The one who gives to charity is seen as having an elevated status compared to those who receive from the charity. These power dynamics can soften as we open ourselves to give and receive as part of life's flow.

Then there are the personal and ancestral wounds that make us close ourselves off to letting things in. If bad things, traumatic things, overwhelming things came in when we were soft and open to receive, then it might feel better to close up our walls and keep everything out. All of these factors give us our own personal threshold for how much receiving feels comfortable.

I became aware of my own threshold for receiving in 2012 at a yoga retreat, back when I only had one child. At a lovely college campus in Missouri, our little family gathered with 150 other folks for a week of chanting, yoga, meditation, and workshops. One morning I woke up feeling energized. An audacious display of summer blooms lined the pathway from our bare-bones dorm room to the dining hall. After filling my tummy with yogurt and fruit, I dropped off my son at the childcare room. That morning I skipped the main event and veered into a side room, where ten other people had pulled their chairs into a circle. The air conditioning was too cold in here, so we put on our jackets and scarves and crossed our arms as we waited for the Heart Circle to begin.

A yogic monk dressed in orange robes with a perfectly wrapped turban led us through a ceremony of his own invention. His turban made him look Indian, but he was American and was trained as a psychologist before his days as a monk. He explained that we would invite one person into the center of the circle, and everyone else would sing mantra music to the divine soul within them. He asked for a volunteer, and I jumped up. I was once again a little girl who had forgotten to raise her hand. I sat in the center, and a young man began strumming his guitar. As the other voices joined in, sending all their love my way, my tears began. My whole body was wracked with sobs. Some people closed their eyes, while others were watching me. But I could feel there was no judgment here, so I let myself cry with abandon.

How long did they sing to me? Five minutes? Fifteen? As the music slowed, we all fell silent. I didn't have any tissues, so my face was wet and sticky. I felt held by the circle; everyone was silently rooting for me to heal, to become my authentic self, to deepen my connection with the Divine.

Then the monk began to speak, inviting me to reflect upon what emotions came up as I received the music. I spoke in circles about my traumas, my depression, etc., etc. But the real reason for my tears felt too difficult to share: deep down I did not feel worthy of so much love. They had offered me the most profound gift, and I could only receive a tiny bit. It was tender and humbling.

When my time in the center was up, I returned to my chair as part of the circle. I met eyes with one of the participants, who was gazing at me with unfathomable love. There was nothing sexual or self-serving in his presence; he was channeling Divine Love straight into my heart. But it was too much for me, so after a few seconds I turned away. It was like looking at the sun. I could not bear the brightness. But he continued to sit in stillness, sending me love.

Later that day, he approached me in a common area while I was watching my toddler play with a new little friend.

"How are you doing?" he asked. But I could tell it wasn't a light, conversational question. He was ready to dive deep with this interaction.

"Pretty good, how about you?" I said with a fake smile. I didn't feel comfortable opening my heart again right now. I had to keep the door closed.

"I'm wonderful," he replied calmly. "Will you be joining us for the Heart Circle again this afternoon?"

"I'd love to, but it's my turn to put my son down for a nap." As we conversed a bit, I felt unable to be truly present or thank him for the blessing he gave me. That darn threshold. Still, his gift has stayed with me. A stranger saw me, all of me, and offered complete acceptance. While I could only open up my protective walls to receive a tiny sliver of that Universal Love, the experience showed me how much potential there was to increase my threshold for receiving. People actually *wanted* to give me more than I could currently take in. My ceiling suddenly felt too low; I needed more space and softness to let good things in.

In the decade since, I have found ways to incrementally increase my comfort with receiving while finding my voice. One practice involves noticing and appreciating the things that we already receive every day. My friend Catherine and I made a two-month commitment to send each other a daily text of something we had received that day. While sometimes they were the things we more readily associate with receiving, like getting a gift, receiving a compliment, or getting paid, we also learned to recognize that we received clean water every day. We received nourishing meals from the Earth. We received sunlight, oxygen, electricity, fossil fuels, and solar energy. We received beauty from seeing a shaft of light coming through the window or from hearing a cheerful birdsong. We received other people's voices, songs, smiles, and tender feelings. We started to see that receiving was a part of living and breathing. When we can take it in with appreciation, Mother Earth and the people and animals and plants can receive our gratitude in return. The energy with which we receive creates a vibrational impact as we move through our days.

We can also increase our threshold for receiving by working with our physical body and energy body to find moments when we can safely soften and open. You may experience a visceral softening in a certain body part that helps you open up to receive; perhaps the crown of your head or your heart or your hands or your womb or your feet wish to become the soft, sensitive space where love and other nourishing things can come nestle in. Perhaps all of the little air sacs in your lungs can be your place of experiencing receptivity as you breathe in the body-nourishing oxygen and soul-nourishing white light. They are just waiting to be filled up! Not only can it feel good to receive, but taking in nourishment is the essential first step before you can send your Goddess Voice outward as a gift to the world.

Send it Out as Love

When you learn to soften and open yourself to receive, you can intentionally make your voice a channel for love. I'm talking about the big, Universal Love for all of creation. It is a kind of unconditional loving energy that brings a feeling of benevolence and goodwill. Just like the sun, it shines on all people, animals, and plants without discrimination or differentiation. Sending love through your voice is a practice that starts with self-love. Knowing you deserve this abundant, ever-flowing Universal Love makes it a no-brainer that all beings deserve it too!

I am well aware that focusing on embodying love with your voice may seem sappy, overly optimistic, or naive. So I want to be clear that I'm not talking about just the *emotion* of love that we tend to associate with romance and affection for family members and friends. That is a part of it. But Universal Love is also the all-encompassing presence and divinity within everything. There may be times when the idea of sending love seems incompatible with the emotions you're feeling. You may ask, "How am I supposed to feel loving right now without shutting down and bypassing my anger and sadness?" During these times you might think of love as being synonymous with wholeness. If you want to write a scathing journal entry with all of your angry thoughts, that can serve your wholeness. It can also serve our collective wholeness for you to honor all your human emotions. If it feels like it will lead to expansion, you are becoming a vessel for the light of your Goddess Voice to come through.

I have been experimenting with how to embody love through my voice for nearly two decades. After the all-night recording session with Jyoshna in my early 20s, I attempted to become a conduit for Divine Love. During concerts and speaking events, I would have moments of being able to focus on channeling love in different ways. At first, I visualized my guru among the faces in the audience. But that often felt forced. When I learned the Buddhist practice of metta meditation, I began to imagine sending light as a vibration of loving-kindness. With practice, it became more natural. Now, I often experience the Universal Love that can be shared through the voice as a stream of energy or light that pours into an expansive circle. This doesn't mean I'm always in some ecstatic flow with no egoic anxieties when I express myself. Embodying your voice as love is not an all-or-nothing end state, but a practice of turning toward the waterfall of abundant Universal Love whenever we are able.

During the coronavirus pandemic in 2020, I began to experience how our voices can send Universal Love across time and space. While previously all of my experiments had been in front of live audiences, I noticed I could have the same impact as a conduit through the medium of video. My husband and I were asked to sing and play mantra music on a sudden slew of Zoom calls and prerecorded videos. Because he can be very particular about tech setup, we usually did the chanting away from my piano in his cozy office filled with haphazardly-hung family photos. His impeccable rhythm on the guitar freed me up to just focus on singing and experiencing the love I wished to express. I noticed that whenever I was trying really hard to send a certain energy or vibration, I would get out of the flow. My mind would start to wander as I sang the repetitive melodies. But when I was able to step into the Goddess Archetype of being a humble conduit for what wants to come through, moments of magic began to emerge. I closed my eyes and raised my hands into the air as I saw us held in a circle of light pouring downwards from the sky. At some point, the light naturally expanded to encompass all of the people who were listening. Even when we were recording a video that would be watched later, through pure grace I was able to feel a connection with all of the people who would be receiving my voice in the future. I felt the huge, all-knowing presence of Mother Earth grounding and anchoring our space. I felt all of our hearts swelling in sacred communion. Eventually, this spontaneous visualization would become a practice with a name: Collective Shining.

Because of the repetitiveness and sacred intentions, this type of chanting was an ideal petri dish for me to practice sending my voice as a gift of love across time and space. I have since discovered that Collective Shining can be practiced in any context when you open yourself to be a vessel for love and release attachment to outcomes. I have practiced the visualization of expanding my circle of love while connecting with my ancestors and descendants. While giving podcast interviews, online summit talks, and small group workshops, I have facilitated the group energy by creating a light-filled communal space. I have used the visualization to help ground the collective nervous system after a scary communal experience on a packed commuter train. I have practiced Collective Shining as silent support while clients are composing music, writing their truth, practicing boundaries, or healing their inner child. I have taught the practice to many of those clients as well, and from their wise and unique experiences, I have learned that there is truly no right or wrong way to show up and allow your throat to be a channel for love.

Unleash Your Goddess Voice Practice No. 11: Collective Shining

Collective Shining is a way to send loving kindness through your voice. I recommend practicing with a trusted friend or coach to feel how your individual body experiences being a conduit for light and facilitating changes in the collective energy. Animals, plants, and trees can make great audiences as you experiment as well.

Each person may have a slightly different way of facilitating collective shining, but the foundation is opening yourself as a humble conduit for light. Allow yourself to serve the highest good of all without attachment to outcomes.

For a recording of this practice, visit saragiita.com/free

1. Invite any divine guides you resonate with into your space. If you don't work with any guides, you can connect to the energy of your highest Self.

2. Open yourself to receive light from the sky or from Mother Earth, whichever feels more nourishing at this moment. Allow the steady stream of light to fill your whole body and your energy field, forming a circle three feet around your body.

3. When you feel ready, allow your energy field to expand so it encompasses your audience as well, however big or small.

4. Allow the light to continue pouring into this much larger circle. Tune into your divine guides offering the light,

rather than your ego having to do any work or make something happen.

5. Begin speaking or singing a simple mantra on repeat, such as "May we all feel worthy." Let your voice be a conduit for love.

6. To close, let your energy field contract back into the space three feet around you. Let the light nourish and cleanse your being.

CHAPTER 12

Final Words

Hands outstretched,
Throats open,
Our bellies Ablaze in Light;
Please join the Circle
Of Loving Voices,
In our uniqueness we Unite.

My Vision for Us All

Looking back on all the territory we have traversed together, I want to share with you a prayer and vision that I hold. I see myself and all of the clients I have worked with and all of the people who have read this book and all of the people who are dedicated to empowering all voices—and we are all standing side by side in a huge circle upon the Earth. We are all deeply rooted in our power, opening ourselves collectively as conduits for Divine Love to be expressed and amplified. We are dancing and singing and soaring. We are quiet and focused and tuned in. We embody all the joyful paradoxes that come with self-expression and deep listening. We are calm yet exuberant; we are dark and mysterious yet filled with light; we are transcendent beings of oneness who are simultaneously reveling in our vibrant bodily pleasures. We are collectively creating space for every single inch of every single person to be seen, heard, and valued. And as the circle of awakened beings starts to expand, our impact naturally ripples outward into the collective consciousness of all humanity. Just by showing up authentically, we are birthing a new era of abundant compassion, passionate self-expression, and collective responsibility.

When I focus on each person in this collective energetic circle, I see so many unique and beautiful expressions bubbling up. Even if you are momentarily in a place of feeling lost, unworthy, or confused, you still belong in this powerful circle. There is space for you here. Your voice is an essential contribution to the whole. Just find the one pathway that calls to you right now. You may feel a little inner pull to turn the whispers of self-compassion into a steady, reassuring voice inside. You may be in the heart-expanding space of acknowledging personal and collective pain and shifting limiting beliefs that keep us mired in those places of stuckness. You may know in your bones that part of your contribution will come through expressing yourself through your beautiful, just-right body. You may sense that you are here to be a light worker grounded in intuitional flow. Or you may find your inroad into authentic self-expression through creating safe places to be seen, heard, and celebrated as you heal your nervous system. Perhaps you are a cackler who is here to help us reveal our wholeness. Or you can be a garden tender who helps all the inner children feel safe to play and express themselves. Through it all, are you an energy alchemist bringing ancient secrets into being with your inexplicable power? Are you a spreader of Universal Love?

Yes. I believe you are. All these visions, all these potentials live inside of you already. You can heed your soul's calling to speak up, sing out, and play big. I know this because we are standing side by side across space and time. Even amid global suffering and upheaval, I see your authentic truth and radiant potential as if it were my own. Because your empowerment is also my empowerment. So step into the circle, my friend. Trust. Listen. Your unshakable Goddess Voice is emerging like a rumble from the Earth.

APPENDIX

Calming Down from Overwhelm

If you are feeling anxious or overwhelmed, consider this a menu of options to assist with calming down. Choose what feels right for you in the moment. In the longer term, the support of a therapist, counselor, or well-trained coach can help episodes of overwhelm to become less frequent and more manageable.

1. Call a Crisis Hotline— Anonymous hotlines are available 24/7, every day of the year, at no cost! Calls are answered by compassionate, trained staff and volunteers. There are also several crisis text services that you can find with a quick online search. These national hotlines are a few of the many available services in the US:

   Rape, Sexual Assault, Abuse, and Incest National Network (RAINN): (800) 656-4673

   National Domestic Violence Hotline: (800) 799-7233

   National Suicide Prevention Lifeline: (800)273-8255

2. If you are feeling overwhelmed but not in need of a crisis service, finding a way to change your physiological state can change your mental state. Consider:

- Engaging in exercise that increases your heart rate, such as taking a walk or run, doing jumping jacks, dancing, or following an exercise video

- Splashing cool or cold water on your face, forearms, ankles, and feet

- Placing a cold pack over your eyes for a few minutes. (If it has been in the freezer, be sure to use a thin cloth as a barrier between your skin and the cold pack or ice.)

- Drinking a glass of water

- Taking a shower or bath

- Eating nourishing food if you are hungry

3. If you feel stuck in a loop of anxious thoughts, it may be helpful to spend a few minutes with a distracting activity such as watching a funny video, reading an engaging book, or looking at old photos that bring back pleasant memories. You can also distract yourself by counting backward, solving math problems, or finding objects in your environment that match each color of the rainbow. After the distraction, bring your attention to a resource that helps you feel safe or stable, such as:

- Imagining a safe place in nature or indoors

- Focusing on an area of the body that feels neutral

- Thinking of a supportive or loving person in your life

- Sensing what celestial support is available to you (angels, guides, your own Inner Flame)

- Noticing an interesting object in the room

- Bringing your attention to a pleasing sensory experience in the present, such as a calming movement or listening intently to birdsong, crickets, music, or any other calming sounds.

- Focusing on pleasing scents such as essential oils or candles

4. Engage in rhythmic movements that feel calming to you, with or without music. You may wish to try:

   - Gently tapping your thighs with each hand, first on the right side, and then on the left side, over and over again for as long as you wish.

   - Marching in place or stomping to music

   - Shaking your right hand ten times as you count out loud, followed by shaking your left hand ten times. Continue alternating between the hands for a few minutes. You can also experiment with a faster or slower pace as well as a different number of counts.

5. Use your vocal cords. Speaking full sentences, chanting, singing, humming, and even making a sustained groaning sound will change our breathing pattern. Our exhale will naturally lengthen as we vocalize, which has a calming effect on the nervous system. If you speak or sing with someone you trust, it may also provide social connection, companionship, and solidarity.

6. Write in a journal to express your feelings and let your body settle into a more relaxed state. You may wish to write freely, or you could write down the self-critical thoughts or worst-case-scenario fears that are running through your mind. Once they are on paper, it is easier to evaluate them with a rational eye and determine what is accurate and what is exaggerated or overly harsh. To finish, write down some helpful thoughts or beliefs you wish to strengthen.

7. Engage your senses to help you notice the present moment.

- Sniff beautiful scents such as essential oils or incense.

- Notice your sense of touch by walking barefoot in the grass, hugging a tree, putting on soft yummy clothing, or cuddling with a beloved pet.

- Listen to music, nature sounds, or a funny podcast.

- Keep your eyes occupied by taking a walk and noticing your surroundings, gazing at artwork you love, or taking a Google Earth tour of a national park.

- If color is important to you, you may also try color therapy glasses or put on clothing that represents a new mood for you.

A Note about Taste: While we all love delicious flavors, I don't recommend using the sense of taste as a calming down strategy because it could lead to unhealthy associations. However, if you are hungry, that can contribute to a volatile mood so keep your body nourished!

8. When you wish you had more control over life, find a corner of your home or office that you can clean and organize. You could also consider pulling some weeds in the garden or picking up litter in a local park. Creating

order can give us a sense of peace. While the law of entropy tells us that disorder will creep back in, consider cleaning or decluttering as a worthwhile practice even if the results are not permanent.

ACKNOWLEDGMENTS

It takes a village
to honor a voice
to tend a fire
to support a soul.
With gratitude I see
How I came to be
Who I am
Because of you.

To my husband, Paco, thank you for always supporting my healing. In so many ways this journey of self-actualization has only been possible due to your grounded presence.

Amy Rose, thank you for providing your expertise on healing trauma and the nervous system. Your encouragement and kindness is a gift that keeps on giving.

Maria Blon, thank you for helping me feel seen, heard, supported, and known. Your unwavering belief in me kept me motivated through the challenges of completing this book.

To my first editor, Amanda Hendrix, your expertise helped me move forward and see how the book wanted to evolve. Thank you for your generosity, kindness, and solidarity.

To my second editor, Zhenya Goma, thank you for helping me understand the impact of my words. The messages that you channeled were encouraging and life-giving.

Christy Caudill, your reactions to the sections I read out loud to you were magical. Thank you.

I am so grateful to all the people who read and tested out early versions of the written practices: Nancy Orrantia, Nydia Barone, Kathleen Rosenberg, and Macy Miller. Every time you asked me how the book was going, your interest helped me keep going!

To my students and clients, especially Julie, Jesse, Jordan, Janae, Madhuri, and Elle, thank you for your dedication and for helping me grow my life's work of blending voice work and personal development.

Eileen Maxwell, I want to give you a special thanks for reading the practices early on and helping ensure they were trauma-informed. I am grateful for your expertise and guidance.

Carolyn Elges, thank you for coaching me to deeply believe in myself and this book.

To my past therapists, Maggie Kerrigan and Janet Green, you gave me life. Thank you.

I want to share my gratitude for everyone else who supported me during the long journey of making this book a reality: Anastasia Canfield, Terry Joiner, Catherine Cole Hobbs, Melia Bisbee, Amanda Testa, Victoria Robson, Jodi McLaren, Charlene Schik, Wanda Gronhovd, Joanna Metcalf, Danielle Cohen, Rebekah Moan, Mirra Price, and the TMS Lions group.

Thank you to the many teachers and authors who have informed my work: Tina Lynn-Craig, Sue McBerry, Carol Biel, Rachael Maddox, Kristine Kaoverii Weber, MJ Glassman, Mirabai Starr, Peter Levine, Bessel van der Kolk, Ruth King, Brené Brown, Tarana Burke, Glennon Doyle, Caroline Myss, Matt Khan, Sonya Renee Taylor, Kristin Neff, Christina Lopes, and Tosha Silver.

To my parents, I am eternally grateful for all you have given me throughout the years, and especially for supporting my musical education.

To my sister, thanks for being a great listener.

Diego, thank you for always making my life an adventure.

Amalina, thank you for inspiring my creativity day after day.

Finally, I wish to express my gratitude for Mother Earth, Baba, and the many forms of the Goddess for filling me with light so that I could bring these ideas and stories into the world of form. I am yours.

BIBLIOGRAPHY

Ben-Shahar, Tal. Audio Recording of Positive Psychology 1504 Course. Harvard University, 2006.

Brown, Brené. *Atlas of the Heart: Mapping Meaningful Connection and the Language of Human Experience.* New York, NY: Random House, 2021.

Capaccione, Lucia. *Recovery of Your Inner Child: The Highly Acclaimed Method for Liberating your Inner Self.* New York, NY: Touchstone, 1991.

Cardozo, Peter. *Live Music Therapy: Audible Pure Tones.* Burnet, TX: Live Music Therapy Press, 1988.

Dupree, Ulrich E. Ho'oponopono: *The Hawaiian forgiveness ritual as the key to your life's fulfillment.* Translated by Tony Mitton. N.p.: Earthdancer GmbH, 2012.

Early, Jay and Bonnie Weiss. *Freedom from Your Inner Critic: A Self-Therapy Approach.* Louisville, CO: Sounds True, 2013

Gibson, Lindsay C. *Adult Children of Emotionally Immature Parents: How to Heal from Distant, Rejecting, or Self-Involved Parents.* Oakland, CA: New Harbinger Publications, Inc, 2015.

Johnson, Kimberly Ann. *Call of the Wild: How We Heal Trauma, Awaken Our Own Power, and Use it for Good.* New York, NY: HarperCollins Publishers, 2021.

Levine, Peter A. with Ann Frederick. *Waking the Tiger: Healing Trauma.* Berkeley, CA: North Atlantic Books, 1997.

Linn, Denise. *Energy Strands: The Ultimate Guide to Clearing the Cords That Are Constricting Your Life.* Carlsbad, CA: Hay House, 2018.

Maddox, Rachael. *ReBloom: Archetypal Trauma Resolution for Personal & Collective Healing.* N.p.: 2021.

Maheshvarananda, Dada. *After Capitalism: Economic Democracy in Action.* Puerto Rico: InnerWorld Publications, 2019.

Mark, Thomas. *What Every Pianist Needs to Know about the Body.* Chicago, IL: GIA Publications, 2003

Monk Kidd, Sue. *Traveling With Pomegranates: A Mother daughter Story.* New York, NY: Viking, 2009.

Myss, Caroline. *Defy Gravity: Healing Beyond the Bounds of Reason.* Carlsbad, CA: Hay House, 2009.

Neff, Kristin. The Space Between Self-Esteem and Self-Compassion: Kristin Neff at TEDxCentennialParkWomen. YouTube, Uploaded by TEDx Talks, Feb. 6, 2013.

Pinkola Estes, Clarissa. *Women Who Run With the Wolves: Myths and Stories of the Wild Woman Archetype.* New York, NY: Ballantine Books, 1995.

Powell, John. *How Music Works: The Science and Psychology of Beautiful Sounds, from Beethoven to the Beatles and Beyond.* New York, NY: Little, Brown Spark, 2010.

Silver, Tosha. *It's Not Your Money: How to Live Fully from Divine Abundance.* Carlsbad, CA: Hay House, 2019.

Stone, Hal and Sidra Stone. *Embracing Our Selves: The Voice Dialogue Manual.* Mill Valley, CA: Nataraj Publishing, 1989.

Stone, Sidra. *The Shadow King: The Invisible Force that Holds Women Back.* Mill Valley, CA: Nataraj Publishing, 1997.

Taylor, Sonya Renee. *The Body is Not an Apology: The Power of Radical Self-Love.* Oakland, CA: Berrett-Koehler Publishers, 2018

Van der Kolk, Bessel. *The Body Keeps the Score: Brain, Mind, and Body in the Healing of Trauma.* New York, NY: Penguin Books, 2015.

Wall, Joan. *International Phonetic Alphabet for Singers: A manual for English and foreign language diction.* Dallas, TX: Pst...Inc., 1989.